The THOMAS family

The 300 year history of 11 generations of the
THOMAS family of Devon and New Zealand.

by Trevor N Price

John Thomas born 1829

Other family history books by Trevor N Price

MORGAN PRICE & family… Wales & Southland, NZ.
The THOMAS family … (John & Uncle George) Devon & Auckland, NZ
WILLIAM THOMAS & Family (John's brother). Devon & Auckland, NZ
The STEVENS family… Devon, England and Canterbury, NZ
          (Author received The Kevin McAnulty Award, from NZSG)
The WOODS family … Wales, Norfolk UK, & Auckland, NZ
NELSON PRICE … World War 2 Diary

First published 1993 (in hardback) by the author.
ISBN # 0-473-01939-6

This paperback edition published 2022 by:
Starting Gun Books, Auckland, New Zealand

National Library of New Zealand Cataloguing-in-Publication Data

Price, Trevor N. (Trevor Nelson), 1937-
The Thomas family : the 300 year history of 11 generations of the Thomas family of Devon and New Zealand / T.N. Price. Pbk. ed.
Previous ed.: Auckland [N.Z.] : T.N. Price, 1993.
Includes bibliographical references and index.

ISBN 978-0-473-66537-1

Cover by Xanthe Price
Printed by Lightning Source
Authors website: **www.tnprice.co.nz**

This book is dedicated to the memory of
MICHAEL STANLEY THOMAS
who held a strong attachment for the family
and printed the 1970 John Thomas Family Tree.

1907... PHEBE and JOHN THOMAS family photo.
L to R, rear........ SYDNEY, PERCY, ELSIE, FREDERICK, GEORGE;
L to R, front...... JACK, JESSIE....JOHN (V) and PHEBE.....ALFRED,
CHARLES, and young ROY.   (Chapter four)

We have searched everywhere for a ***POLLY and GEORGE THOMAS***
family photo, but one does not seem to exist. (Chapter five)

4

CONTENTS:

AUTHOR'S NOTE:

The following pages have been compiled from information received from many Thomas descendants, historical books and official documents. We acknowledge most of these on page 304, however, we thank you all for your interest and help.

The **LIFE STORIES** run from that person's birth to their death, and we show as many photos as were made available.

The NEW ZEALAND FAMILY TREES. We apologise for any spaces.

--oo0Ooo—

A brief explanation of the **FAMILY TREE LAYOUT.**
There were two brothers who came to New Zealand........
JOHN AND GEORGE THOMAS.
We have nominated them as 1st Generation New Zealanders, their children are 2nd Generation, and this continues to today's 7th Generation.

1st, 2nd and 3rd New Zealand Generations are shown in the
BRIEF FAMILY TREE on pages 8 and 9.

JOHN...... His family's detailed trees appear after each of his 2nd and 3rd Generation descendant's life stories, in Chapters 3 and 4.

GEORGE.... His family's detailed trees appear after his 2nd Generation descendant's life stories in Chapter 5.

The Tree detail is printed in vertical columns, starting with the first born and completing their children's and grand-children's details before moving on to the next eldest's details.

**A look at your own immediate family will show you how easy
to read this system is**. (Ladies are under their maiden names.)
b = Birth date.   m = Marriage date.   d = Death date.
at = Town of Birth or Marriage.
Bur at = Town where buried.....not town where died.

CHAPTER ONE

THE THOMAS FAMILY:

This book is about the Thomas Family of Devon and New Zealand.
In fact, it covers nearly 300 years, starting from 1700.

ELEVEN GENERATIONS altogether are followed, and we have divided these up into 4 Devon and 7 New Zealand generations.

Two brothers, **JOHN** (Chapter 3) and **GEORGE** (Chapter 5) of the 5th Devon Generations, came to NZ and they became the 1st New Zealand Generation.

They left behind in Devon, two brothers and two sisters. We follow their sister **ELIZABETH'S** family (starting page 24) whom we have met and who still live in Devon.

In the main this book details the lives of Chapter 3 John's, son **John and wife Phebe** (Chapter 4) and their 15 children and his brother **George and wife Polly** (Chapter 5) and their 12 children.
(There is another book "William Thomas & family" that details the lives of Chapter 3 John's other son William)

BRIEF TREE & INDEX.

Due to there being a large number of people named......
William, John, Elizabeth and George Thomas,
we follow this page with a Brief Family Tree starting at 1700 and depicting the first 7 of the eleven generations. Chapter 2 provides more detail of the Devon families.

Should you still be having trouble deciding where you fit into all this, we suggest you consult the Family Index commencing on page 304....... find your own name..... and work back from there.

THOMAS FAMILY TREE.

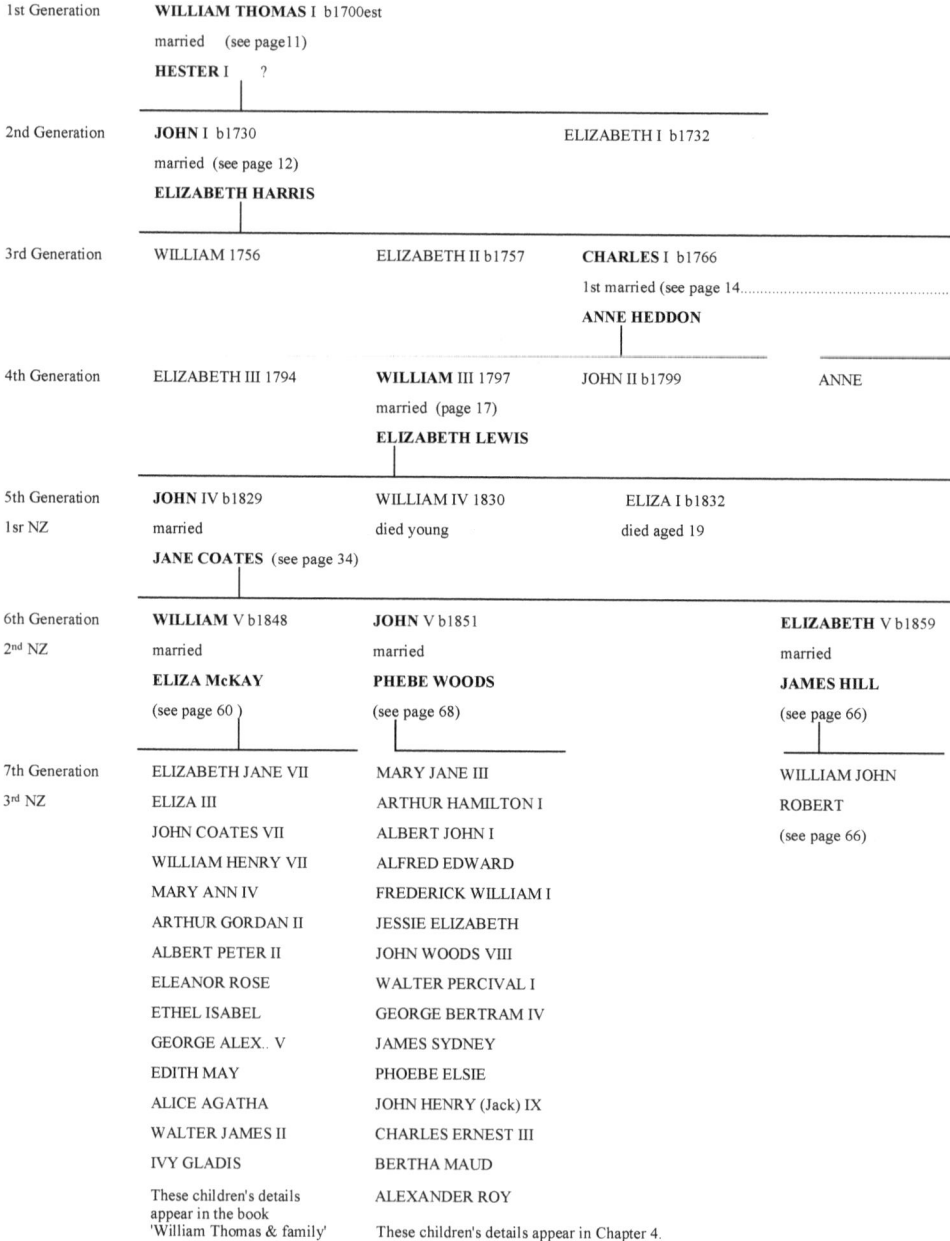

1st Generation	**WILLIAM THOMAS** I b1700est
	married (see page 11)
	HESTER I ?

2nd Generation	**JOHN** I b1730 ELIZABETH I b1732
	married (see page 12)
	ELIZABETH HARRIS

3rd Generation WILLIAM 1756   ELIZABETH II b1757   **CHARLES** I b1766
1st married (see page 14.....................................)
ANNE HEDDON

4th Generation ELIZABETH III 1794   **WILLIAM** III 1797   JOHN II b1799   ANNE
married (page 17)
ELIZABETH LEWIS

5th Generation **JOHN** IV b1829   WILLIAM IV 1830   ELIZA I b1832
1sr NZ married   died young   died aged 19
JANE COATES (see page 34)

6th Generation **WILLIAM** V b1848   **JOHN** V b1851   **ELIZABETH** V b1859
2nd NZ married   married   married
ELIZA McKAY   **PHEBE WOODS**   **JAMES HILL**
(see page 60)   (see page 68)   (see page 66)

7th Generation **3rd NZ**		
ELIZABETH JANE VII	MARY JANE III	WILLIAM JOHN
ELIZA III	ARTHUR HAMILTON I	ROBERT
JOHN COATES VII	ALBERT JOHN I	(see page 66)
WILLIAM HENRY VII	ALFRED EDWARD	
MARY ANN IV	FREDERICK WILLIAM I	
ARTHUR GORDAN II	JESSIE ELIZABETH	
ALBERT PETER II	JOHN WOODS VIII	
ELEANOR ROSE	WALTER PERCIVAL I	
ETHEL ISABEL	GEORGE BERTRAM IV	
GEORGE ALEX.. V	JAMES SYDNEY	
EDITH MAY	PHOEBE ELSIE	
ALICE AGATHA	JOHN HENRY (Jack) IX	
WALTER JAMES II	CHARLES ERNEST III	
IVY GLADIS	BERTHA MAUD	
These children's details appear in the book 'William Thomas & family'	ALEXANDER ROY	
	These children's details appear in Chapter 4.	

ANN b1774

.... 2nd married

JULIAN HEDDON

JOHN III   ROBERT   CHARLES II   GEORGE I   MARY I   HESTER II   GRACE

ELIZABETH THOMAS IV b 1834   **GEORGE** II b1837   RICHARD I

solo mother (see page 24) Wales   Married   **(Polly)**   b 1840 Wales

                                       JANE MORRIS   Died aged 10

FREDERICK PALMER I   SELINA ANN

married   ELIZA JANE II

ALICE SING   ELIZABETH VI

(see page 26)   MARY ANN II

                                       JOHN   VI

RICHARD III   WILLIAM   VI

WILLIAM VIII   GEORGE   III

WALTER BROWN III   RICHARD HENESY

LEONARD PALMER   HESTER (Esther)   III

ELIZABETH VIII   EDWARD ERNEST

                                       ALFRED SAMUEL

details page 31   HILDA JANE

                                       details in this book Chapter 5

CHAPTER TWO

DEVON.

The THOMAS FAMILY BEGINNINGS.
In Chapter One we provide a brief family tree to show the
generations at a glance and follow the earliest known seven
generations starting from 1700.
In this Chapter we provide greater detail of the first six
generations, and follow one line via Family Tree, down
to the present day.
(i.e. Elizabeth Thomas ----5th to 11th Devon Generations)
+++

Situated in the north of Devon, England, are the small villages of
BERRYNABOUR, BITTADON and WEST DOWN and the larger town of
ILFRACOMBE. All are known to feature in our Thomas family beginnings, but
West Down is the village and district in which they spent the greatest amount of
time...... from 1730 until 1991.

BERRYNABOUR: The 1887 "Gazetteer of the British Isles "describes this parish
as *"a coastal Parish and Village in north Devon, 2.5 miles east of Ilfracombe, having
4982 acres and 534 population, a Post Office and Telegraph Office."*

BITTADON: The Gazetteer advises "this small Parish centers around the village
and is situated 5.5 miles NW of Barnstaple". A population of 47 is recorded in it's
1841 Census Return. Unfortunately, we have found that all Church of England
records before 1812 were lost to fire.

WEST DOWN: We do not know how large the village was in the early 1700's but
the Gazetteer describes it as *"both a Parish and Village in Devonshire with a total
population of 461 and has 4082 acres. The village is seven miles north west of Barnstaple
(and seven miles south of Ilfracombe) and there is a Post Office and a Telegraph Office."*

In 1990 we found the district still contained a few hundred village residents and
the surrounding rural population.
Our inquiries at West Down revealed that the first part of their St Calixtus,
Church of England, was erected about 1320.

1st Generation

WILLIAM THOMAS .. married .... **HESTER ????**
b 1700-10   est 1729   b1700-10
Both possibly buried at Bittadon but no headstone erected.

They had two children we know of:-
JOHN THOMAS baptised 19 May 1730 at West Down.
ELIZABETH THOMAS bapt 11 June 1732 at West Down.

We have researched the Parishes surrounding West Down, for William and Hester's baptisms and marriage. These were not found in records for West Down, Ilfracombe, Berrynabour, East Down, Marwood, Georgeham and Braunton. No records have survived for Morthoe and Bittadon for the estimated time frame 1690-1730.

As these events were not found in the other Parishes, we believe they occurred at Bittadon. People did not travel very far in those days, so we strongly think the few miles covered by the four Parishes of Berrynabour, Bittadon, West Down and Ilfracombe were the "home grounds" of our Thomas family beginnings.

An earlier generation ... ?
Purely speculative and not provable because records lost in fire.

FACT: There was a John Thomas living in Berrynabour in the late 1600's. He had two daughters .. Mary bapt 10 Feb 1691 and Helena 16 June 1695. There were no more Thomas children baptised in this Parish until 1730. There were no burial records for these people and no marriages were found either.

GUESS: We think this John Thomas was ours and he took his family to work in nearby Bittadon about 1696. Additional children would have followed, possibly including a son William baptised 1700-10 who married Hester about 1729.

2nd Generation

JOHN THOMAS ....married .... **ELIZABETH HARRIS**
bapt 19 May 1730   4 May 1755   bapt 20 March 1730
at West Down.   at Ilfracombe.   at Ilfracombe.
John died and buried... possibly 1801 at Ilfracombe.

        They had four children ......
WILLIAM   T bapt 24 March 1756 Ilfracombe C of E.
ELIZABETH   T bapt 3 August 1757 at West Down.
CHARLES THOMAS bapt 26 May 1766 at West Down.
ANN   T bapt 19 June 1774 at West Down.

Our research of the West Down, Church of England records commenced at 1600. There were no Thomas people baptised or married in this church until our 2nd generation John was in 1730. John and Elizabeth married in Elizabeth's home town of Ilfracombe where John described himself as 'John Thomas of Berrynabour'. Their first child William was baptised at Ilfracombe where many of Elizabeth's family were.

In 1757 it would seem they were living in Bittadon ... possibly near the West Down boarder. It is possible the West Down church was closer to them than the Bittadon one as this is where their second child Elizabeth was baptised. Their third child Charles was baptised at West Down and father John described himself as 'John Thomas of Bittadon'. John did not record his residential address at any of the other three children's baptisms. Although there are large gaps between the children's baptisms, we could find no record of additional children's baptisms or burials.

We have searched the Bittadon Land Tax records for the 50 year period 1780-1830. (the only years available). There were 9 properties in the Parish that paid tax and none were owned by any person named Thomas. John would not be able to describe himself as 'Farmer'. There were three large farms and John and his family were probably living on one of these, where John would be employed as a general farm-hand known at that time as an Agricultural Labourer.

ELIZABETH HARRIS:

2nd generation John Thomas' wife Elizabeth Harris was a twin.
Her parents THOMAS HARRIS and BEATRIX SOMERS were married at Ilfracombe on 20 Oct 1718 and 11 children were baptised at the Ilfracombe Church of England.

Their children were…

John　　H bapt　6 August 1719, died the same month.

Esther　H bapt 17 July 1721, died on 15 Aug 1721.

Esther　H bapt 16 August 1722.

Thomas H bapt　7 December 1724, died aged 10, 13 April 1734.

John　　H bapt　2 August 1727, died aged 3 on 5 October 1730.

Sarah　　H bapt　20 March 1730. (twin)

ELIZABETH HARRIS　(twin) bapt 20 March 1730.

Mary　　H bapt　26 June 1732.

John　　H bapt　5 June 1733, died on 11 June 1733.

William Thomas H　bapt 19 May 1734.

John　　H bapt　27 October 1738.

Father…　Thomas Harris died 22 July 1750 and was buried at Ilfracombe.

Mother…　Beatrix Harris died 7 May 1748 and was buried at Ilfracombe.

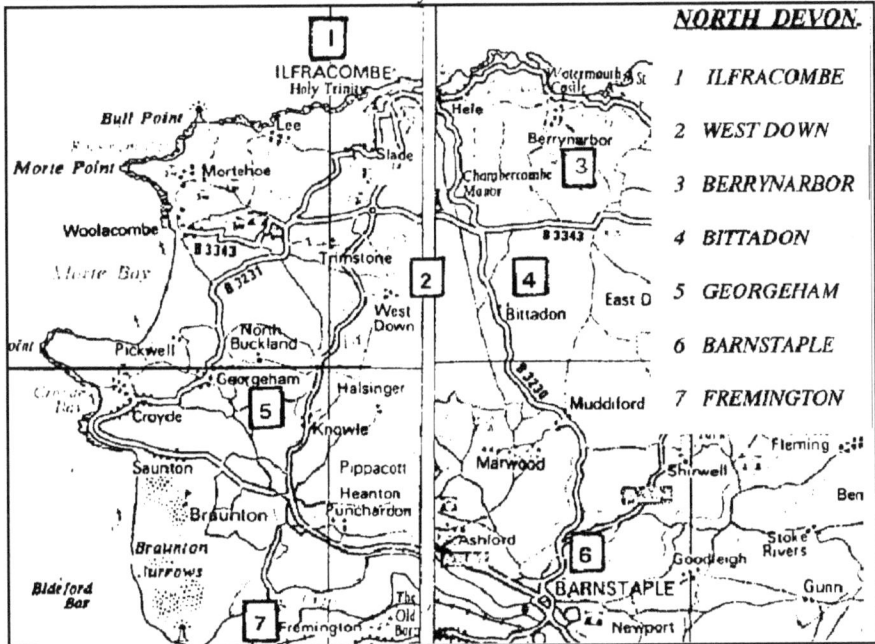

NORTH DEVON.

1 *ILFRACOMBE*

2 *WEST DOWN*

3 *BERRYNARBOR*

4 *BITTADON*

5 *GEORGEHAM*

6 *BARNSTAPLE*

7 *FREMINGTON*

13

3rd Generation

CHARLES THOMAS .... first married .... **ANNE HEDDON**
bapt 26 May 1766   10 Jan 1794   bapt 27 Dec 1772
at West Down.   at West Down.   at West Down
died 28 August 1831 (65)   died 1 July 1799 (27)
Buried at West Down Cof E.   :   Buried at West Down.
                   :

second marriage ...... **JULIAN HEDDON**
4 June 1800   bapt 15 June 1768
at Stoke Damerel.   at West Down.
            died 6 June 1844 (76)
            Buried at West Down.

CHARLES and ANNE had three children.....
> ELIZABETH T   bapt 12 October 1794 at West Down.
> **WILLIAM THOMAS** bapt 12 January 1797 at West Down.
> JOHN   T bapt 21 April 1799 at West Down but
>   died 27 April 1799 and buried at West Down.

CHARLES and JULIAN had eight children.....
> Anne   T bapt 22 March 1801.   John   T bapt 8 August 1802.
> Robert T bapt 2 January 1804.   Charles T bapt 9 August 1806.
> George T bapt 2 April 1808.   Mary   T bapt 7 January 1810
> Hester T bapt 16 June 1811.   Grace   T bapt 3 January 1813.
> These children were baptised at West Down, Church of England.

--oo0Ooo —

The **HEDDON** family ....

ANNE and JULIAN were sisters.
Their parents, ROBERT HEDDON and MARY TUCKER were married
28 March 1762 at West Down and had six children......
> Mary   H   bapt 5 March 1763.   Elizabeth H   bapt 4 August 1764.
> Robert H   bapt 19 June 1766.   **JULIAN H**   bapt 15 June 1768.
> John   H   bapt 24 May 1770.   **ANNE H**   bapt 27 Dec 1772.

Father Robert Heddon died 30 Mar 1806 and was buried at West Down.
Mother Mary Heddon died 14 Oct 1806 and was buried at West Down.

--oo0Ooo--

We have researched the West Down Land Tax records of 1780-1830 and none of the large number of estates were owned by any person named Charles Thomas. We do not know his occupation ... he may have followed his father and became an agricultural labourer or, like his son William, learnt the trade of a mason.

Mentioned on the headstone of this Thomas burial plot in the West Down Church grounds, is Charles, his two wives Anne and Julian, plus daughter Anne (wife of Thomas Hill) and daughter Hester (wife of Richard Collins).

It also carries this phrase.....

> "They lived in Peace, They died in Love,
> In hopes to live with God above.
> No worldly wealth did they require,
> To live with Christ was their desire."

WEST DOWN'S...... ST CALIXTUS CHURCH of ENGLAND.
This Church played a large part in the lives of our Thomas family,
for at least six generations and from at least 1730.

JOHN THOMAS' BAPTISM 1829 at West Down's Church.

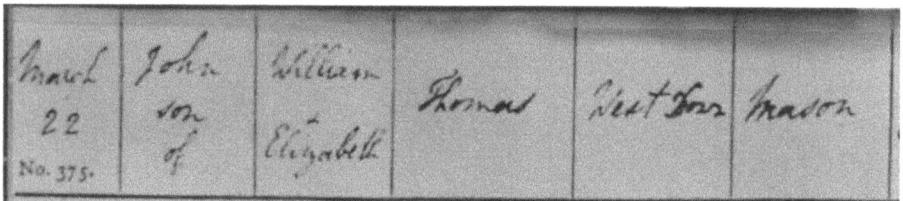

4th Generation

WILLIAM THOMAS married ELIZABETH LEWIS

bapt 12 February 1797   1 January 1821   bapt 1 June 1794
at West Down.   at Ilfracombe.   at Ilfracombe.
died 14 December 1866 (69)   died 29 November 1866 (72)
Buried at West Down.   Buried at West Down.

They had six children all baptised at West Down......
JOHN THOMAS bapt 22 March 1829.   (Came to New Zealand
     and full details of his life and descendants are in Chapter Three)
WILLIAM T. bapt 26 December 1830   (thought to have died young.)
ELIZA T. bapt 29 April 1832,and died aged 19 on 14 February 1851.
ELIZABETH THOMAS bapt 16 March 1834. (She never left Devon.
     Full details of her life and descendants are in Chapter Two)
GEORGE THOMAS bapt 10 Sep 1837.   (Came to New Zealand
     Full details of his life and descendants are in Chapter Five)
RICHARD T. bapt 23 August 1840, and died 19 February 1850. (10)

We have searched many parish records for baptism and death details of children who may have been born during the eight years between their marriage in 1821 and John's birth in 1829, but have found none.

--oo00oo—

ELIZABETH LEWIS family :

William's wedding details show his wife's name as Lewes but all other references found, use the spelling LEWIS.

Elizabeth Lewis' parents were JOHN LEWIS (Husbandman of Ilfracombe) and JOANNA RICHARDS. (Spinster of West Down)

Banns were called at the West Down Church of England on March 14 + 21 + 28 and records show that neither of them could sign their name. They married on 29 March 1784.

We have found four children mentioned in the registers.....

John Lewis   bapt 23 May 1784 at West Down.
Mary Lewis   bapt 13 April 1788 at Ilfracombe.
ELIZABETH LEWIS bapt 1 June 1794 at Ilfracombe.
William Lewis bapt 12 September 1798 at Ilfracombe.

WILLIAM'S OCCUPATION:

The 1841 Census Returns have only one Thomas family at West Down.
William and Elizabeth Thomas and all 6 children detailed above, were living at
Bradwell Mill, West Down at that time.

Over the years William changed his occupation as the need arose, but we believe
he learnt the art of a mason first and probably worked around the West Down
district. At the age of 24 in 1821, no occupation was listed on his wedding
records. When he baptised his children John, William and Eliza (1829 to 1832) he
gave his occupation as *'Mason'*. When he baptised his children Elizabeth, George
and Richard (1834 to 1840) he gave his occupation *'Miller'*. In 1841 he described
himself as a *'Farmer'*.

BRADWELL MILL:

The two storey building in the centre with a chimney is the family home. Hiding
part of it's roof is a very old pear tree. At the right of this building and attached
to it, was the grain Mill. The long building to the left of the home, was once a
bake-house and the other two were general farm buildings.

On the extreme left of our photo is another farm complex ... originally
part of the Bradwell community.

BRADWELL MILL... 1990:

upper...   The main front entrance to the house. On the right
behind the pear tree, the steps up to the Mill room can be seen.
lower... Standing at, and looking away from the house's front door,
the bake-house is on the right and the two farm buildings on the left.

19

BRADWELL MILL and WILLIAM THOMAS :

The deeds of Bradwell Mill show that William Thomas bought the Bradwell Mill ruins in 1825 and this was his immediate family's home for the next 41 years until he died. Future generations lived there and even in 1990 (166 years later) when we arrived at West Down, we found it still owned and occupied by William's descendants.

William paid 65 pounds for the ruins, containing two cottages, one with the corn mill attached, and foundations of numerous other buildings, all on one third of an acre, a short distance from the West Down township.

LAND TAX :

Our search of the West Down Land Tax records from 1780 to 1832 showed only one person by the name of Thomas in this entire Parish, who owned or occupied land and paid taxes during this 52 year period. Although William officially bought the property in 1825, it was not until June 1830 that he first paid tax of three shillings on this property. He was recorded as being both the 'Proprietor' and 'Occupier' and paid the same amount of tax in 1831 and 1832. No more records are available.

Over the 52 year period Bradwell was in three sections. The large Bradwell Barton (farm), Bradwell and Bradwell Mill, all being shown as three separate taxable units. Bradwell Barton was divided into five smaller units in 1810, but Bradwell Mill is the property we are interested in.

From 1780 to 1790 Phillip Challacombe rented the 'Bradwell Mill' property to William Kidwell. From 1791 to 1801 he rented it to John Harris. From 1802 to 1805 he rented it to John Coats of Willincott Estate. In 1806 he put himself down as 'Occupier'. From 1807 to 1826 he rented it to John Heddon, then the proprietorship changed to Avery Berry who continued to rent it to John Heddon until 1829.

The next year (1830) William Thomas became the proprietor / occupier.

HISTORY :

Mr John Longhurst of the Ilfracombe Museum was interested in the history of the district and in 1979 wrote to George Thomas of Auckland, (great great grandson of 1837 George, and our John Thomas' brother.) In his letter he detailed some ancient history of Bradwell Mill that he had uncovered. In part he says:.....
"There is no trace of Bradwell Barton (a large farmyard...... not let with the rest of the Manor) *which was situated about 1.5 miles west of West Down Church.*

All that is now on the site are a few agricultural buildings however, the Mill situated about a quarter of a mile to the east, still stands. Prior to the Conquest this land had been in the King's hand.

Bradwell is mentioned in the Doomsday Book. The name is of Saxon origin meaning BROAD STREAM - Brade Wielle.

Ralph de Limesei, a nephew of William the Conqueror had, in 1086, four estates in the Braunton Hundred, one of which was Bradwell. At that date it was spelt Bradevilla and of 873 acres.

In the Book of Fees of 1242 it is recorded as Bradwill when Ralf de Pyn was the Lord and held it for a half fee for the honour of Gerard de Odingeseles. He was succeeded by Augustin de Pyn in 1303.By 1316 the estate was called Bradewille Pyn.   In 1346 William de Pyn held the estate for the honour of Braneys because both honours were then in the hands of the Prince of Wales (Richard) whose head manor in Devon was Bradninch. William Pyn's daughter Joan carried Bradwell to Robert Yoe the elder, of Heanton Satchvil, who died in 1409. It then passed to Robert Yoe the younger who died in 1428, it passed to his grandson William Yoe and when he died in 1481 it passed by a female heir to the Rolle family who held it for many generations.

Bradwell then passed to the Walpole family in 1810 and thence in 1822 to Lord Clinton by inheritance."(end of quote)

> Described here is the property next to the Mill, but the Mill may have been part of the same title in earlier years and enjoyed a similar interesting background.

In 1825 William Thomas became the owner of Bradwell Mill.

RESTORATION :

From 1825 to about 1833, William Thomas the Mason, restored the ruined Bradwell Mill site and he and his wife moved into the cottage with the Mill attached. All their children seem to have been born here.

On a beam inside the Mill is carved the date 1830 and we wonder if William Thomas did this to record for posterity, the year he got the Mill operating and grinding again. Further improvements were done to the Mill with the present overshot wheel installed in 1893 and a new pit-wheel was cast by Raffels in 1900. The cogs of this mill were made in the old style out of apple tree wood. The remains of the crown wheel, pinion, hopper etc, were still there for Mr Longhurst in 1979 and he advises the building beside the road was the bake-house and the pear tree near the door to the Mill is over 100 years old.

He aged the present house as being built in the early 1800's, possibly by William Thomas as he bought 'only ruins'.

This author is 6 feet tall and had to stoop to pass through all the doorways on the property. There is no sign today of the 'broad stream' but Mr Longhurst could still trace to the north of the Mill, nor the leat and millpond.

William was soon earning enough money from this Mill to replace his mason activities with those of a miller. It is believed he milled corn for his closest neighbours too. We are advised that the restored Mill was worked for a further hundred years but was not worked after William's grandson, Frederick P Thomas, died in 1938.

We know William taught his sons John and George, the milling trade, as this was the occupation that gained them both assisted passage to New Zealand.

After 10 years of Mill operation the 1841 Census was taken and William, described as a Farmer, employed a full time agricultural labourer named John Brown. This Census return seems to depict Bradwell Mill as a 'Hamlet' of seven residences, with eight families totalling fortysix people.

The KITCHEN AREA at BRADWELL MILL in 1990.
Jill Price (centre) with Elizabeth (nee Thomas) and Alfred Newcombe.

Included in the 1841 Census at Bradwell were, William and Ann Coates and 2 children, George and Sarah Lewis and 4 children, William and Mary Robins and 5 children, Elizabeth Kift and 4 children, George and Ann Guard and 2 children, Richard and Jane Edwards and 5 children, John and Mary Winser and 2 children and our William and Elizabeth Thomas and their 6 children.

All but two of the men were described as agricultural labourers. William Robbins was a mason.

In 1990 there were only three houses left in the area and William Thomas descendants still had ownership of a few paddocks near the Mill upon which sheep roamed and orchard trees grew. It is thought that William gained access to some of these during the years prior to 1841 and that he continued with the milling as well.

William died two weeks after his wife in 1866 and the property was put up for auction early in 1867 at the West Down Public House .... but was not sold. By this time son Richard and daughter Eliza had died and it is thought young William had also died.

Sons John and George had emigrated to New Zealand and daughter Elizabeth was the only one left at West Down.

Soon after the auction failed, she became the owner, paying William's estate £265.

--oo0Ooo--

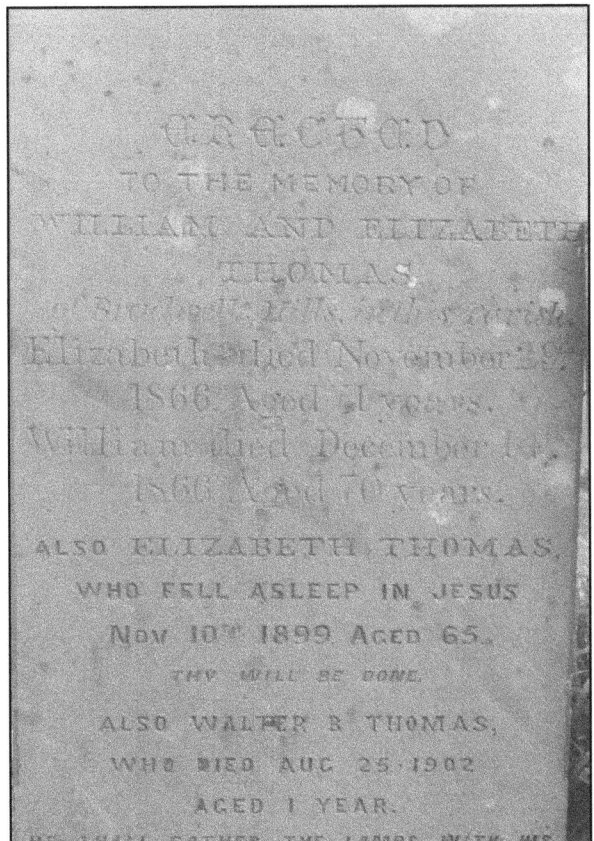

William & Elizabeth's WEST DOWN HEADSTONE.

23

ELIZABETH THOMAS: (1834-1899)

Elizabeth was the fourth child of William and Elizabeth Thomas of Bradwell Mill, West Down. She was baptised 16 March 1834 and, as a solo parent raised three children. She died aged 65 on 10 November 1899 and was interred at the West Down Church of England cemetery.

--ooOOoo--

The 1841 Census shows her at age 6, living with her parents and all five brothers and sisters at Bradwell Mill, West Down, Devon.

The 1851 Census shows that at age 16 she had left home and was living and working elsewhere. Only her younger brother George, then aged 13 was still at home with his parents. During the past 10 years, brother William may have died. In 1850 her brother Richard died, and her sister Eliza died 2 months before the Census. Now she only had two brothers, John and George. In 1848 brother John married Jane Coates and went to live in Ilfracombe.

The 1861 Census shows Elizabeth returned to live at Bradwell Mill and at age 26 was unmarried. During this 10 year period her elder brother John emigrated to New Zealand in 1854. The following year his wife Jane and their two children (William and John), together with Elizabeth's younger brother George emigrated to New Zealand also. Elizabeth was now the only surviving child of William and Elizabeth left in Devon.

The 10 years between the 1861 and 1871 Censuses were busy for Elizabeth.
A story passed down the generations starts around the New Year of 1865 when a man named Frederick managed to get two local girls pregnant. Unfortunately for Elizabeth he decided to marry the other young woman. This appears to have hardened Elizabeth's attitude and although she continued to have male companionship and two more children, she never married. The Thomas name therefore continued on at Bradwell Mill.

1865... October 18: Elizabeth's first child **Frederick Palmer Thomas** was baptised at the West Down Church of England. (His life details page 26)
1866... November 26: Elizabeth's mother Elizabeth died aged 72.

1866... December 14: Elizabeth's father William died aged 69.

In 1867 Bradwell Mill and lands went up for auction but were not sold. Later that year Elizabeth became the owner. Mortgages were held over the property most of the time she and her parents owned the Mill and land.

1868 **Bessie Thirza Tucker Thomas** was born. (Dec Q reg Barnstaple) During the 1891 census aged 22 Bessie was a domestic servant for the Francis family in Roath, Cardiff. In the 1901 Census Bessie aged 32 was single and working as a servant at 58 Newport Road, St German, Cardiff for Eliza Moxey.. In 1901 she married a gentleman named William Legg, (Sept Q reg Cardiff) and died aged 37 on 19 November 1905 without children.

The 1871 Census shows Elizabeth aged 35 and her two children (Frederick 6 and Bessie 2) living at Bradwell Mill with a gentleman named William Tucker aged 38. His occupation was stated as 'Miller'.

1872 Elizabeth's third child was born (Mar Q reg Barnstaple). **Kentley Sydney William Tucker Thomas**.

In the 1891 census aged 19 he was single and a domestic servant for John Cook farmer at Pentyrch in Glamorganshire.

In 1990 the descendants of Frederick advised us that his half-brother Kentley was very upset when he heard his mother had remained unmarried. It appears he changed his name ... dropping the Thomas ... and left Devon. They believe he travelled to Wales, married and raised a family.

We found Kentley. S. W. Tucker married Mary Jenkins in Wales in 1892 (Dec Q reg Pontypridd) The 1901 census show Kentley 28 and Mary 28 have 4 children... Beatrice M 7, William J 6, Olive G 3, and Sidney A aged 1 mth. Mary was born 1873 in Pentyrch. The family were living at 143 Victoria Terrace, Pontyclun, Wales. He may have been employed on the Railways.

> We wonder if this Tucker family has any idea of their connection to
> Bradwell Mill and to this Thomas family of north Devon.

The 1881 Census shows Elizabeth 45 and William Tucker (head) 49 still at Bradwell Mill. with Frederick 16, Thursa 12 and Kently 9 plus 2 lodgers.

> Elizabeth signed her Will on 7 May 1888 and it remained unchanged for the next 11 years. Son Frederick was made sole Executor and Trustee and the simply written Will left everything to the three children.

On 7 September her estate was valued at £286.

> 10 November 1899 Aged 65, Elizabeth died and was buried in the West
Down Church grounds along with her parents and her grandson Walter.

FREDERICK PALMER THOMAS: (1865-1938)

Frederick was born at Bradwell Mill and baptised at West Down Church of England on 18 October 1865. His mother Elizabeth remained unmarried and raised him on her own. Both his grandparents William and Elizabeth Thomas died soon after his first birthday. We assume he was educated at West Down and believe he later worked with his 'foster father' William Tucker at the Mill and on the farm paddocks owned by Bradwell Mill, as he was still there at age 16 for the 1881 Census.

Alice Sing became his wife in 1893. (Mar Q reg Barnstaple) Alice and Frederick had five children... Richard, William, Walter, Leonard and Elizabeth. Full personal details follow in the Family Tree page 31. Their children Richard and Leonard never married. Walter died at the tender age of one. Elizabeth married but there were no children, and son William married and had one child named Beatrice May Thomas known as May. (She told me she was supposed to be called April but arrived a bit late. T) William never saw his daughter May as she arrived after he had departed to take part in World War One. He was killed 3 December 1917 at Folka, only six miles from Jerusalem. May was just 7 months old.

Alice had been a school teacher before she married Frederick and later became the organist in the Wesleyan Chapel on the other side of the road near Bradwell Mill in 1890. This Chapel was erected in 1861 (complete with burial ground) and Alice's son Richard recalled attending Sunday School there before it was closed and demolished in the early 1900's.

In April 1938 Frederick wrote and signed his Will. He divided his property and stock up into five parts for his wife, three surviving children and daughter-in-law. When Frederick died in October 1938 the estate comprised Bradwell Mill, house and other buildings, over 34 acres of land and some stock. It was then valued at £1,943.

In 1990 we visited Bradwell Mill. It was a thrill to find Frederick's daughter Elizabeth (aged 81) still living in the old house with her husband Alfred Newcombe. We toured the grounds, looked at the now disused Mill and sat in the kitchen where the author's great great grandfather John (who brought his family to New Zealand) must have sat and eaten meals as a little boy and young man, nearly 150 years ago.

1992... Ownership of Bradwell Mill buildings and land has changed again since Frederick's Will was executed, but is still in family hands with May Verney. Until 1991, her aunt Elizabeth and husband Alfred lived in the old Mill house but soon moved to Ilfracombe. Expenses are high these days and May had the building complex up for sale as none of her children were able, financially or physically, to take over the property themselves.

2000... May has recently advised us that seven acres of the farm land is still theirs, but the house, Mill and other farm buildings have now been sold.

So, after 170 years and six generations of Thomas occupancy.......
Bradwell Mill has left the family.

We acknowledge gratefully the assistance provided by Elizabeth Newcombe and May Verney of Devon, and George Albert Thomas of Auckland, New Zealand in gathering these facts.

1990 ... TREVOR PRICE with PAMELA MORGAN,
ELIZABETH NEWCOMBE & MAY VERNEY in DEVON.

27

FREDERICK PALMER THOMAS
and wife ALICE nee SING
at BRADWELL MILL.

RICHARD, LEONARD and WILLIAM THOMAS
of BRADWELL MILL in Devon.

1918
ELIZABETH THOMAS
(Newcombe) age 9
and
MAY THOMAS
(Verney) age 1

4 GENERATIONS.
JENNIFER, GWEN, MAY and
HELENA THOMAS.

5th Generation ELIZABETH THOMAS
FAMILY TREE of descendants of Elizabeths first son
6th Generation FREDERICK PALMER THOMAS
+++++++++++++++++++++++++++++++++++

FREDERICK PALMER THOMAS ………..…......	married …………….…...	ALICE SING
bapt 18 October 1865	March Q 1893	b
at West Down, Devon	at Barnstaple	at Landcross, Devon
died 13 Oct 1983 (73)		d 13 Nov 1950
bur West Down.		bur West Down

Alice was the daughter of Richard Walter Sing and Ann Brown

Frederick & Alice had 5 children … Richard, William, Walter, Leonard & Elizabeth

+++++++++++++++++++++++++++++++++++

7th Genertion	8th Generation	9th Generation	10th Generation
RICHARD THOMAS b 8 June 1894 at West Down, Deven died 30 March 1983 (89) remained single			
WILLIAM FREDERICK THOMAS b 6 Oct 1895 at West Down, E d 3 Dec 1917 (22) buried at Jerusalum, Israel. WW1. m ========= at Barnstaple HELENA BADDICK b 1888 at Stratton, England d Aug at Woolacoombe, E bur Morthoe, E She was daughter of Elizabeth Baddick they had 1 child, May	BEATRICE <u>MAY</u> THOMAS b 14 May 1917 at West Down, E m ========= at Barnstaple FREDERICK VERNEY b 1 Feb 1916 at Infracombe, E d 30 June 1997 (81) bur Ilfracombe, E He was son of Frederick George Verney they had 7 children Gwen, Patricia, Sheila William, Pamela, Andrew & Kentley	GWEN VERNEY b 13 Dec 1934 at West Down, E m ======== at ROGER AVERY b at Marwood, E PATRICIA VERNEY b 16 Oct 1935 at Ilfracombe, E m ========= at ALAN ROY WHITELOCK b 11 Dec 1933 at Stoke Cannon, E 3 children …	JENNIFER ANN AVERY b at NICHOLAS WHITELOCK b at ELIZABETH WHITELOCK b at REBECCA WHITELOCK b at
		SHEILA VERNEY b 26 March 1936 at West Down continued	RICHARD SMITH b at continued

7th Generation	8th Generation	9th Generation	10th Generation
William & Helena cont.	Frederick & May cont.	Sheila Verney cont	Richard Smith cont.
		m =========	m
		at Stoke Cannon, E	at
		MICHAEL TOM	CATHRYN
		SMITH (Mick)	
		b nov 1930	b
		at Exeter, Devon, E	at
		d June1997 (67)	
		bur	They have twin boys
			11th Generation
		1 child, Richard	b Jan 1992
			PHILLIP &
		WILLIAM	FIONA VERNEY
		FREDERICK	b
		THOMAS VERNEY	at
		b 28 Feb 1942	
		at West Down, E	
		m =========	
		at	
		PAULINE ADAMS	
		b	
		at Newton Abbott, E	
		they had 1 child	
		PAMELA VERNEY	?
		b31 May 1943	MORGAN
		at Wesr Down, E	b
		m 21 Oct	at
		at	
		DAVID MORGAN	?
		b 1 Jan 1942	MORGAN
		at Exeter, E	b
			at
		they had 2 children	
		ANDREW VERNEY	JAMES VERNEY
		b 16 June 1944	b
		at West Down	at
		m =========	
		at	SARA LOUISA
		JILL	VERNEY
		b	b
		at	at

7th Generation	8th Generation	9th Generation	10th Generation
William & Helena cont.	Frederick & May cont.	KENTLEY VERNEY	PAUL VERNY
		b 1 Jan 1951	b
		at West Down, E	at
		m ========	
		at Ilfracombe, E	TONY VERNEY
		PAT COLES	b
		b 18 May 1952	at
		at Ilfracombe. E	
			JOHN VERNEY
			b
			at

WALTER BROWN
THOMAS
b Aug 1901
at West Down, E
d 25 August 1902 (1)
bur West Down, E

LEONARD PALMER
THOMAS
b 2 Dec 1904
at West Down, E
d 25 June 1981 (76)
bur West Down, E
remained single

ELIZABETH THOMAS
b April 1909
at West Down, E
d 6 June 1995
at West Down, E
m July 1934   (both were cremated and ashes acattered
at West Down, E   at Bradwell Mill, just along the road,
ALFRED JAMES   in the field around the christling tree.)
NEWCOMBE
b 13 Jan 1912
at Buckington, E
d 16 June 1951

We are sorry there are so many gaps in this tree.   The family still live in Devon.

We believe this to be a photo of **JOHN THOMAS born 1829** at West Down. We were given this photo during our visit to Bradwell Mill in 1990 by descendant Elizabeth Newcombe nee Thomas. She had been told that this was a photo of one of the two brothers that went to New Zealand..... that is, either John aged 25 or George aged 17. To the author this is a photo of a man much closer to 25 than to 17 years .

The photo was taken in London, we presume just before he departed from England in 1853, and was left with his parents. We wonder if the long side-burns and moustache were fashionable at that time, or, whether he grew these so as to appear older and closer to his wife's age.

CHAPTER THREE

5th Generation

JOHN THOMAS and JANE

1829... BIRTH:

JOHN THOMAS, baptised 22 March 1829 the first child of William Thomas (a Mason) and Elizabeth Lewis. He was named after his maternal grandfather, and baptised in the Church of England at West Down, Devon, England.
John was also a popular Thomas family name.

1841... CENSUS:

He lived all his childhood years at the family home known as Bradwell Mill in the Parish of West Down. He would have attended the School and Church in the West Down township.
In 1841 during the Devonshire Census he was aged 12 and shown as the eldest child of six and already has left school and was working at home.

1848... WEDDING:

In the township of Ilfracombe, Devonshire, on 16 March 1848 **JOHN THOMAS** aged 19 married **JANE COATES** aged 24.
They were married at the Holy Trinity Church of England in Ilfracombe. John's occupation was shown as "Miller".
They had three children...... William, John, and Elizabeth.

The COATES Family ....

JANE was born and baptised at West Down on 19 October 1823, a daughter of farmer **PETER** and **ELIZABETH COATES**. Peter Coates is described as "Yeoman" in our copy of Jane's baptismal record. According to Collin's Dictionary a Yeoman is ... *"A small landowner, a person of middle class engaged in Agriculture, a Farmer."*

Jane's baptism and death certificates spell the name, Coats. and a NZ Grand child was given the name spelt Coates. It would appear as if either form of spelling is acceptable.

More Coates family information on page 56.

The 1887 "Gazetteer of the British Isles" describes Ilfracombe as "an Urban District, Parish, Seaport and Market -town, with a Railway Station,

35

Ilfracombe, c. 1899

15000

Lower photo **ILFRACOMBE ... 1990**
Looking across the inner harbour at St Nicholas Seaman's Chapel
and the Lighthouse built in 1320, on the hill.

ILFRACOMBE CHURCH OF ENGLAND
Exterior and Interior ... 1990.

and Lifeboat Station, on the Bristol Channel, 14 miles North West of Barnstaple, having 5627 acres and a population of 9275. It is an ecclesiastical district of Holy Trinity. It's Lighthouse of 29 foot height has a fixed light 127 feet above high water that can be seen from five miles."

The Directory "White's Devon of 1850" records on page 594 .....
       `JOHN THOMAS-- Flour Miller-- of Fore Street.'

1851...CENSUS:
This shows our family has grown and that they have left West Down and are now living in the Ilfracombe Township.
Census District 295/4 Ilfracombe, Page 25, Item 97 shows that living in rented rooms at Sea View House in Fore Street, Ilfracombe were:-
        JOHN THOMAS .. Head of house. 29 yrs. Born at West Down.
                           Occupation ...... Miller, employing one man.
        JANE THOMAS .. Wife. 26 yrs. Born at West Down.
        WILLIAM THOMAS .. Son. 2 yrs. Born at Ilfracombe.

        For some reason they lied about their ages.
        John was actually aged 22 and Jane now 27 and a half.
John and Jane had a second son born 1st May 1851, some four weeks after this Census was taken, whom they named JOHN THOMAS.
This John Thomas came to New Zealand with his parents in 1855 when aged 4 and later married Phebe Woods. (This book contains John's life story, and brother William's life story is in another book "William Thomas and Family")
At the beginning of the 1851 Census details, there was a description of the district. It read :-- *"All that part of the town of Ilfracombe which lies between the Millhead and the Barnstaple Inn, including the North side of Fore Street, from the Millhead to the Bank."*

SEA VIEW HOUSE:
We visited Ilfracombe in 1990 and from this Census detail were able to locate Sea View House which was still there. Above the Fore Street doorway was a small sign ... "SEA VIEW HOUSE...erected 1700".
Our page 39 photo shows this four story, tall narrow building, which operated as a boarding house or series of small apartments in 1851. Also can be seen are the 1990 road markings which lead down to Millhead Lane. This was their home for 6 years 1848 to 1854. John Thomas had only a short walk to his place of employment. The Mill was situated immediately below and behind Sea View

House. In 1990 the present owner showed us a photo of the exterior of the Mill, as it was years ago... a round-fronted building with "TOWN FLOUR MILLS" written above the windows of the Milling-room. He showed us the location of the Water Race and Mill Pond sites, still partially visible. We stood in the circular milling-room where John would have ground grain 140 years ago, but now is the present owner's lounge.

SEA VIEW HOUSE .... erected 1700

1854...EMIGRATION:,

JOHN and JANE THOMAS and family emigrated to New Zealand during the years 1854-5.

They may have seen the New Zealand Company's advertisement on page 56.

John Thomas (25) came first, arriving at Wellington on board the `Duke of Portland' on 12 February 1854. He obviously found work, liked the country and got word back to Devon, because his wife Jane (34) together with their children William (6) and John (4) and John's younger brother George Thomas (17) arrived at Wellington on board the `Sea Snake' on 25 May 1855.

Unfortunately, both the official sets of shipping papers have been lost to time but some of the passenger's names were recorded in the local newspaper.

THE DUKE OF PORTLAND.

One of the finest sailing ships sent out to New Zealand in the early fifties was the 533 ton, ash timbered ship, *Duke of Portland*, which brought many honoured passengers to New Zealand, including Bishop Selwyn and Mrs. Selwyn, who landed at Auckland in 1855.

The *Duke of Portland* made her first appearance in the colony in 1851.

In **1854** the ship, under the command of Captain Seymour, with cargo and 48 passengers, made the record passage to between Plymouth and Nelson ... 88 days. She sailed from Plymouth on the 19th November, 1853, crossed the equator on December 1st, rounded the Cape 26 days later, and made the New Zealand coast at Cascade Point, South Island, on the last day in January—82 days from Plymouth, arriving at Nelson on the 5th February, and reaching Wellington on 12 February 1854.   (Wings V11)

"The NZ Spectator & Cook's Strait Guardian"

The *"Duke of Portland"*
Details in issue
15 Feb 1854.

Same day—Ship *Duke of Portland*, 800 tons, Seymour, from London, via Nelson. Passengers—Rev. A. Baker, Miss Brett, Messrs. C. J. Hewson, J. Ferrie, B. Wilson, Miss Greenhead, Miss Matthews, Miss M. Carner, Mr. and Mrs. Fox, Mr. J. F. Hodgkin, Mr. and Mrs. Burney, two Misses Reid, Mr. and Mrs. Brown, Messrs. W. Pharco, J. Thomas, and 25 in the steerage.

----->

"The NZ Spectator & Cook's Strait Guardian"

The *"Sea Snake"*
Details in issue
26 May 1855.

----->

ARRIVALS.
May 24—Barque *Douglass*, Hedgcock, from Geelong.
May 25—Ship *Sea Snake*, 500 tons, Gilbert, from London and Otago. Passengers—Mr. J. Bennett, Mr. and Mrs. Deacon, Mr. J. Deacon, A. M'Kay, Miss E. Miller, Mr. J. Laing, Miss E. Scally, Jane Thomas, W., J., and G. Thomas, Mr. and Mrs. Ward and 2 children, Mr. A Todd and 2 children.

The *Sea Snake* left London on 6 January 1855 and arrived at Dunedin on 21st April where a considerable amount of her cargo was unloaded.

The 19 passengers were all bound for Wellington and finally disembarked on 25 May 1855 after a trip of 129 days. She was skippered by Captain Gilbert and was a metal sheathed ship of 500 tons.

--ooOOoo--

WELLINGTON:

The 5 members of the Thomas family arrived in NZ February 1854 and May 1855. We do not know how long the family lived in Wellington or where else they lived and worked for the next four years. Father John must have visited Auckland and picked a site for his Four Mill, then they moved to Auckland.

MAP of AUCKLAND

AUCKLAND MAP showing............

A....Site of the STAR FLOUR MILL
    and two houses, and across the road
    the Mill Dam on the Oakley Creek.
    See pages 44, 69, 72.

B...Thomas Channel refer page 47

C...George's Homesite for 20 years

D...George's 8 Acres in Whau

E...George's Rosebank Rd section

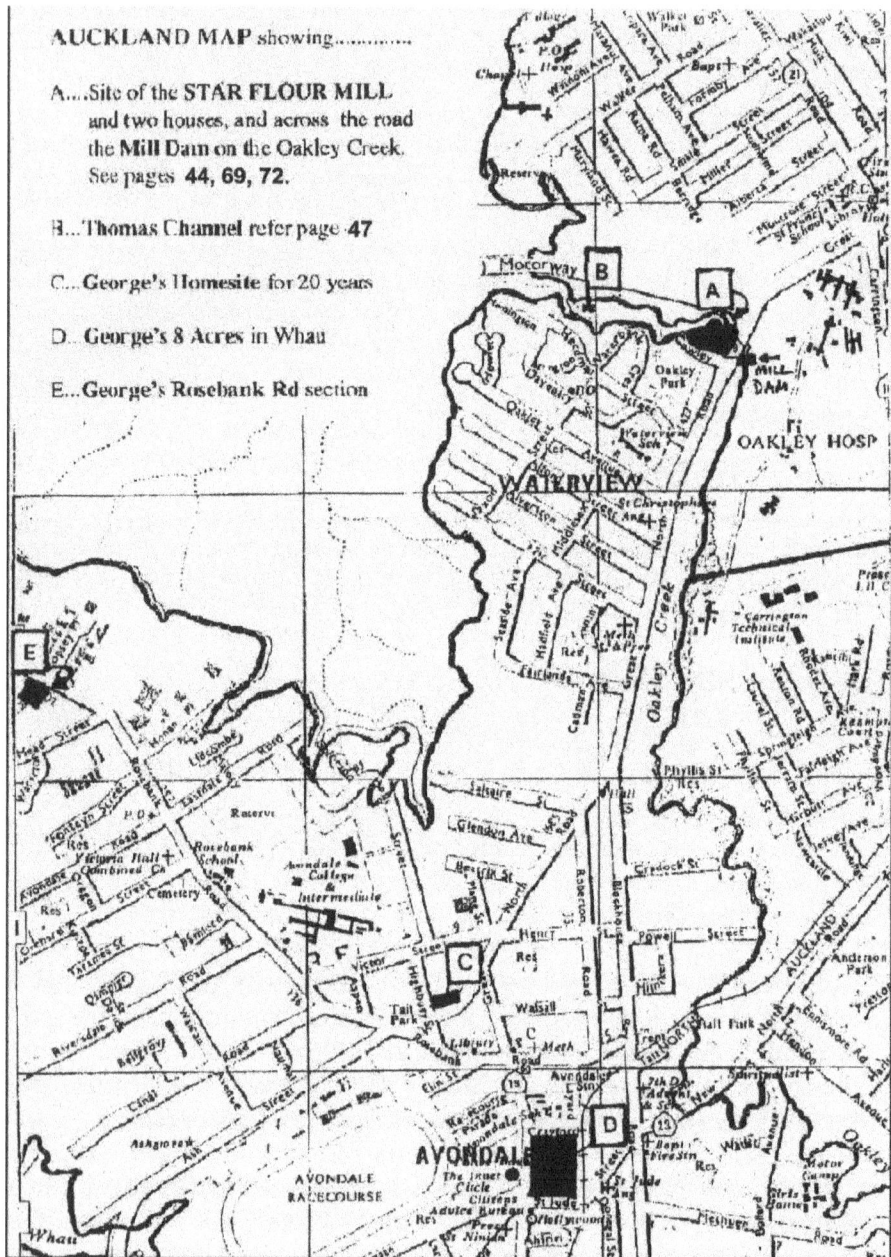

AUCKLAND: The WHAU District.

1859... We first find John Thomas and family living in Auckland beside the Oakley Creek, Whau, in 1859.

John & Jane's third child was born at Whau in March 1859, John became owner of the Oakley Creek land in April 1859, and brother George was married at Whau in July 1860.

John and Jane and brother George may have shifted to Auckland for employment, for better climatic conditions or to escape the Wellington district's frequently occuring earthquakes of that period.

Maybe John and Jane went directly to Auckland, because John had found a good spot to erect his flour mill. At 17 George probably stayed with them.

The Whau name changed between the elections of 1884 and 1887 to Avondale but it remained an independent Borough until amalgamation with Auckland City in 1927.

In the 1860's the road from Auckland to the Whau Village was unmetalled and when travellers arrived they went there by foot or on horseback to the houses and farms.

1875: The Whau district of Auckland was described in the 1875/6 Wises NZ Directory and a reduced version follows.....

"The Whau Village is 6 miles from Auckland on the Great North Road. Another road via Mt Albert Highway connects it with the Mt Eden side of Auckland. A Presbyterian Church is in the center of town and the Episcopalian Church meets in the Public Hall which was built in 1864. The school has a roll of fifty pupils and two teachers. There is a Hotel providing accommodation.

The Whau Creek is navigable to small vessels and on it's banks the manufacture of bricks, tiles and pottery is carried on. There are 3 stores, a Carpenter, two Smithy shops, Messrs Gitto's Tannery and the Star Flour Mill.

A train does the Auckland to Whau trip once a day each way via Great North Road, and an omnibus twice each way via Mt Albert. The land provides large quantities of butter, potatoes and oaten hay and the view from the rising ground beyond the township is one of the sweetest English and homelike scenes."

1859... ELIZABETH:

On the 1st March 1859 John and Jane Thomas' third child was born, at Oakley Creek, Whau, a district near Auckland. She was named after both her grand-mothers. John registered her and spelled Jane's maiden name as Coates. He also gave his occupation as Miller. (The Star Flour Mill)

1859... AUCKLAND LAND: 20 April Purchase...DEED 9D:389 #15423.

Before the early months of 1859 John Thomas (a Miller) had searched for and negotiated to buy some land in Auckland, as, registered in his name on 20th April was the purchase of Part Lot 18A measuring 3 acres and 10 perches and Part Lots 31, 32, 33. John paid 195 pounds for the nearly 8 acres of land situated beside the Oakley Creek and the Great North Road on the border of Whau and the Point Chevalier districts of Auckland. (location map on page 42)
(Today in 1993 the land is in the Auckland City suburb of Waterview.)

John erected a home here for his family. He also erected a Dam on the Oakley Creek, and down-stream and beside the creek he erected his Grain/Flour Mill. He built it four stories high and of similar operating design as his father's mill in Devon where he learnt the milling trade.
He traded under the name "STAR MILL."

We were advised in Devon in 1990 by descendants of the family still living at Bradwell Mill, *"that the brothers in New Zealand (or one of them) had sent out to NZ, a Water Wheel produced in Barnstaple of similar construction to that used at Bradwell Mill."*

1859... Mortgage...,,DEED 6M:400 #15424.

Also on the same date (20 April) John handed over 20 pounds and signed a Mortgage for 175 pounds, with the land's seller Andrew Rooney.
The document states *"..agree to pay the sum of 175 pounds on the 1st January 1864 with interest thereon in the meantime commencing from 1st January last at the rate of 8 pounds 10 shillings per centum per annum, (8.5% PA) payable half yearly, the first payment to be made on the 1st July next."*

1860... 26 January...,,DEED 6M:793 #16280
"The original Mortgage, principal and interest and costs due having been fully paid and satisfied..." the property was transferred into John's name.
However he immediately remortgaged it.

We feel the 175 pounds of the original mortgage was not enough to cover costs to erect all the Mill and housing needs he had.

44

1860... Mortgage...DEED 6M:793 #16281.

"All land with all buildings thereon erected.... also all the Machinery and Mill stones in and about the Mill erected upon the land hereby conveyed ....remortgaged for the sum of 450 pounds until 25 January 1863 with interest of (12.5% PA) paid quarterly."

Another addition to the mortgage was ... *"during the continuance of this security keep the buildings comprised ... insured against damage by fire to the amount of 300 pounds at least, with the New Zealand Insurance Co or other....and within 7 days after each premium shall become due, will deliver the receipt to Andrew Rooney."*

1860... ADVERTISEMENT advises the mill is open for business (see p 304)

A H WALKER... Author.

In *"The Story of Pt Chevalier 1861-1961,"* A H Walker mentions John Thomas and the Star Mill quite a lot. Included here are excerpts which we are most grateful he recorded and for the research time he put in.

1860... OAKLEY CREEK:

Oakley Creek was named after Mr Edwin Oakley, a civil engineer who advocated utilizing the fresh water creek as a source of the water supply for Auckland. Mr Walker advises that *"In 1860 a prize of 50 pounds was offered by the Provincial Council for the best design of a water supply for the growing city. Four were submitted...and after considerable discussion and investigation the prize went to Mr Stewart for his Onehunga scheme. Both the Western Springs and the Oakley Creek schemes had almost equal merit, but the biggest obstacle to their acceptance was the amount of compensation which would have had to be paid to either Low & Motions or to John Thomas for the loss of power for their Mills."*

> This must have been an anxious time for John Thomas... wondering whether he did or didn't have a business.

THOMAS FLOUR MILL:

In the "New Zealander" on 27 April 1861 an article written by J C Loch described all he saw on a trip from Queen St Auckland, out the Great North Road to Henderson and on passing John Thomas flour mill he says.....

..."*We then passed over the Oakley Creek with it's sparkling waters high on either bank and Thomas' Mill, for whose special use it's aqueous treasures have been hoarded up."*

FIRST BORN:

At one point Walker records that *"In the middle 1860's residents of Pt Chevalier were the Walkers, Dignan, Blagrove, Thomas (Star Mill) and Josiah Dell."* He also felt that the first white children born in the district were Thomas, Richard and Elizabeth Walker. However the Walkers did not settle here until new years day of 1861 and were not to know that John and Jane Thomas of the Star Flour Mill had enjoyed the arrival of their daughter Elizabeth on 1st March 1859 and whose birth certificate clearly mentions her birth place......Oakley Creek.

MILL SITE:

Walker described the position of the mill as...

"On the bank of the Oakley Creek John Thomas erected a flour mill, just to the right of the bridge which crosses the creek when traveling towards Waterview, using the water coming though the Mental Hospital grounds for driving the water wheels."

THOMAS CHANNEL:

The roads at the time were almost non existent and Mr Walker mentions them as... *"no more than rough tracks"* and that *"during the middle 1860's and 1890's the upper harbour must have been a very busy sea lane. The many brickyards and lime kilns on the Whau and Henderson Creeks were all operated by sea transport. Thomas' Mill on the Oakley Creek was also worked in this way and hence the name 'Thomas Channel' which runs past the end of the shell bank and which was sealed off when the northern motorway was formed a few years ago.."*

Thomas Channel allowed the Mill's own boat and the customers' boats to enter the lower tidal waters of the Oakley Creek to deliver wheat and coal etc to the Mill and to collect the Mill's finished product for delivery to its customers.

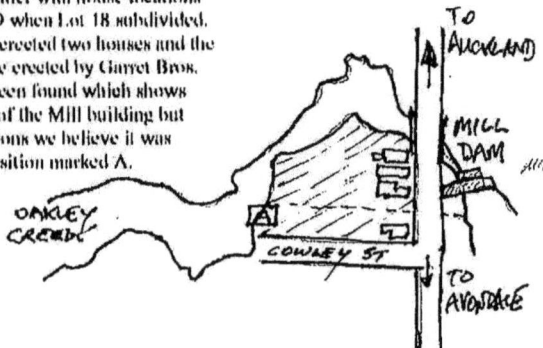

STAR FLOUR MILL SITE.
Lot 18a (3 acres) on Oakley Creek
and bounded by Oakley Avenue
(now Cowley St) and Great North Rd.

We have joined the original 1859 plan showing the Mill Dam on Lots 31, 32, 33 (4 acres), together with house locations shown in 1949 when Lot 18 subdivided. John Thomas erected two houses and the other two were erected by Garret Bros. No plan has been found which shows the exact site of the Mill building but from descriptions we believe it was sited at the position marked A.

1864... BRICK BURNER sought for John Thomas' brick-yard.   (see p 305)

1864... COURT CASE John Thomas V Jeremiah Casey, re lost wheat. (p 305)

1864... The Whau Public Hall was opened on the 14th Nov and a good account of the occasion is recorded in the "Daily Southern Cross" newspaper.

1865... 21 February... **DEED** 11M:72 #28831.
On this date John fully paid off Andrew Rooney's Mortgage and the land was once again debt free but only for a few minutes as John took out another Mortgage that day.

1865... Mortgage... **DEED** 11M:72 #28832.
New Mortgage from David Nathan, Auckland Merchant, of 350 pounds until 21 February 1867 plus interest at 12.5% PA payable quarterly.

BRICKS & MAORI WAR:

In his book *'The City of Auckland'* John Barr wrote…
"During the years 1863-64 the entire adult male population of Auckland was enlisted for compulsory service in the militia, volunteers or fire brigade, and had to undergo military training. … On 22 July 1863 the Auckland First Class Militia and Volunteers joined the force and did duty on the Wairoa River. In February 1864 the Second Class of Militia, comprising business and trades-people were ordered onto active service."

In 1863 the Government set aside land for the Auckland Mental Hospital. Building of the hospital was completed in 1867.

1864... Jan 5th: During the non-harvesting period, the flour milling business must have been too quiet for John Thomas for we found Mr A H Walker producing detail of our John making bricks.... *"In 1864 John Thomas successfully tendered for the making and supply of bricks for the erection of the new Mental Hospital,* (on the other side of Oakley Creek from Star Mill. T) *his price of £3- 16 shillings per thousand, being 18 shillings less than the next tender."*

Dulcie Twizell (nee Dove), John Thomas' great granddaughter, helped us locate four items referring to the brick contract, at the Auckland Library.

1. A copy of John Thomas' Letter of Tender, dated 5 January 1864 and showing an address of *'Oakley's Creek'*. In it John states….. *"I have no bricks to deposit as sample but would guarantee them as good and suitable quality…"*

2. A copy of a letter from Robert Graham, Superintendent of the Auckland Provincial Council of 11 January 1864, which reads in part ….

"I have the honour to inform you that your tender for supply of bricks for the new Lunatic Asylum has been accepted…"

3. A copy of the Contract Bond document dated 20 January 1864 including a completion date of seven and a half months.

4. A copy of the December 1863 detailed Brick Specification written by James Wrigley the Architect, which our John agreed to meet.

Mr Walker continues… *"Mr Thomas entered into a contract to supply 900,000 bricks at a rate of 180,000 per month for five months. The bricks were made at the present day (1961) entrance to the Northern motorway. He was under a penalty if he failed to fulfil his undertaking and this clause in the contract read… 'If the contractor fails to deliver the bricks as specified, the Superintendent of the Provincial Government, through Mr Wrigley the Architect, have the power to purchase bricks elsewhere and charge the difference to the contractor'."*

"Mr Thomas also ordered machinery for making bricks from Vickery, Masefield Co, prominent Auckland engineers at that time."

"The Maori War was at its height… and after supplying the first monthly quota, Thomas, his foreman, and four workers were called for military service."

(A lot of time has been spent trying to find where our Thomas men served but with no result. **We think they probably qualified as Second Class Militia, called up in February 1864, but no proof can be found.** Unless they were required to mill or bake bread then sons William (aged 15) and John (aged 13) may not have been called up as the age limit was 18 to 60.)

In *"Armed Settlers"* by H C M Norris we found this comment…
"The Militia of the Second Class were allotted duties in the town, but most of the other militia and the volunteers were sent on active service."

The 3 February 1864 *New Zealand Herald* issue states…
"100 Second Class Militia left that afternoon for duties at Otahuhu".

Did they carry guns? The Second Class Militia did not. It seems that had our men carried guns and gone in to battle, they would have been eligible for the New Zealand War Medal and none of our Thomas names appear on that list.

Did they work in the Ngaruawahia flour mills? John's brother George's descendants tell us that *"George set up a mill and bakery at the junction of the Waikato and Waipa Rivers at Ngaruawahia to bake bread for the Red Coat soldiers and the Maori they were fighting."*

(No known 'Thomas mill' was ever at Ngaruawahia, but brother George could well have set up and managed one of the flour mills there at that site.   T)

(Mr Walker continues…) *"When their term of service was completed, Mr Thomas found that the architect had purchased 500,000 bricks from Pollen's yard on the Whau Creek and 100,000 from Boyd's Grey Lynn works at a price of 18 shillings above his contract price. His guarantors, Messrs Macky and Thomas Milne Machattie, Merchants of Auckland, who had given bond of £500 had received payment for the first consignment, less the extra money that had been paid to the other suppliers. Messrs Vickery, Masefield had been unable to supply the brick making plant as they had to fulfil urgent Government orders for the steamers on the Waikato River, which were required to facilitate the movement of troops. This work could not therefore be postponed."*

"Mr Thomas petitioned the Provincial Government for some relief," His Petition number 44, was first heard in Session 18, October 1864. (Only newspaper records available. T)
Mr Walker continues… *"stating, the Superintendent Mr Robert Graham, had given him an undertaking to see that he and his workers would be exempt from militia duties."*

His petition stated… *"That owing to loss of time sustained by your Petitioner and his Servants on account of such Militia duties and the no- supply of machinery as agreed upon by Vickery, Masefield, your petitioner lost the benefit of the fine weather, and was driven into the winter, before he was able to make any progress, whereby your Petitioner has been unable to fulfil his contract."*

The *New Zealand Herald* on 8 March 1967 produced an article written by E.W.G. Craig celebrating 100 years of existence for Oakley Hospital. (formerly known as the Auckland Asylum.) In part he wrote… *"Mr Thomas had to forfeit £497. He petitioned the Government, only to be told that the Government's needs had been a matter of life and death, while his problems affected only himself."*

Mr Walker continues… *"The hearing of the appeal was a long drawn out affair, several witnesses were called and just as the enquiry was terminating, John Thomas died suddenly at his mill on 5 April 1865. The strain and worry had taken its toll and he died at the age of 36, leaving a wife and young family.*

When finally the Auckland Provincial Government released its findings it granted £ 250 to the wife and family of the deceased, stating that the unfortunate Mr Thomas had met with unexpected and unavoidable difficulties in the execution of his contract."
(End of quote) (see p307)

--ooo0ooo--

TIME AT WAR:

The contract to supply the bricks was signed 20 January 1864. John supplied the first 180,000 bricks. The Second Class Militia were called up early in February 1864. John petitioned the Government in October 1864. This leaves eight months, less time to supply the final 120,000 bricks, time to take advice from his guarantors, time to prepare his petition and time to await the date set down for the hearing of the petition. We believe John Thomas and his four men served time-at-war of five to maybe six months.

1865... DEATH: The Weekly News, 8 April on page 8 advised everyone ....

"John Thomas died aged 35 at his residence 'STAR MILLS.'

Medically he died of Dysentery, and had lived 11 years in NZ.
Son William was aged 16, son John 14 and daughter Elizabeth aged 6.
His funeral costs included Dr Aickin's fee £ 9-15 shillings, 2 nurses
for £ 5, his Undertakers Carson and McCulsky charged £ 32-5/-
and £ 27 was spent on 'Mourning and Refreshments' at his funeral.

No Will was found, and John was declared Intestate.
The family stayed on at Oakley Creek and milled flour for the next five years.
> The next record of property transfer occurred in 1870
> when son William turned 21 years of age.
John Thomas died during the course of Mortgage 11M:72 #28832.
Who ran the mill during this period?   Who was legally responsible?

With John's death, the Mortgagor, David Nathan would have reconsidered his mortgage. He seems to have taken a kindly view to the family and extended his mortgage until William's birthday in 1870.

THOMAS BARRACLOUGH:

Tom lived nearby and was a close friend of John and Jane's. We think that whilst still operating his Oakley Creek Store he may have became an 'on site' financial and business adviser to Jane and her young sons William and John, until uncle George Thomas became available for the Mill's management.
However, we have found Thomas Barraclough ('Engine Fitter') married Jane in 1867 and, in 1870 became a Miller and Mill Engineer and was a one third shareholder in the business.

50

By July 1865 brother George seems to have moved from his home in Napier St, Auckland, to the Star Flour Mill site, as this is the address he gave at that time. We think the family must have decided that John's two sons would take over the mill when legally old enough, and that brother George supplied his labour and milling knowledge for the operation of the mill. He would have prepared his 16 and 14 year old nephews for ownership.

The records show that George received wages and we feel he became the Manager of the Mill. We have found no evidence that George had any financial interest in the mill until much later ... until 1874 when he purchased the Star Mill from his nephews.

1865... JOHN's WILL: (Part 1)
25 April 1865. A statement signed by Jane Thomas to the Supreme Court of New Zealand, accompanied what Jane believed to be John's last Will dated 4 April 1865, (the day before he died,) which appointed her executrix of his estate, thought to have a value of not more than $ 2,800. On the same date a sworn statement from a merchant named Thomas Milne Machattie of Auckland, declared that he knew John Thomas when he was alive.

3 June 1865.
Another sworn statement signed by Jane, accompanied an 'Inventory of Assets' and

Jane Thomas

values seem to have been overstated at $ 1,800, covering debts owing to the company $ 400, machinery to make bricks $ 300, bricks $ 400, wheat and flour $ 450, third share of cargo boat $ 100, horses, drays etc $ 150.

Jane pleaded for authority to (a) collect the debts owed, (b) sell the bricks and (c) sell the wheat and flour... *"as I believe the same will sustain great damage and deterioration in value by keeping and that it would be greatly for the benefit of the estate that the same should immediately be sold and disposed of."*
She advised the court that *"John has left her and three children surviving who are of the respective ages of 16, 14 and 6 years".*

It appears the 25 April statement and Will were not proved to the court's satisfaction, as in this document Jane said she believed he left a Will in England and that she had done all in her power to obtain that Will and hoped... *"it will be forwarded to New Zealand in the course of a few months."*

10 June 1865. Success at last. Another paper shows that Jane was given Court authority to administer John's estate (ie, collect the debts and sell the stock) until the Will of John Thomas could be produced and proven.

However, two sureties had to be sworn.

11 July 1865. An official Document of Bond shows that Jane, plus T M Machattie and George Thomas (John's brother) were bound to the Registrar of the Supreme Court for the sum of £ 5,600 (three times the estate value) as security for the administration of the estate. They had to produce an Inventory before 10 September 1865 when Jane would be eligible to commence the administration of the estate. She also agreed to supply the court with an account of actions taken for the estate, by 10 June 1866.

(Neither of these reports have survived to the year 2000.)

Continues in later entry… **28 May 1870** … (JOHN's WILL: (Part 2)

1865… Five acre **ALLOTMENT SALE mention's** the Star Flour Mill. (see p 306)

1865… BRICK YARD TO LET at Oakley Creek, 4 miles from town. (see p 306)

1867… FLOUR COSTS:

On 2 November 1867 the newspaper, *Daily Southern Cross* recorded the wholesale prices for flour… *"Imported flour from Adelaide £15 per ton, and from Chile and California £13 per ton. Local miller's price. First quality £15 a ton,   Seconds at £ 11 for one ton and Sharps … £7 per ton.   Baker's price per pound weight = 3 pence, baker's bread 2lb loaf = 4 pence."*

1867… MARRIAGE:

On 29 August, Jane aged 44, a widow for two years and with children aged 18, 16 and 8, married Yorkshire man Thomas Barraclough aged 35, at the dwelling house of Rev. J Wallis in Newton, Auckland. They had a child.

At Oakley Creek, on 14 January 1869, Jane (now aged 45) and Tom had a son they named Thomas Coates Barraclough. Thanks to research by Carina Bowring, Joan Bridges and Linda Gomas, we have learnt that young T. C. Barraclough sadly died aged 6, during 1875 in Melbourne, Australia.

Thomas Barrac lough was mentioned in the Raglan Electoral Rolls for 1869/70 giving an address of 'Oakley's Creek' and in the Rates Assessment for the Whau district 1868 and again in 1869. He paid rates on two acres of Lot 18A at 12 pence per acre, a total of 2 Shillings (20 cents) each year.

1873: It seems Jane and Tom Barraclough's marriage broke up in 1873.

Tom remarried in Onehunga on 23 December 1873 and shifted to Melbourne with a younger lady named Charlotte Cutter nee Kendall, taking his son Thomas and probably Jane's share of the Mill money. This will be one of the reasons why the Star Flour Mill was sold in September 1874 with Tom wanting out and wishing to sell his share of the property and business.

Charlotte, a coloured South African, born in Capetown, had given James Cutter three children and with Tom she had four more, the last in 1880.
Charlotte died aged 35 on 28 February 1882 at Euroa, Victoria, Australia.

Tom died at Euroa, aged 56 in August 1888 after a fourth marriage.

1870... Son WILLIAM married ELIZA McKAY in May in Auckland.

28 May 1870... JOHN's WILL: (Part 2)
There is no knowledge of the English Will ever being produced to the court.
Three pages of Inventory and Final Account of the Assets and Disburse-ments of the £ 1,398 Estate of John Thomas, prepared for the Court on 28 May and signed by Jane Barraclough. They show the wheat and flour sold to I. S. Macfarlane & Co. Henderson & Macfarlane bought the third share in the cargo boat, George Thomas and the Workmen received wages, the Ironmonger and the Saddler were paid, and large debts due to I. S. Macfarlane, Henderson & Macfarlane and Alfred Buckland were paid.

GRIST MILL:
In 1870, John Thomas' sons, who then owned and operated the Mill, described the mill as a Grist Mill. *"the only grist mill in Auckland."*
A Grist Mill, was explained in the *Auckland Star* 11 May 1887 as..."*generally the first type of mill to be established, with local farmers having their flour ground by the mill, the Miller taking one tenth of the flour or charging about one shilling per bushel. These mills usually only worked during the harvesting season to satisfy the needs of the rural population. They were mostly small, water powered mills run by the Miller and one or two assistants.*"

1870... STAR MILL:
The story of the Star Flour Mill continues from page 69, 70-----.
Son William must have worked at the mill in his late teenage years but developed a liking for carpentry. His son Jack told his son-in-law George Wright, he worked for some time at the Wheelwright's Shop situated on Great North Rd opposite the Auckland Asylum. Most records show he took very little part in the Star Flour Mill's operation after his marriage but continued to hold his share of the investment until the mill was sold in 1874.

1870... George Thomas' advertisement for **NEW SEEDS** ... on 10 March & 3 October.

1870... **13 July MAIZE MEAL** ... (p308) Thomas & Barraclough advertisemnt.

1870... **STAR MILL:** 15 Oct 1870 advertisement ....

1871... **FIRST GRANDCHILD for JANE:** Elizabeth Jane (Lizzie) Thomas was born 14 February to William and Eliza at Oakley Creek.

1872... Son **JOHN married PHEBE WOODS,** December at Whau. Details (pages 69 & 308)

1873... **MAIZE MEAL PRIZE**
21 June. Thomas & Barraclough won a prize for their Maize Meal entry at the Auckland Market-house opening exhibition. (*Daily Southern Cross.*)

1874... Thomas & Barraclough **DISOLVE PARTNERSHIP** and Barraclough with new wife Charlotte, sail to Australia. (p305)

1877... Son JOHN and family **LEFT AUCKLAND** for the South Island.

1878... Daughter **ELIZABETH married JAMES HILL** in May at Auckland.

1893... **JANE DIED:**
Jane died in Auckland a widow on 25 July 1893 aged 72....
at the Costley Home in Epsom. Jane's death certificate is in the Thomas name and her Barraclough name is not mentioned on that document.

      Costley Home was erected with funds bequeathed by Mr E Costley and was opened on 23 April 1890 for Auckland's 'Aged Poor' administered by the Auckland Hospital Board. It is possible that Jane was a 'founder inmate' because at the National Archives in Auckland we found a set of minute books for Costley Home starting at July 1890. It seems the inmates gave the home everything they possessed (even rings) and the Hospital Board provided for them, for the rest of their lives. A committee met once a month to arrange staff hire, wages (the cook earned 30/- [£1.10/- or $3] a week in 1892), they reviewed inmate's eligibility to stay, and to approve expenditure. The only item that mentioned (Jane) Thomas was on 29 March 1893, four months before she died. The committee authorised *"the purchase of material for white washing and timber (?) for beds, as recommended by Sister King for inmates Thomas, Oates and Hurley."*

(Photo Costley Home see p307)

Jane Thomas was buried at Grafton Cemetery, Auckland.

We have not been able to locate either John or Jane's grave site due to the fact that around 1930 the Grafton Cemetery records were destroyed by fire. In recent years the Auckland motorway has carved through Grafton Gully and a lot of the graves had to be shifted. Before this happened the authorities had every grave site drawn in a plan and all legible names recorded from headstones still standing. Unfortunately less than one third of the sites were able to be recorded and John and Jane's names are not amongst them.

We have also searched records at 'Waikumete', 'Purewa' and 'Rosebank' Cemeteries operating at that time and unfortunately they are not there.

Jane died one year after sons William and John sold their Allenton Nursery. At that stage they were extremely short of cash and daughter Elizabeth was married with two children, somewhere on a farm. We do not think Jane's children abandoned her but it would appear she took poorly at a time when none of her children were able to assist her financially.

--oo0Ooo—

We continue with detail of…

wife **JANE'S ……. COATES** and **CHAPPELL** families on pages 56 to 59.

then **JOHN & JANE THOMAS' THREE CHILDREN**

ELIZABETH THOMAS page 66.

WILLIAM THOMAS   A brief summary page 60. His life and descendants are fully documented in the book…   *"WILLIAM THOMAS & family"*.

JOHN THOMAS   Chapter Four starting page 68.

Information concerning the life and descendants of John's brother **GEORGE THOMAS** are fully detailed starting page 210 in this book..

--oo0Ooo--

The COATES family of North Devon.

There always seems to have been people named Coats or Coates, living in the north Devon parishes of West Down, Ilfracombe and Georgeham. There are quite a lot of people named Peter, John and Elizabeth Coates and the records prior to 1700 are very faint and almost unreadable. We are still researching this name but feel confident that our lineage is as follows...

PETER COATS, born in the late 1600's, had a son PETER in 1715.

PETER COATS junior, was baptised 18 January 1715 at Ilfracombe, he married **ELIZABETH FLEMING** on 11 December 1753 at West Down.

Elizabeth was baptised 1 May 1725 at West Down, the daughter of Charles Fleming of West Down. She died 8 August 1792 and buried at West Down.
Peter and Elizabeth Coates had four children that we have discovered .....

JOHN	baptised 31 July 1754 at West Down.
ALICE	baptised 9 February 1758 at West Down.
	(She may have married Richard Chugg in 1774)
JULIAN	baptised 8 June 1760 at West Down.
ELIZABETH	baptised 14 July 1764 at West Down.
	(She may have married William Heddon in 1784)

JOHN COATES was baptised 31 July 1754 at West Down and
married **ELIZABETH LAWRENCE** on 28 February 1775 at Ilfracombe.
Elizabeth Lawrence was baptised 16 December 1749 at
Ilfracombe, daughter of Richard Lawrence and Elizabeth
Chugg who married 16 Februarry 1747 at Ilfracombe.
More detail of Elizabeth Chugg's family ... see page 55 .....

John and Elizabeth had seven children all baptised at West Down. (WD)

PETER	baptised 6 August 1776.
RICHARD	baptised 28 May 1778.
ELIZABETH	baptised 12 June 1780.
MARY	baptised 25 October 1782.
JOHN	bapt 25 May 1784, died 28 Sept 1784, buried WD.
GILLIAN	bapt 19 Jan 1786, died 2 Nov 1789 buried WD.
JANE	baptised 7 June 1788.

ELIZABETH CHUGG was the eighth and final child of William and Joan Chugg of Ilfracombe. Their children were Mary baptised 27 February 1696, Jane 7 May 1698, John 29 July 170, Edward 17 August 1702, Pruscilla 3 September 1704, Joane 4 March 1706, Thomasine 1 May 1709 and Elizabeth baptised 8 May 1711. At the time of the baptism registration of the first seven children, their mother's name was spelt Joane, however her name was spelt 'Joan' when daughter Elizabeth's baptism was recorded.

      Father William died 8 April 1747. Buried at Ilfracombe Church-yard.

      Mother Joan died 17 April 1758 and is buried with her husband.

PETER COATES was baptised 6 August 1776 at West Down. He described himself as 'Yeoman of Georgeham'. Aged 36 he married ELIZABETH CHAPPELL (27) 11 April 1812 at Church of England in Fremington, Devon. Elizabeth was the first daughter of George Chappell's second wife Susanna, and was baptised 11 November 1783 at Fremington.

A brief CHAPPELL TREE follows on page 57.

Peter and Elizabeth Coates had seven children …

HANNAH	bapt 25 April	1813 at Georgeham.
ELIZA	bapt 23 October	1814 at Georgeham.
PETER	bapt 16 June	1816 at " (he died 4 August 1853.)
SUSANNA	bapt 25 May	1818 at West Down.
JOHN	bapt 1 August	1819 at West Down.
MARY	bapt 21 October	1821 at West Down.
JANE	bapt 19 October	1823 at West Down.

Jane married JOHN THOMAS at Ilfracombe
on 16 March 1848 and they later came to New Zealand.

In the 1841 Census, Peter Coates, 65, listed himself as 'Independent'. His wife Elizabeth, son Peter (Agricultural Labourer) and daughter Mary lived on Dean Farm. All the other children had left home.

The only Jane Coates of the correct age in this Census, a servant on a farm named 'Tarak', for Sarah Howard 'farmer'. Sarah's 4 year old daughter Mary.

Father Peter Coates died aged 69, at Dean Farm on 18 December 1845 and is buried at West Down.

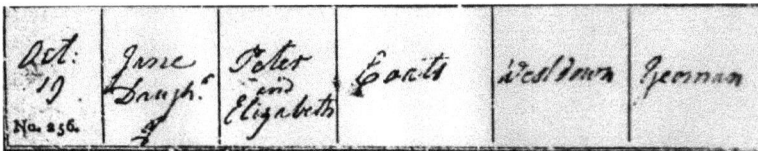

1823 West Down baptismal record of JANE COATS.

57

New Zealand Company advertisement to entice people to New Zealand from England, Wales, Scotland & Ireland.

EMIGRATION
TO
NEW ZEALAND.

The Directors of the New Zealand Company, do hereby give notice that they are ready to receive Applications for a **FREE PASSAGE** to the

TOWN OF WELLINGTON,
AT LAMBTON HARBOUR,
PORT NICHOLSON, COOK'S STRAITS,

NEW ZEALAND,

From Agricultural Laborers, Shepherds, Miners, Gardeners, Brickmakers, Mechanics, Handicraftsmen, and Domestic Servants, **BEING MARRIED**, and not exceeding Forty years of age; also from **SINGLE FEMALES**, under the care of near relatives, and **SINGLE MEN**, accompanied by one or more **ADULT SISTERS**, not exceeding, in either case, the age of Thirty years. Strict inquiry will be made as to qualifications and character.

Apply on Mondays, Thursdays, and Saturdays, to **Mr. JOSEPH PHIPSON, 11,** Union Passage, Birmingham,

AGENT TO THE COMPANY.

TOWN and **COUNTRY SECTIONS** of **LAND** on sale, full particulars of which may be had on application as above.

The Fremington Church in Devon where ELIZABETH CHAPPELL married PETER COATES in 1812.

The CHAPPELL's of FREMINGTON, Devon.

1   **SAMUEL CHAPPELL**   married **MARY HEYMAN** at Northam on
    born c1600   15 Aug 1621 and moved to Fremington to live.

2   **JOHN**   m   **JOAN BARWICK**
    b 1636   1662   1639   (daughter of George Barwick of Fremington)

3   **SAMUEL**   m   **MARY BERRY**
    b 1672   1698   1670   (daughter of John Berry of Chittlehampton)

4   JOAN   JOHN   **SAMUEL**   ROGER   WILLIAM   MARY   MARY
    b 1699   1701   b 1703   1705   1707   b&d 1710   1716
                 m 1730
             CHARITY BIDGOOD

5   SAMUEL   CHARITY   MARY   ROGER   GEORGE
    b 1731   1734   1737   1743   1748
      WILLIAM   JOHN   THOMAS   JAMES
       1732   1735   1740   1745
                                  2 marriages

    m 1770   m 1780
    Hannah Harding   **SUSANNA CANN** was born 1751,
                       the daughter of James and
                       Elizabeth Cann of Barnstaple.

6   CHARITY   SARAH   SAMUEL: GEORGE   ROGER
    b 1771   1773   1775   1781   1782

6   ELIZABETH   JAMES   WILLIAM   JOHN   MARY   HANNAH
    b 1783   1785   1787   1789   1790   1792
    m 1812
    PETER COATES

6th Generation

WILLIAM THOMAS: (1848-1923)

1848... WILLIAM THOMAS was born at Ilfracombe in Devonshire England, on the 26th December 1848, the first born and eldest son of John and Jane Thomas. He was named after his paternal Grandfather. We could find no record of his baptism at West Down or Ilfracombe but his birth certificate shows his parents living in Ilfracombe at this time. He arrived in New Zealand aged 6 with his parents and brother John aged 4 in 1855.

1859... We know that his family arrived at Wellington and later moved to Auckland's district of Whau, where his sister Elizabeth was born on 1st March 1859. William was then aged ten.
He must have completed his education at Whau and then like his brother John, followed his father into an occupation of "Miller", at his father's Star Flour Mills on the Oakley Creek at Whau.

1865... William was only 16 years of age, when his father (John) died.

1865... STAR FLOUR MILL:
In those days a lad of 11 or 12 was considered old enough to do a man's job. Aged 16 William would have had 5 years experience working as a Miller's assistant for his father. However, at his father's death he would not have been legally allowed to carry the management or ownership of the mill, but seems to have continued working there under his Uncle George's guidance.

1870... MARRIAGE:
William aged 21 married **ELIZA McKAY** (Euphemia Eliza Ramsey McKay) aged 19 on 28th May 1870, at the residence of the Rev William John Dean in Beresford Street Auckland.
William listed his occupation as Miller and signed with an educated and firm hand. Eliza signed with an X. Eliza was born at Dundee, Scotland in 1850.
William and Eliza had 14 children. Refer page 8 brief tree.

1870... MILL OWNER:
Soon after he was married and had turned 21, joint ownership of the STAR MILL was bestowed upon William.

Purchase... DEED 23D:486 #41575.

This 1st June 1870 Deed of Conveyance was between David Nathan, Gentleman (now on a visit to England) and William Thomas and Thomas Barraclough of Oakley Creek, Storekeeper. Mr Nathan appears to have extended his Mortgage #28832 of 350 pounds to five years instead of the original two because of father John's death. It reads in part, "..........and whereas default has been made in the payment of the principle 350 pounds and the same still remains unpaid together with the sum of nine pounds interest thereon, David Nathan agrees to sell to WT & TB (all the land and buildings) for 360 pounds, purchased as tenants in common.....,....with two thirds to WT 240 pounds and one third to TB 120 pounds."

Mortgage... DEED 14M:439 #41576.

The new Firm of Thomas and Barraclough, trading as The Star Mills, on the 1st June 1870 raised a Mortgage of 450 pounds at 10% PA to June 1872 with David Nathan, over all the land and buildings plus Machinery, Tools of Trade, Goods, Chattels and Effects as contained in schedule (A).

(Schedule A) 1 Water Wheel with driving shaft, drums, cogs, wheels etc; , 2 pairs of 4ft 6" Mill Stones; 1 Dressing Machine; 1 Smutting Machine; Hoisting Gear and chain; 2 pairs of trucks; 1 Mill proof Weighing Machine with 11 weights for same; All belting required for driving above machinery all fixed and in good working order; All other Machinery which may during the continuance of the security be fixed on the land.

Transference... DEED 24D:195 #41755.

On the 5th July 1870, only one month after the above two deeds were signed, "William Thomas (Oakley Creek, Miller) signed over to his brother John Thomas (Oakley Creek, Miller), one of his third shares in the Mill for the consideration of 10 shillings."

This entitled John to one third ownership and one third of the 450 pound Mortgage debt. Young John had only turned 19 on the 1st May just past. William and John signed in the presence of Eliza Thomas. (We believe this would have been William's wife Eliza.)

Mortgage... DEED 13M:825 #46624.

The three man partnership raised further funds from David Nathan, now residing in London, of 100 pounds to 18 Jan 1875 at 10% PA.

1873... MILL FIRE:

On the 8th January the Star flour Mill was razed to the ground by fire.

... Details of this disaster continue in brother John's chapter on page 70 and ends in George's chapter 5, page 221.

... The family rebuilt the Mill on a larger scale and continued milling.

From 1871 to 1874 William was living in the Waikato, milling flour, and therefore was not mentioned in any of the newspaper reports about the fire.

1874... MILL SALE:

DEED 27D:684 #49858. Dated 22 July 1874 this "Equity of Redemption" records the sale of William Thomas' one third share of everything to John Thomas and Mr T Barraclough for 150 pounds.

WILLIAM'S CHILD: *When we researched this family in 1993 we only found one child to William and Eliza. We knew there were more and now (we know they had 14 children. See the* William Thomas *book.)*

1875... JOHN COATES THOMAS born 6 January 1875 at Whau. The baby was baptised on the 9 March 1875 by the Rev W Harris of the Edwards St Auckland, Primitive Methodist Church. William recorded his address as Great North Rd, Waterview, Auckland. (= The Star Mill address)

1874 - 1882:

William and Eliza stayed in the Whau district for the next eight months until their son was born and baptised. His brother John and shifted to the South Island mid 1877 and we think William and family travelled soon after. They were in business together at Christchurch before moving to Ashburton.

1882... CHRISTCHURCH:

William, aged 34, was involved in a Christchurch joint venture business with his brother John for an unknown short period, up to September 1882. On that date they gave their occupations, "Corn Dealers from Christchurch" when purchasing together an eight acre property at Allenton, near Ashburton.

William and John ran a Nursery on these 8 acres for up to 11 years, until the property was sold on 10 March 1893.

1885... In the 1885/6 NZPO Directory we found mention of one.....
"William Thomas...Nurseryman...Ashburton" but no mention of John and there was no mention of either brother in the 1893/4 issue.

1892/3... NGAWAPURUA:

At the time of signing the Ashburton sale document, we find William and family living at Ngawapurua (near Woodville) and he gave his occupation as Nurseryman.

Brother John was already in business in Ashburton as he gave his occupation as Produce Dealer. We wonder when they both left the Allenton Nursery ?

1890/3... Phoebe Ching (Grand daughter of John & Phebe) recalls her mother telling her that about this time William and John had a great argument and they separated. It appears William strongly felt John was being inconsiderate to his wife Phebe, by getting her pregnant so often.

(By this time Phebe nearly 38, had been married 21 years, given birth to 14 children and seen 5 of these die.)

Bertha Maud Thomas aged 9 months died 1st February 1891 and this could have been the point where William said something to John.

In 1988 when talking to all of John and Phebe's grandchildren, we found only Phoebe Ching had any knowledge of John having a brother. It was as though there really had been a difference of opinion and the two families had not communicated from that time on.

1893... William's mother Jane Thomas died in Auckland on 25 July 1893 aged 72, and William was aged 44 and still alive at that time.

1899... On 25 December 1899 their son John Coates Thomas (a farmer) was married to Alice Mary James. Eliza was now aged 49 and William 51 and he was described as a Nurseryman on the wedding certificate. We have been unable to trace a photograph of William and Eliza and to date have not been able to trace a living descendant.   (Sorry, That was the situation in 1993.)

1898... About this year William left Ngawapurua and bought 88 acres of New Lynn in Auckland known as Riverview Farm. Here he grew grain, had orchards, a small forest and a large building for a hen-house.

He also erected a Brick-Works which was serviced by road and sea. Today's Rata St and Queen Mary Ave have been built on this land.

WILLIAM THOMAS died 25 February 1923 aged 74 at his Rata St, residence. His wife **ELIZA** died 6 March 1953 aged 83.

They are buried together at Waikumete Cemetery, Auckland.

--ooO0oo--

JOHN COATES THOMAS: (1875-1955)

1875... William and Eliza's son John Coates Thomas was born on the 6th January at Whau, Auckland. His birth certificate shows his father was a "Miller" and Eliza recorded their residential address as Waterview. He was named John after his Grandfather John Thomas and Coates was his Grandmother Jane's maiden name. As we already have 2 John Thomases we have decided to refer to this one as JCT. He is John Thomas VII.

1880... JCT would have moved south with his parents and no doubt enjoyed the company of his first-cousins in Ashburton even though he was a few years older than them.

1890... We wonder if aged 15 he was working at the Allenton nursery with his father and uncle, or already involved in Carpentry or Farming.

1893... At the age of 18 JCT was in the North Island, in the Palmerston North / Levin area. His father was living at Ngawapurua (near Woodville) when JCT (a farmer of Levin) married in December 1899.

1899... JCT aged 24 on 25 December, married **ALICE MARY JAMES** aged 26, at the residence of Mr Ivor James in the Horowhenua Village Settlement, Levin. Alice, the daughter of farmer Ivor James & Mary Ann Howe was born in Wellington in 1873. Rev H.E. Bellhouse officiated. The wedding certificate gives his age as 23 but he was a couple of weeks off his 25th birthday.(?) His mother's maiden name has been recorded as Eliza Carrie and we know it was McKay (?) Alice was attended by Amy R James...probably a sister and JCT's best man was first cousin Frederick William Thomas, then a Labourer in Levin. They must have become good mates in the Allenton days. Fred was three years younger than JCT.
We wonder if JCT hated his middle name of Coates.
His marriage certificate records him as only John Thomas and he signed his name without the Coates, too!

CHILDREN: JCT and Alice had five children, a girl in 1899, a son in 1901, and three more girls in 1903, 1904 and 1906. We have no names.

(NB...A Frederick Thomas died 8 Sept 1921 and Kate Thomas died 7 March 1938. They are buried at Rosebank Rd Cemetery Auckland, in the plot containing JCT's cousin William Thomas and wife Lily. They could be two of JCT's children.)

JCT and Alice were living in New Lynn, Auckland when Alice Mary Thomas died 6 December 1909 aged only 37. Her children were now aged 10, 8, 6, 5, and 3, and husband JCT was aged 35. Alice was interred at Waikumete Cemetery, Auckland. There is no headstone on her grave in the `Non Conformist' section D..Row 1..Plot 47.

Phoebe Ching in 1988 still had her mother's handbag, in which was a 1909 Death Notice for Alice Mary Thomas and it is from the small amount of information on this card that we have been able to find and accumulate the detail for JCT plus details of William and Eliza Thomas.

We do not know anything more of the following 28 years but can not imagine an overly happy time for either JCT or the children.

1937... JCT aged 63 was remarried by a Presbyterian Minister at Whakatane, to **ROSE MYRTLE CAMERON** aged 58. Rose outlived JCT and there were no children by this marriage living when JCT died.

1955... APRIL: JCT (retired Farmer) signed his Will on the 12th and left all his estate of 3500 pounds to his wife Rose. There were no children mentioned. We wonder what happened to the five of them!

1955... JULY: John Coates Thomas died on 4th July aged 80 years. His card at the Waikumete Cemetery Auckland, states that he was a retired Carpenter and his last address was Old Main Road, Orewa. He was not with either of his two wives...but interred in `Protestant' Section A..Row 6..Plot 57, without headstone. The Cemetery records show that there is only one person in both his and Alice's graves.

1976... ROSE died 22 March. Her Will left a Grandfather Clock and all personal items (including Rings) to her friend Martha Banks of Main Rd, Orewa. The balance of her estate valued at $3900 went to her children from her first marriage, Mary Frances Ryan, Winifred Myrtle Bayes and Morton Kennedy Cameron. William's children were not mentioned.

We have not found a photograph of JCT, Alice or Rose and to date we have been unsuccessful in tracing any living relations. (T ..1993)

ELIZABETH THOMAS: (1859-1928)

1859... ELIZABETH THOMAS was born at Oakley's Creek, Whau in Auckland on 1 March 1859, the first daughter and third child of John and Jane Thomas.

1865... Elizabeth's father John died when she was only 6 years old.

1870... We wonder if Elizabeth when aged 8, 11 and 13, had any part in the wedding groups when her mother married Thomas Barraclough, or when her brother William married Eliza McKay, or when her brother John married Phebe Woods ?
She must have completed her education at the Whau School.

1877... On 15 May 1877 Elizabeth was aged 18 and on this day she signed and dated an inscription inside a Bible she gave to her brother John and Phebe Thomas when they left Auckland for the South Island.

1878... Elizabeth aged 19 married **JAMES HILL** aged 23,
on 28 May 1878 in Auckland. James was a 'Labourer'
and was born in County Tyrone in Ireland.

1879... A son was born 6 March 1879 at Richmond in Auckland.
They named him **William John Hill.**

1883... A second son was born 25 January at Paeroa, in the Kaipara District near Helensville. He was named **Robert Hill.** James aged 28 was still described as 'Labourer' (equaled farm labourer). Elizabeth was 24 years old.
A letter in June 1989 from Mr D.R. Monk solves the location of Paeroa problem. *"My father lived in the area from 1860 to 1950. The area was called Paeroa by the Maori until about 1884 when the railway to Thames and Paeroa was built. To avoid confusion the name of this area was changed to Wharepapa, that being another local name. The only two farms occupied in this area were those of Monks and Phillips."* We think that this Hill family worked and lived on one of these two farms for a time.

Robert Hill served with the World War I Expeditionary Forces.

1903-1906... James Hill purchased a farm at Poi Poi and worked it with his son Robert for about thirty years.

Michael S Thomas (a 5th New Zealand generation, John Thomas' family) corresponded in 1972 with a Mr Duncan Inkpen of Ramarama and gained the following information which is still being investigated....

    1.   The family of four lived on a farm near Te Kuiti.
    2.   Son William, known as Bill, went to Peru, married
and fathered two daughters called Dorothy and Gwen.
          a... Dorothy had one daughter.
          b... Gwen married a Scotsman named McLean.
          He was an Ambassador in Peru for Great Britain.
          They had two children Pat (Patricia?) and Donald.
    3.   Son Robert (known as Bob) married Edie (Edith) ..?..
and took over the farm. There was no issue.
It is thought that Robert died at Manurewa in November ..?..
and Edie died in Auckland in December 1971.   (End MST)

1928... New Zealand Herald 18 July:
          "Elizabeth Hill, in her 70th year,
    died 16 July 1928 at her residence in Forbes Street, Onehunga".
She was buried at Hillsborough Cemetery on the 18th July.
At the Cemetery "Area 4, Row 27, Plot 2191" we found that she is buried with husband James Hill who died aged 79.

1933... James Hill died 6 September.
          He was a retired farmer, then living at Forbes Street, Onehunga.
James' Will left his half of the Poi Poi farm to son Robert... who owned the other half. The farm was 1611 acres, section 11 and 12 in Block 6 of Maungamangaro District, about 50 miles south west of Te Kuiti.
          When James signed his Will in 1923, Robert was described as of Haku
          in the County of Kwakino, NZ.   (No mention of son Bill)

          We have not found any photos of Elizabeth or James Hill and to date
          have been unsuccessful in tracing any living descendants of Bill.

CHAPTER FOUR

6th Generation.

JOHN THOMAS and PHEBE.

1851... DEVON:

JOHN THOMAS was baptised at Ilfracombe, Devonshire on the 1st May 1851 and emigrated to New Zealand with his mother Jane Thomas, and elder brother William and Uncle George Thomas, arriving at Wellington during 1855. His father, also named John Thomas, came to New Zealand the year before to prepare for their arrival. John would not have remembered Devonshire much, as he was only aged four at the time they travelled.

1859... AUCKLAND:

We believe young John and his family did not live in Wellington but travelled north, finally settling near the Whau district in Auckland. (now called Avondale.) They were living at Oakley Creek, in March 1859 when John's sister Elizabeth was born. His father owned the Star Flour Mill. John was probably educated by his mother, and later at the Whau School.

1865... FATHER DIED:

John was nearly 14 years of age in 1865, when his father died at Oakley Creek, Whau. John would have been working for his father full time for the past two years or so, at the flour mill learning the art of Milling.

At this time his Uncle George Thomas and family moved to the mill-site and young John would have continued working at the Mill.

1867... JOHN'S MOTHER REMARRIES:

John, now aged 16 would have attended his mother's marriage to Thomas Barraclough who was employed as a Storekeeper at Oakley Creek. Three years later Barraclough purchased a third share in the Star Mill. When John's mother married, Uncle George moved to a house he had purchased on an 8 acre block in the Whau township but he returned each day to work at the mill.

1870... STAR MILL:

During this year John's father's estate was finally settled and ownership was transferred to John's 21 year old brother William and step-father Barraclough.

William's pages 58 to 60 detail, (a) this ownership change, (b) the 2 mortgages taken out, (c) the July 1870 transference by William to a now 19 year old John, of a third share in the Star Mill's ownership and debts.

1870... ADVERTISEMENT:
Throughout June & July a STAR MILL advertisement advises.....

We have not found any photos, nor the exact location of this Auckland Produce Store. Later in Ashburton, John opened another Produce Store that continued in the family for three generations.

MESSRS. THOMAS & BARRACLOUGH are now prepared to receive WHEAT, MAIZE, BARLEY, &c, for GRISTING, either at their Produce Stores, Queen-street, a few doors obove Wellesley-street East, or at the Star Mills, Oakley's Creek, Great North Road, the only Grist Mill in Auckland.
On Sale at the Store,
Flour, retail only
Sharps
Bran
Maize, whole or crushed
Maize Meal, always fresh
Barley, crushed for pig feed
&c., &c., &c.

N.B.—Highest cash price given for provincial-grown Wheat.
Star Mills, Great North Road, and at Wellesley-street East, a few doors from Queen-street

1872... WEDDING:
On 31st December 1872,
JOHN THOMAS aged 21,
married **PHEBE WOODS**
aged 17 1/2 years, at the Whau Presbyterian Church by the Rev David Hamilton. John was a Miller. He had a new cottage for them erected on the three acre Mill land. (The Church renamed St Ninian's, Avondale, 63 years later.)

See an article in *The Daily Southern Cross* newspaper 22 Jan 1873 ... page 308

PHEBE's PARENTS:
Phebe was born second of 10 children to John Woods and Mary Ann nee Lowe on 14 May 1855 at their Hobson St home, Auckland, according to family records. The registration of her birth was overlooked
Some **WOODS & LOWE** family details are recorded at the end of this chapter starting on page 104 and in the book "The WOODS Family".

CHRISTENING: At the Edwards Street Primitive Methodist Church in Auckland, on 3 June 1855, Mary Ann and John Woods' second child Phebe Woods was christened by the Rev Robert Ward.

PHOEBE or PHEBE...

Her name is spelt Phoebe on her Marriage Certificate and on her Death Certificate. However, as her Headstone at Coromandel Cemetery, and the Certificate of Title to their property at Coromandel, and the listing for her in the Parliamentary Rolls, and the Bible gifted to her by sister-in-law Elizabeth, all spell it Phebe........... so then, we will call her **PHEBE**.

CHILDREN:

John and Phebe had 15 children known as.....

Mary, Arthur, Albert, Alfred, Frederick, Jessie, John, Percy, George, Syd, Elsie, Jack, Charles, Bertha and Roy.

Their full names are listed under the date of their birth and their life's story together with lists of descendants are detailed following this section.

John and Phebe lived in a number of houses and towns in New Zealand.

They lived in Auckland as husband and wife for five years, (December 1872 to late 1877) which saw four children born and two die.

1873... AUCKLAND DIRECTORY:

This Directory lists only NINE families living in the Point Chevalier district in 1873. They were named Isaac Carrie, Patrick Dignam, William Motion, Capt Seymour, Richard & Thomas Henry Walker, Barraclough & Thomas, Star Mill... Oakley Creek, and W Edgecombe.

Our family certainly were pioneer settlers of Auckland.

1873... FIRE at STAR MILL:

The newspapers advise us ....

"The City firebells rang out an alarm about one o'clock this morning (8 January 1873) as if the whole town were afire. A number of slumbering citizens were induced to forsake their virtuous couches and venture out into the drenching rain. The rival fire brigades under Superintendents Asher and Matthews also mustered at their engine sheds. It was soon discovered that the fire was some miles from the town and most returned to their respective domiciles. Mounted Police constable Bullen was dispatched to the spot.

The scene of the conflagration was the Star Flour Mills, situated at the Whau. The property belonged to Mr Thomas Barraclough and his step-son Mr John Thomas, and included besides the mill, a small dwelling house, some out-buildings and a new cottage in which Mr Thomas lived, on four acres of land.

The Mill which was erected some 13 years ago, by Mr Thomas' father, stood by itself, and there was therefore no likelihood at any time that the fire would spread.

Later that morning, pursuant to instructions received from Inspector Broham, Detective Tornahan proceeded to the scene of the late fire. He found that the Mill, which was a four story building, was burnt to the ground, in less than one hour after the discovery was made by the man in charge. The entire mill, a portion of the waterwheel and all the machinery were destroyed.

It is very difficult to account for the probable origin of the conflagration, which has destroyed a valuable property and entailed a serious loss on the owners. It is possible that the machinery of the mill, which had been working almost constantly night and day, had become heated by friction to such an extent as to cause ignition, or it may be that a spark dropped unperceived from a sperm candle placed on some sacks whilst some of the hands were at work on the evening of Tuesday started it all.

A servant named John Lowndes, states that he had been working to about 10.30pm, in company with Mr Thomas who had been hoisting up maize for putting through the hopper. In consequence of the recent dry weather, the water supply was getting short and Lowndes says he stopped the mill and lay down on some sacks, intending to rest until the dam got a little fuller and Mr Thomas went to his home nearby.
Mr and Mrs Barraclough also reside close to hand and Mr Barraclough had been confined to his bed for some days past.

Lowndes states that he remained on the ground floor resting on the sacks, until about 12.30pm, when he perceived the smell of smoke and immediately jumped up and proceeded to search the mill.
He found the fourth floor on fire.

It was filled with sacks of wheat and already the fire had made considerable progress. He immediately gave the alarm and called Mr Thomas who came promptly, and by their united exertions they endeavoured to extinguish the fire by throwing buckets of water at it.

They soon perceived that their efforts were useless and they turned their attention to save some of the bags of flour and wheat and the books. By this time the floor began to give way and they deemed it therefore inconsistent with their personal safety to remain any longer.

The building which was valued at about 900 pounds was insured in the Royal Insurance Company for 400 pounds but the stock was uninsured.
Three sacks of flour and 100 sacks of wheat were all that could be saved.

The loss consists of the mill, machinery, and the stock stored at the time....known to be 400 sacks of wheat, three ton of flour, eight sacks of bran, one ton and a half of meal, and fifteen bags of sharps, all estimated as worth 600 pounds.

Heavy rain fell during the time of the conflagration, but had not the slightest effect upon the flames. (end quote)

1873... MILL REBUILT:
The Daily Southern Cross newspaper on the 20 June announced that the Star Mills at the Whau were again set in operation, after having been rebuilt on a more extended scale by Mr H Palmer, the contractor for the Hamilton Mill in the Waikato.
The building is substantially supported by a strong brick foundation.

On the wheel side of the mill a thick scoria and brick wall, surmounted by a solid beam of heart kauri, give the necessary strength for supporting the enormous weight here bought to bear. The sides elsewhere are weatherboard with heart kauri. The waterwheel is on the high-breast principle, and measures 20 feet in diameter by 5 feet on the face. It is composed of iron and kauri, with inverted segments.
There are two pairs of stones of English manufacture. The mortice-wheels are furnished with wooden (pohutukawa) teeth and work noiselessly.
A creeper of ingenious formation contains the latest improvements, and will convey the grist to the silk.

The work of grinding was commenced yesterday, in order to exhibit some maize-meal at the Show at Auckland.
The trial working was in every respect satisfactory but a short time will necessarily elapse before everything is in perfect working order.
About 15 tons of flour can now be turned out each week.
(end quote)

The new STAR FLOUR MILL of 1873:
.... as shown in NZ Graphic 10 Sept 1898
"Auckland Public Library (NZ) photo A1683.

Mr Walker records in his book, the Star Mill's maize meal entry at the NZ Market Exhibition on the 21 June 1873, was a winner.   (DSthC) The above record of the fire and rebuilding comments are a condensed version of newspaper items, as reported in 1873 in the copies of the Auckland Star 8th January, NZ Herald 8th and 9th January, the Weekly News 11th January and the Daily Southern Cross on the 20th June.

1874... MILL SOLD:
There were three Deeds used for John to sell the Star Flour Mill to his uncle George Thomas.

1874... 22 July **DEED** 27D:684 #49858
This "Equity of Redemption" records the sale of William Thomas's one third of everything, to John Thomas and Thomas Barraclough for 150 pounds.

1874... 22 July **DEED** 18M:568 #4985922
John Thomas and Thomas Barraclough both of Star Mills, raised a new mortgage with George William Binney, Auctioneer and Merchant, of
800 pounds at 12% PA calculated upon monthly balance and which was secured ever everything.

1874... 26 Sept **DEED** 29D:76#50323
Two months after William sold his one third share to his partners the business changed hands.
G W Binney (the mortgager), John Thomas and Thomas Barraclough (joint owners) sold to George Thomas, a miller of the Whau.
George paid 1300 pounds for the new Star Mill and equipment, 2 houses with contents and the lands.

Full details of the transaction appear in George's chapter 5, page 217. Included is a list of items from John and Phebe's cottage which they must have decided were easier to replace in Christchurch, than to try to transport them to the South Island.

Although ownership of the Star Mill transferred to George Thomas we think that John and brother William may have stayed on and rented the houses and worked for wages at the mill, for the next two years before shifting their families south.

1874... MARY JANE THOMAS was born 5th February 1874 at Whau in Auckland. The informant was Thomas Barraclough of Whau ... a Miller and father John was a Miller too.
Mary died 30th November 1878 at Papanui, Christchurch, of Diphtheria aged 4 years. She was buried at Papanui Cemetery by a minister of the Church of England. John gave his occupation in 1878 as "Miller".

74

1875... ARTHUR HAMILTON THOMAS was born 17th 1875 at Whau in Auckland and died aged 3 months at Auckland on 19 April 1875 and possibly is buried with Albert.

1876... ALBERT JOHN THOMAS was born 2 January 1876 at Whau in Auckland. Albert died 13th October 1876 aged 9 months, of Congestion of the Lungs from which he had suffered for 8 days according to Doctor Aicken.
He was buried at 'Grafton` Cemetery, Auckland on the 15th by Rev William Tinsley of the Primitive Methodist Church. The informant was his Aunt Martha Woods of Chapel St, Auckland.

1876... MILL CLOSED:
On 25 March uncle George Thomas sold the Star Mill to the mortgager Mr G W Binney and after 17 years it left the Thomas family. Mr Walker notes that deteriorating economic conditions forced the closing of the mill.
Mr Binney sold the mill, land and houses to the 5 Garrett brothers who converted it into a Tannery and built two more houses on the land for their tannery workers.
      The Mill building was demolished between 1910 and 1912.
The land (section 18a) was purchased by Samuel Henry Todd in 1913 and subdivided in 1949.   (2021, the land formed part of Waterview Heritage Park.)

1877... ALFRED EDWARD THOMAS was born 21 March 1877 at Whau in Auckland. More detail page 110.

CHRISTCHURCH and SOUTHBROOK:
1877... On the 15th May 1877 the family (John, Phebe, with children Mary and Alfred) left Auckland and moved to Christchurch.

On this day John's sister Elizabeth gave John and Phebe a Bible which she had inscribed, dated and signed on the fly leaf.

This Bible, was in 1988 with John's brother Roy's son Mervyn's wife ....
Beatrice <u>Mary</u> Thomas.

Presented To
John. & Phebe. Thomas.
On Their departure from Auckland
May 15" 1877
By Their affectionate sister
Elizabeth Thomas

The question of why John and Phebe left Auckland and went to Christchurch may never be factually answered. We have found that Canterbury was a rapidly expanding area and not hit as hard as other parts of New Zealand by the world-wide depression of 1875-1895.

Auckland suffered severely from the falling prices, and falling interest rates and profits. Because of this slump and the closure of the flour mill we believe that John and his brother William may have had difficulty in gaining flour milling jobs or may have been more forward looking, seeing bigger opportunities in the South Island with greater security for their families.

1878... FREDERICK WILLIAM THOMAS was born 13th May 1878 at Styx in Christchurch. More details page 130.

1878... Mary Jane Thomas died at Papanui, Christchurch aged four years on 30 November 1878. John gave the answer of "Papanui" when asked what his usual address was.

1878... SOUTHBROOK: John and Phebe moved to Southbrook, near Rangiora, some 25 miles out of Christchurch, in December 1878 or early 1879.

D N Hawkens book "Rangiora" has a good account of Rangiora and touches on nearby towns.
Southbrook was two miles away and first settled and farmed in 1860.
In October 1863 Edward Steggell began construction of the first flour mill there and by the end of 1864, he also owned a Hotel a few yards downstream from the Mill.
Late 1864 saw the second flour mill built at Southbrook for Robert Grimwood. Other businesses followed.
1886 a store for John and Joseph Thompson, Frederick Thorn a Fellmongery, and a Tannery for McHaig.
1869-70 saw the start of a very big Flax Industry.
In 1869 Thomas Dench opened a Butcher Shop and a builder's yard was opened by James Withers.
1870 saw a General Store started by Robert Grimwood and another Butcher Shop opened 1872 for 3 men named Wearmouth, Sutherland and Watson.
The Post Office opened in 1872 and the Railway line from Christchurch arrived at Rangiora, passing through Southbrook and all upward and downward rail traffic passed each other in the Rail yards at Southbrook.

In 1873 the Wesleyan Chapel was shifted from Rangiora to Southbrook. Most of the people living at Southbrook at that time were Wesleyans and their leader David Graham (a farmer) arranged for the building's removal.

There was a strong Wesleyan bond between Southbrook leaders Graham, Withers, Watson and the Thompson, Grimwood and Seed families. The Rangiora Methodists belonged mainly to the United Free sect and had their own Church. Most of the services were taken by Laymen.

The Wesleyan and United Free Churches united in 1896.

In the daytime the Southbrook Chapel was used as a Primary School until the official Southbrook Primary School was built and opened on Oct 1874. It started with a roll of fifty-eight children.

In February 1874 Rangiora was advised that a thousand Immigrants were expected to arrive in Canterbury in March 1875 and that it would receive its share of these.

In 1874 a Library opened. The Anglicans started a small church in 1880.

The Fire Brigade was formed in 1883.

1878 Southbrook seems to have everything John & Phebe needed....

(a) "Employment" in a Flourmill... John was a Miller.
The 1878 Canterbury Census shows that there were 107 men working in 33 Grain Mills throughout Canterbury within a dozen miles of Rangiora.

(b) There was a strong "Methodist" Church group.

(c) A "School" for their children

(d) Ample "support businesses" such as Butchers, Carpenters etc.

The Rail went there, the Post Office was there and the big town of Christchurch was only a short distance away.

The map on page 78 of the Rangiora District was drawn soon after 1877 and shows both Flourmills at Southbrook. Grimwoods was bought in 1875-6 by Harry Archer and Steggell's Mill sold to William Moir 1876-7.

The book "Rangiora" also has a map showing the site of these two mills in relation to the Southbrook Stream and Southbrook township, plus photos of the two local mill buildings.

It is very probable (but not provable unfortunately) that our John Thomas found work at one of these Southbrook mills or at nearby Styx where a mill was established in 1874.

77

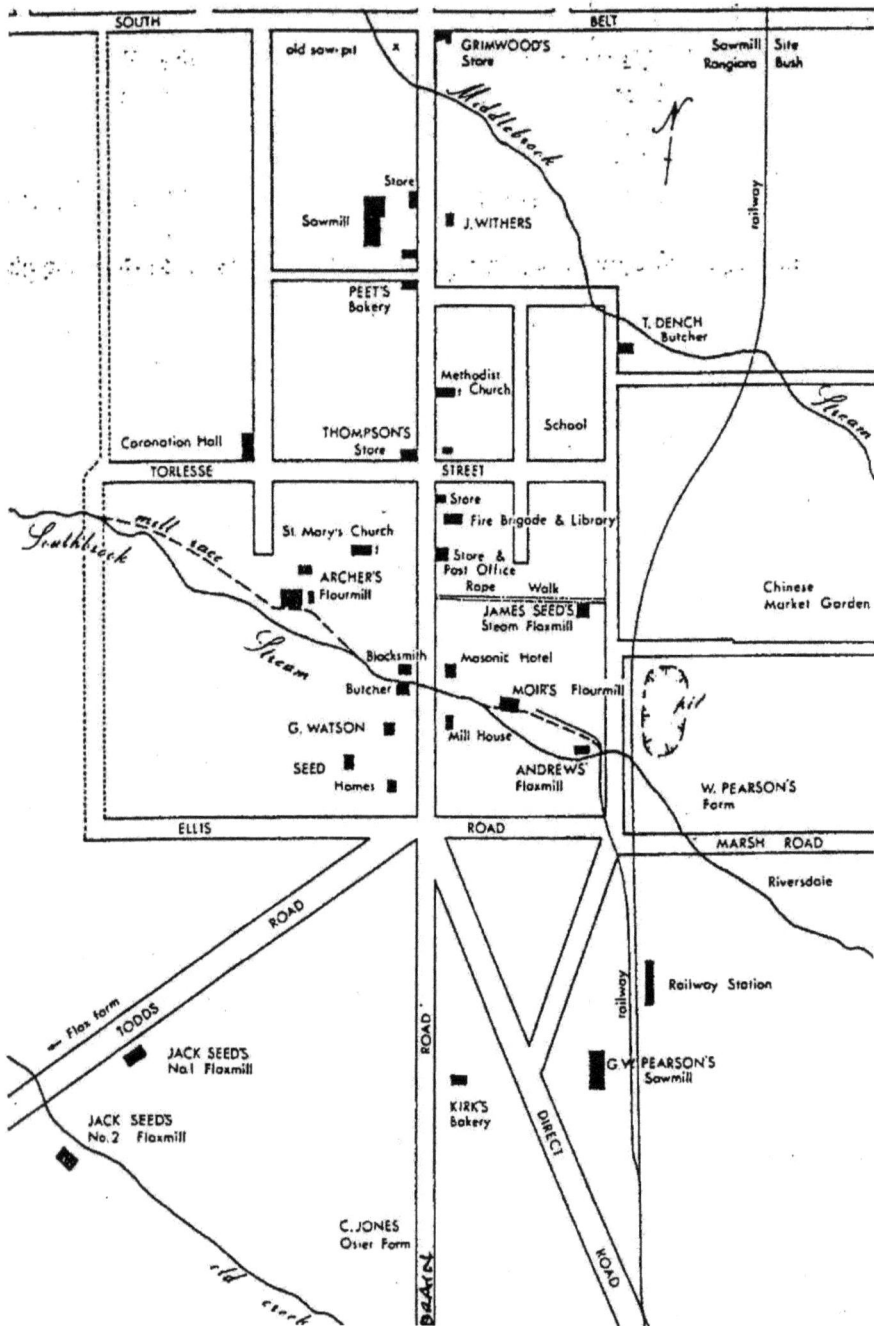

SOUTH   BELT
old saw-pit   x   GRIMWOOD'S   Sawmill   Site
                                Store   Rangiora   Bush
                                             Middlebeck
                    Store
        Sawmill   J.WITHERS   N

                                                            railway
        PEET'S
        Bakery   T. DENCH
                                                    Butcher
                          Methodist
                          Church
        THOMPSON'S   School   Stream
        Store

Coronation Hall
TORLESSE   STREET

                      Store
Southbeck   mill race   St. Mary's Church   Fire Brigade & Library
                                        Store &
        Stream   ARCHER'S   Post Office   Chinese
                            Flourmill   Rope   Walk   Market Garden
                    Blacksmith   JAMES SEED'S
                    Butcher   Steam Flaxmill
                                Masonic Hotel
        G. WATSON   MOIR'S Flourmill   Pit
                            Mill House
        SEED   ANDREWS'   W. PEARSON'S
        Homes   Flaxmill   Farm
ELLIS   ROAD   MARSH   ROAD
                                                    Riversdale

        ROAD
Flax farm   TODDS   railway   Railway Station

        JACK SEED'S   G.V. PEARSON'S
        No.1 Flaxmill   ROAD   Sawmill

JACK SEED'S   KIRK'S
No.2 Flaxmill   Bakery   DIRECT

        C. JONES
        Osier Farm
old creek   ROAD

78

1879... JESSIE ELIZABETH THOMAS was born 23 June 1879 at Southbrook, and the birth was registered at Rangiora. Jessie never married, and, after many months of Lung and Intestinal illnesses, died aged 28, on 6th Sept 1907 at her parent's home in Grey St Ashburton. Rev H E Bellhouse of the Weslyan Church buried her at Ashburton.

1880... JOHN WOODS THOMAS was born 7 October 1880 at Southbrook and on 2 March 1881, when aged 4 ½ months, he died of Diarrhoea. Although his death was Registered at Rangiora, he was buried at the Church of England Cemetery at Papanui Christchurch.

John gave the family residential address then as "Southbrook" and stated he was employed as a "Miller".

We believe he is with his sister Mary Jane Thomas who was buried there in November 1878.

1881... CORN DEALERS:

After March 1881, John and his brother William, must have started a business in Corn Dealing in or near Christchurch, (maybe a Styx) as this is how they described their occupations when purchasing eight acres of land near Ashburton in September 1882.

1881... WALTER PERCIVAL THOMAS was born 17th November 1881 in Barbados Street, Christchurch. He was known as Percy.

John described himself as a "Produce Dealer of Christchurch".

Percy told everyone he was born at Styx, but this may have been where the family lived at that time. More detail page 142.

At the most, John, Phebe and family lived in the Southbrook and Christchurch area for five years before moving on to Ashburton in mid 1882. A five year period that saw four children born and two die.

ASHBURTON:

1882... John and Phebe now had four living children, Alfred, Frederick, Jessie and Percy.

1882... FREEHOLDERS:

The October 1882 edition of "Freeholders of NZ" records William and John Thomas as joint owners of 8 acres of freehold land in the Ashburton district with a value of 1000 pounds.

1882... ALLENTON.

The Land Act was passed by the NZ Government in 1877 and land purchases began to be Registered. In September 1882 John, with his brother William, purchased a property of eight acres at Allenton, which at that time was just outside the boundary of the township of Ashburton.

An article recently published in the Ashburton Guardian by Ray McCausland, states that on the property were old stables, barns and men's quarters and three cottages, before Mr W H Collins bought it in 1893.

We wish to call the attention of our readers to the sale of trees by Mr T. Bullock, at Mr J. Thomas' nursery, North belt, on Monday next. The apple trees are proved good sorts, as Mr Thomas has over 200 varities in his orchard, but his experience has made him confine his nursery stock to about 50 of these, they being found most suitable for the district for bearing properties, quality, and value as a crop.' Some of these are blight proof both roots and branches, and some are long keepers and suitable for export, viz.—Lord Wolseley ; Stone, Golden, Sturmer, and Allonsbury pippins ; Scarlet, Nonpariel, Majstin,' and many others, both early and late varieties for kitchen and dessert use. A number of specimen fruits from this orchard were exhibited this season in Mr Page's windows and much admired for their color, size and symmetry.—(Advt.)

We found this advertisement in the **Ashburton Guardian 10 July 1890**, for the sale of trees in the Ashburton Guardian for J Thomas's Nursery. (No mention of William, was he a junior partner or had he left Allenton by then?)

The auctioneer Mr T Bullock advises John had 200 varieties of Apple trees in his Orchard. The advertisement makes interesting reading when compared to the wording of adverts of today.

These acres were in their joint names for 11 years until officially sold on 10 March 1893 to William Henry Collins. This gentleman (a local Timber dealer) erected a very large and beautiful house on the property and called it "Menorlue". The building still exists in 1989 and is occupied by the Ashburton College Community Division.

Allenton in 1989 is now a northern suburb of the Ashburton township.

William and John paid 1000 pounds for these 8 acres in September 1882 and arranged a mortgage with the previous owner. This was taken over by Dixon Investments in 1886.

In March 1893 Dixon took control of the property for 10 shillings and six months later sold it for 620 pounds to W H Collins.

This sale almost covered the mortgage debt of 700 pounds. When John signed the sale documents on 10 March 1893 he described himself as "Produce Dealer", implying his Ashburton Shop was already in existence at that time.

Brother William also signed that day and described himself "Nurseryman" living at Ngawapurua near Woodville in the North Island.

We are thankful to grandchildren John & Betty who lead us to the Allenton location. John recalled as a lad, sitting in a car eating an ice-cream and his father Alfred telling him as they drove past, that the Thomases used to live there. Betty recalled her father George saying that he had been born on the "Menorlue" property, as it is known today.

In 1882, as we mentioned earlier, John and Phebe had four living children and four had died, and William and Eliza had only one child to our knowledge. John and Phebe had a further 6 children during these 11 years at Allenton and in Feb 1891 Bertha Maud Thomas died aged 9 months.

COMMENTS:

1   Whilst researching John's life his granddaughter Phoebe Ching recalled her mother telling her that during this period William and John had a great argument and they separated. She thought William strongly believed younger brother John was being inconsiderate to his wife Phebe, by getting her pregnant so often. I January 1883 John and Phebe had been married 11 years, had 9 children and saw 4 of these die.

William and Eliza who had been married longer at nearly 13 years, had only 6 children and all had survived. Maybe William did say something to John. In 1988 when talking to all of John and Phebe's grandchildren, we found only Phoebe Ching had any knowledge of John having a brother. It was as if there really had been a difference of opinion and the two families had not communicated from that time on.

Alternatively, it could have been the Allenton nursery financial problems which caused the men to go their separate ways. The nursery may have earned John a wage , but it did not seem to have made a profit for them at the time of sale, and William as an investor would obviously not be too happy having lost a lot of money

2   We wonder, as their nursery was heavily into trees, if the special Gingko tree on the Menorlue site in 1999 was planted by them. No one knows the exact age of the tree except that it is very old, so it could have ben planted during their 11 year ownership of the property.

The Collin's house appears to have been designed to enjoy this lovely tree.

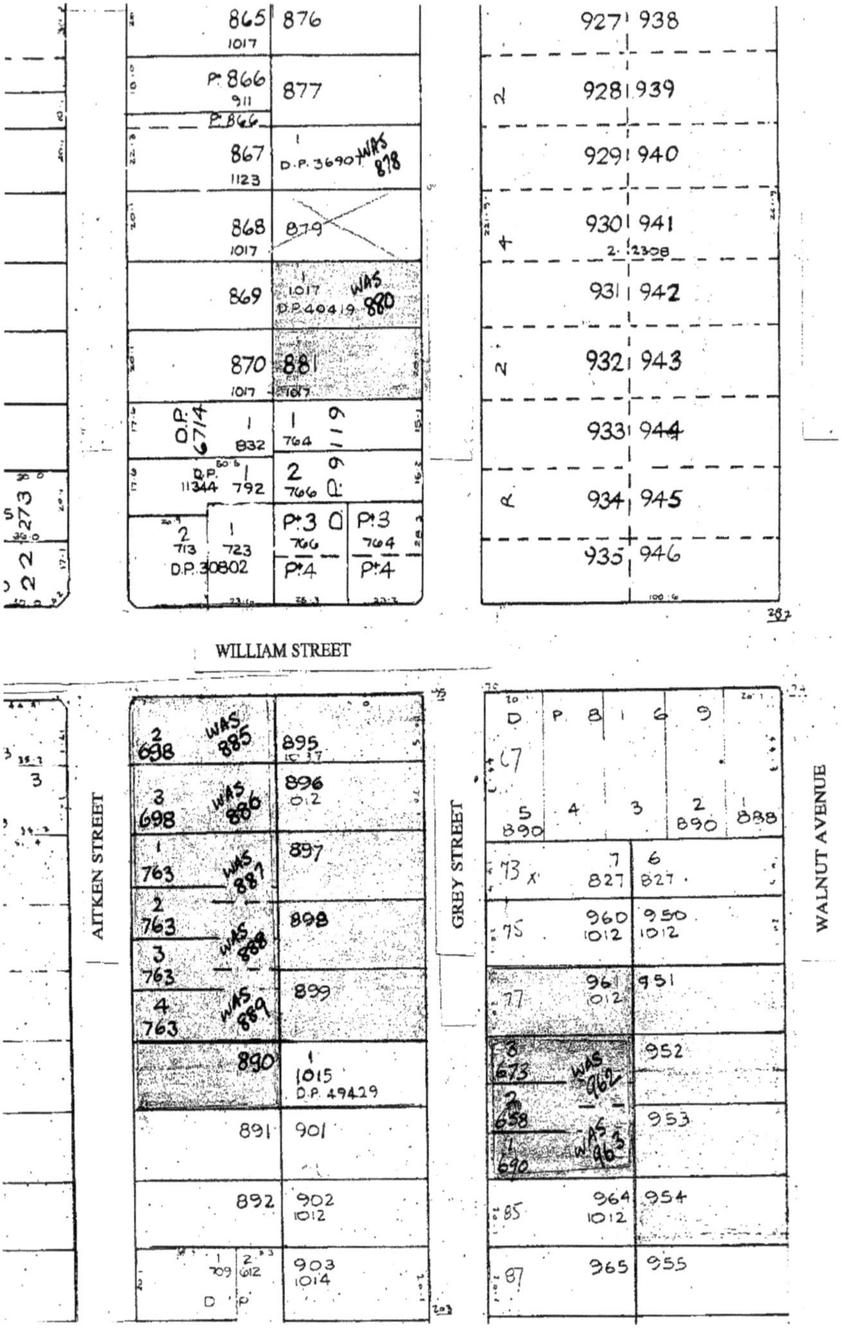

Top block (above William Street):

Left parcel (William St side):

865 / 1017 | 876

P.866 / 911 | 877

P.866

867 / 1123 | D.P.3690 WAS 878

868 / 1017 | 879 (crossed out)

869 | 1017 D.P.40419 WAS 880

870 / 1017 | 881 / 1017

D.P. 6714 | 832 | 1 764 / 9119

D.P. 11344 | 506 792 | 2 766 D.P.

2 713 | 1 723 D.P.30802 | P.3 766 P.4 | P.3 764 P.4

Right parcel:

927 | 938

928 | 939

929 | 940

930 / 2 2308 | 941

931 | 942

932 | 943

933 | 944

934 | 945

935 | 946

100.6   287

522 273

WILLIAM STREET

Bottom-left block (between Aitken Street and Grey Street):

AITKEN STREET

2 698 WAS 885 | 895 15 17

3 698 WAS 886 | 896 0 12

1 763 WAS 887 | 897

2 763 WAS 888 | 898

3 763

4 763 WAS 889 | 899

890 | 1 1015 D.P.49429

891 | 901

892 | 902 1012

1 709 | 2 612 | 903 1014

GREY STREET

Bottom-right block (Grey Street to Walnut Avenue):

D. P. 8 1 6 9

67

5 890 | 4 | 3 | 2 890 | 1 888

73 x | 7 827 | 6 827

75 | 960 1012 | 950 1012

77 | 961 1012 | 951

8 673 WAS 962 | 952

2 658 | 953

690 WAS 963

85 | 964 1012 | 954

87 | 965 | 955

WALNUT AVENUE

82

ASHBURTON PROPERTIES:

After the Nursery at Allenton, John and Phebe moved into the township of Ashburton. The following summary shows the years John paid rates on Ashburton properties. Purchases and sales of these may or may not have taken place in that year. Our map shows the position of the sections.

1894...John first paid rates on section Lots 880/881 with one dwelling, in Grey Street in 1894. They possibly moved into the house after March 1893 when the Allenton sale concluded. Circumstances may have meant they had to pay Rent and the Rates to the previous owner for a couple of years, as it was not until 21 September 1895 that the ownership of the property was officially transferred to him.

The 1894 Rateable Value of these two sections was 21 pounds and John paid one pound one shilling in Rates that year.

This property with a house on Lot 880 and empty section Lot 881, became their home for 15 years until they moved to Coromandel in 1908. The only photo we have found of this home was taken about 1935 during a snow storm and is printed on page 160.

John was the third owner of the one Rood and two tenths of a pole property. He stopped paying rates in 1908. JTM Priest started paying in 1909 and continued to rent and pay rates for 5 years until John Thomas sold the property to him on 14 April 1913. Seven years later it was back in Thomas hands when son George Bertram Thomas purchased it on 17 July 1920.

In March 1978 the original house was demolished and a block of four flats was erected. In February 1989 John and Phebe's granddaughters, Betty and Valmai Thomas, lived at 54 Grey Street..(Lot 881) the house next door to where John and Phebe had lived fifteen of their lives.

1896... John made additional purchases on 23 December 1896 of lot 886 on Aitken Street and Lots 896,7,8,9, all unoccupied land in Grey Street. These were a block away from his home and were debt free for the 16 years he owned them. In 1897 he paid rates on these five sections of ten shillings.

1897... Registered to John Thomas on 11 June 1897 was the purchase of house and shop on a double section site of two roods, being lots 183 & 184 in Havelock St, Ashburton. Mr John Orr, a merchant, was the owner of this site for 13 years before our John purchased same.

In 1898 John paid rates on this house and shop site of 2 pounds 10/-.

1901... On 28 January John sold part of these two sections to his rear neighbours ---- the Ashburton Club. His property was now reduced to 1 Rood and 39 Perches.

No Mortgage was ever raised on the property during the 28 years it was owned by John Thomas and the Thomas Brothers.

After Thomas Bros, George Bertram Thomas continued the business on this site and his son Allen followed him into ownership.

In 1953, after operating for 60 years and three generations, the business and property (Store and House) were sold to the Ashburton Club for 500 pounds.

In 1963 the Club pulled the building down and increased their member's carpark. Today in 1992 it is still a carpark.

1898... He purchased two more unoccupied sections in 1898, Lots 885 on Aitken St, and 895 on Grey St. Rates on the seven unoccupied sections was twelve shillings.

1899... More unoccupied paddocks were purchased. Lots 951/2/3/4 facing Walnut Avenue and 961/2/3 facing Grey Street.

1902... John now had twenty-one properties and the Rates Demands give different descriptions:-

> Lots 183 and 880 had dwellings.
> Lot 184 had the shop building.
> Lot 881 beside his home was now a Garden.
> Lots 885/6/7/8/9 unoccupied sections and stable.
> All other 12 were unoccupied sections.

1904... Lot 890 facing Aitken Street with a dwelling was purchased.

1905... John sold lot 961 in Grey Street to son George B Thomas.
> It was still an unoccupied section.

1908... John sold Lots 888 & 889 and this year moved to Coromandel.

1909... There were now 18 properties left. Lot 880/1 known as his home at 64 Grey Street, was leased or rented out. He sold Lot 954.

The Rates on the Havelock St shop were first paid by Thomas Bros this year.

1912... John sold Lot 885/6 Stable and unimproved section to Thomas Bros. He also sold Lots 896/7 to P G M Gourdie, a local builder, on 18 August 1912 and Lots 898/9 to son Percy Thomas on 14 May 1912.

1913... Ownership of their Ashburton home property Lots880/1 was now transferred to J T M Priest.
As well as the Freehold property at Coromandel, John still owned 10 properties in Ashburton, being Lot 183 Havelock St with dwelling plus unoccupied Lots 887/8: 951/2/3/4: 895 and 962/3 all about Grey Street.

1917... John sold Lot 889.

1918... Thomas Bros bought Lot 183, the dwelling next to the shop. John bought back Lot 889.

1919... John sold Lots 962/3, empty sections.

1920... He appears to have bought back Lot 183 with Dwelling from Thomas Bros. He sold section 951.

1925... John sold his last seven sections to Thomas Bros in this year.

The sketch map on page 82 is provided to help locate these sections.

-ooO0oo--

J THOMAS GRAIN & PRODUCE STORE:
1893... We believe the business was commenced before or immediately John and Phebe moved into the Ashburton Township from Allenton.
We think he rented the shop premises for the first five years as it was not registered to him until 11 June 1897, and he first paid rates as owner in 1898.

The shop was the third building from Cass Street on the southern side and not too far from East Street, the main retail shopping area.

--ooO0oo--

1896 ADVERTISEMENT

The Ashburton Guardian carried this advertisement on the 10th July, exactly to the day six years after his previous advert for a Tree Sale at Allenton.

We wonder if there is any significance in the double use of the 10 July date !

SHOP DELIVERIES:

Son Alfred told his son John Hunter Thomas that on the first day the shop was open, they sold one bushel of Wheat to be delivered. Then aged 16, Alfred delivered this Wheat by handcart. Soon daily deliveries were made by Horse and Cart around Ashburton and later in 1943 a truck was purchased.

The shop obviously started small but grew and prospered over the next 15 years to 1905, when taken over by John's sons, Alfred, Percy, George and Jack. Jack soon decided to try his luck in a business at Otautau in Southland, so the other three bought him out fairly early in the partnership's days.

1906... This issue of NZ Post Office Directory, shows the listing changes to Thomas Bros Grain & Produce.

POSTCARD: Between 1905 and 1925 a writer using the name SINBAD, wrote and illustrated a verse called `The Scroll of Fame` It contained all the names of the business people of Havelock Street at that time and of course the Thomas boys are mentioned.

Copy of the postcard verse is enclosed, compliments of Lillian Price.

THE SCROLL OF FAME

AN
HAVELOCK STREET
ZIG ZAG
BY SINBAD
MARK
TWO

In Havelock Street Many people we see
Who drink every lotion from beer to cold tea
But whatever their notions, whatever they drink
There are folks who are thoughtless and people who think

There is Sarney & Co., making shirts in galore,
And soft drinks at Bushell's the fruit shop next door,
Mister FERRIMAN next with his land and estate,
Or a nice little home with its name on the gate,

Then a Coach factory next where bodies are made
While Matheus The butcher is plying his trade,
Of the Counties ELECT allow me to say,
The Clerk of the Council, lives over the way.

Then all of a sudden you come unawares
On Mister Mont Baker with tables and chairs,
We have dressmakers too, who may like you to call,
For a Costume de Parrie, or a Silk à la ball.

While Mathieson Dyes any colour you like
AT STEPHENSONS AUCTION, you're sure to see IKE,
With auctions on Saturday every week
While CATES does the plumbing or solders a leak,

No Doctor Divinity answers the roll
But THOMPSON the bootmaker fixes the Sole
With sprigs and protectors and stitches and pegs
And keels made of rubber for saving your legs

Then there's KNOWLES who is famous
For GROPER and COD,
And Bundy with bread and a wink or a nod,
And LITHGOW the painter with coaches to paint
When a howling nor wester would anger a saint,

And the THOMASE'S too with plants by the score
And fruit and potatoes and seeds in the Store,
They are corn merchants too,
Deacent Boys, on me soul,
Then over the road Mister ARGYLE Sells Coal,

And McELREA, Buyer of Wool, Skins and Fat,
With his Cash and his Cart and his Dog and all that,
Then a painter named TERRIS,
But Never A WAN
From the Courthouse Corner
To Mister DEVANE

Who can sell yez TOBACCO a Pipe or a Knife,
Like poor Unkle Tom, who is crippled for life.

THOMAS BROTHERS, HAVELOCK ST SHOP.
Brothers Percy and Roy with Alfred on the cart.

SCOTTISH CATTLE on THOMAS BROS 1913 CALENDAR.
Supplied to their bigger customers, it measured 53cm x 32cm.
The sample held by Trevor Price was given by Betty and Valmai Thomas.

We have three different photos of Thomas Bros, Havelock Street shop-front and in 1989 one of these was on display with other historical records at the Ashburton Library.

1908... FIRE at the SHOP:

A fire threatened Thomas Bros store on 27 April 1908, an account of which appeared in the Ashburton Guardian that day on page two. It started at night in the boarding house next to the shop. The fire leapt the gap between the two buildings and caused 50 pounds worth of damage.

On the same page as the Fire story is an advert for Thomas Bros products.

--oo0Ooo--

WISES N. Z. P. O. DIRECTORY:

William Thomas was listed as Nurseryman in Ashburton only once, over the 11 years the Allenton business was operating ... in the 1885/6 issue.

John Thomas does not appear until;-

1887-8 as John Thomas...Ashburton. (That is all ...no occupation)

1890-1 as John Thomas ...Storeman...Ashburton.

      (Maybe the shop started 1891/2 and the Nursery only legally
        ended in March 1893 !)

1892-3 as John Thomas...Storeman...Ashburton.

1896-7 as John Thomas...Seedsman...Ashburton.

1901   as John Thomas...Grain and Produce Merchant...Ashburton.

1903   John same as 1901 but now also listed are sons ... Alfred (aged 26) and Charles (aged 15)... the occupation given for both of them is .... Storeman...Ashburton.

--oo0Ooo--

NZ ELECTORAL ROLLS:

John and Phebe are recorded as follows:-

1884...No 1565..Thomas John. Resident.. Ashburton..Nurseryman.

1887...No 1804   "   "   "   "   "

1890...No 2463   "   "   "   "   "

1893...No 4072..Thomas John. Resident.. Ashburton..Nurseryman.

.........No 4077..Thomas Phebe   "   " Domestic Duties.

1896...No 3569..Thomas John   "   " Grain & Produce Dealer

.........No 3577..Thomas Phebe   "   " Domestic Duties.

FAMILY:

1882... GEORGE BERTRAM THOMAS was born 21st December 1882, at their Allenton Nursery, Ashburton. More detail page 162.

Michael Stanley Thomas, who printed the 1970 Thomas Family Tree was a grandson of George, via his son George Morris Thomas.

1882... Phebe's father John Woods died in Auckland on 13 Sept 1882.

1884... JAMES SYDNEY THOMAS was born 14 Oct 1884 at Allenton, Ashburton and was known as Syd. More detail page 176.

1886... PHOEBE ELSIE THOMAS was born 11 Jan 1886 at Allerton, Ashburton and was known as Elsie. More detail page 185.

1887... JOHN HENRY THOMAS was born 5 August 1887 at Allerton, Ashburton and was known as Jack. More detail page 190.

1907... JOHN THOMAS aged 56   PHEBE THOMAS aged 52

1888... **CHARLES ERNEST THOMAS** was born 13 November 1888 at Allenton, Ashburton and was known as Charles. More detail page 198.

1890... **BERTHA MAUD THOMAS** was born 14 May 1890 at Allenton, Ashburton and died 1st Feb 1891 aged 9 months. She is buried in an unmarked grave at the Ashburton Cemetery.

1893... John's mother **Jane Thomas** died at Costley Home, at Epsom in Auckland on 25 July 1893 aged 72.

1901... **ALEXANDER ROY THOMAS** was born 28 September 1901 at Grey St, Ashburton. He was known as Roy. More details page 202.

1907... **Jessie Elizabeth Thomas** died aged 28, on 6 Sept 1907. More detail page 140.

--ooO0oo—

PHEBE ... KNITTING/CROCHET:

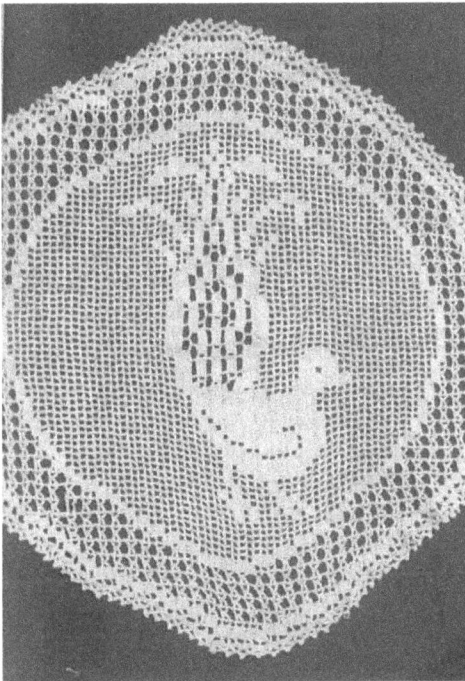

All the grandchildren remember Phebe as being a very active and competent knitter & crochet worker. In fact samples of her work still exist and are scattered all over New Zealand with her descendants.

Jill and Trevor Price have a sample of her crochet.
A circular tray cloth, depicting a Lyrebird and measuring 30cm in diameter. This was placed in their care by Phyllis Rainbow after being in her possession for many years.
Noeline Chappell has a table cloth about 1.20 meters square and worked in 1919 to celebrate Victory and Peace at the end of World War One. This was with George Herrick Thomas until his death.

91

Corner of PHEBE's BEDSPREAD now with Sylvia Ritani.

Corner of PHEBE's TABLECLOTH now with Noeline Chappell.

Corner of PHEBE's TABLECLOTH now with Mary Thomas.

Great Granddaughter Sylvia Ritani now has the Bedspread that her mother Phyllis Rainbow treasured. On special occasions Phyllis also used the bedspread as a table cloth on her extended table.

Phyllis recalled Phebe doing her crochet or knitting for the grandchildren at every available moment. Phyllis also received many jerseys.

Son Roy's daughter-in-law, Mary Thomas has a tablecloth crocheted by Phebe about 1.2 meters square. There is a photo of this being used under a wedding cake but no detail on back of photo.

BOOKLET... Mary Thomas also has in her care a 15cmx10cm booklet given to Phebe by her elder sister Martha. "Pansies & Ferns" it is called, by Isabella J Postgate, and contains five pictures and verses.

1907... FAMILY PHOTO: John and Phebe gathered all 10 surviving children and had a professional photographer take a group photo about mid 1907. Most families still have a copy and we have used this photo to provide a view of the children on the opening pages of each of their stories. Daughter Jessie died in Sept 1907 and she is very frail and ill looking in this photo.

We believe that John and Phebe sensed her death was imminent and therefore organised this family photo.

CARDS... John learnt to play 500 from son Frederick and it was a pastime they both enjoyed for many years as Fred's son Clarry recalls.

WESLEYAN METHODIST CHURCH: ASHBURTON.

During their time in Ashburton, John must have spent many hours following his religious interests. He lived within two miles of a Church for the 26 years after 1882 when he arrived at Allenton.

On 15 May 1908 John was involved with the Barring Square Methodist Church in Ashburton, as the staff of the Sunday School presented him with a bible when he retired and left Ashburton, mentioning on the flyleaf his "many years of faithful service."

This 1908 Bible is now with grandson John Hunter Thomas.

John attended the wooden Methodist Church on the Barring Square site before the present brick one replaced it. The wooden Church was shifted to Barring Square in 1879, and the photo was taken in 1877. This Church's records have not been searched and if they are still available, we feel sure there must be lots of information on the John Thomas family to be found.

"Ashburton Country" by W H Scotter.
In this book we found a list of Prominent Office-bearers of the Wesleyan Methodist Church at Ashburton.
Amongst them were three men we recognised ... our John Thomas and
W H Collins who bought the nursery from John in 1893 and
J T M Priest who bought John's home in Grey Street in 1913.

FAMILY BIBLE:
John and Phebe Thomas's Family Bible was in the hands of son Roy Thomas when Michael S Thomas interviewed him on 16 May 1971 and he copied out the Birth, Marriage and Death details it contained of John and Phebe's children. It has not been seen since Roy's death in 1972.

COROMANDEL:

1908... RETIREMENT:
When John and Phebe retired to Coromandel in 1908, with them went 3 unmarried children, Elsie aged 22, Charles aged 20 and Roy then aged 7.

We have a report from grandchildren Hector and Lillian, of John and Phebe touring the North Island looking for the perfect place to retire. On arriving at Coromandel John exclaimed ... "This is it!" John was then 57 and Phebe 53. Since starting this book we have found that living in Coromandel at that time was Phebe's younger sister Agnes, who had married Patrick Petley and this may have influenced them also.

An old identity in Coromandel, Mr Ron McNeil told us (in Jan 1987) he remembered a shop known as "Petley & Thomas". He was sure John had financially aided Patrick Petley to grow from being a Fruiterer in 1908, to being a grocer in 1925 with two shops...one in Coromandel and another in Grey Lynn, Auckland. We have been unable so far to prove this.

Ron remembered John and Phebe's daughter Elsie, who for many years took him at Sunday School. He enjoyed the way she told her stories with pictures on a felt board and described her as a "Quiet and Saintly" person.

THE HOUSE:
Title .. 132/231 (T46947) 24 July 1908
Mortgage .. Pt 1 Allott 1 Kaponga 121/245 Mortgage 33994, 7 April 1909.
John and Phebe found a lovely large house in Rings Road, on a one acre section diagonally opposite the Coromandel Hospital, about 1.5 kilometres north from the town's main shopping centre and it had a view out over the harbour. This large and beautiful house could also be what he exclaimed "This is it" over, as he bought this house on 24 July 1908.

When John died on 4th March 1928 ownership transferred to Phebe and when Phebe died, ownership went to George Bertram Thomas as Trustee for all his brothers and sister Elsie, and the house was occupied by George's sister Elsie until 2nd June 1937 when the family sold it.

This large house had been erected in 1876 and was used by the British Government to house Kapanga Mine managers Capt. Francis Hodge and Capt. W H Argall.

HISTORY OF THE PROPERTY:

1865: The Native Lands Act 1865, granted ownership of a 49 acre block of Coromandel land to a Maori named **PITA TAURUA,** on 2 Dec 1865.

1866: The 49 acres, (including our one acre) was sold by Pita Taurua for 79 pounds and 10 shillings on 2 February 1866. This block was bought jointly by **CHARLES** & brother **FREDERICK RING,** Timber Merchants, Coromandel.

1868: Charles, on 5 August 1868 sold his part of this block containing our one acre to **FREDERICK RING.**

1868-76: The one acre section became jointly owned by **FREDERICK RING** and **Mr W MILLER** a Hotel Keeper.

1876: On 14 November 1876 F Ring & W Miller sold out to W Miller's wife **Mrs MARY JANE MILLER.**

1877: August 26 saw M J Miller sell to **JAMES McMURRAY** a Coromandel Contractor the one acre of "land and premises" for 40 pounds.

1881: Mr McMurray sold to **E.D.WHITE** on 26 August 1881 and on 30 June 1882 Mr White took a mortgage with Mr Richard Laishley. The Mortgage was called in.

1883: On 27 August 1883 **Mr RICHARD LAISHLEY,** solicitor of Auckland and his partner **Mr FRANCIS GREGORY WELCH** of Onehunga, "Gentleman", sold the "Land and Premises" to storekeeper **LEWIS WILLIAM EDWARDS** for 100 pounds.

1888: Edwards sold for 150 pounds, "the land and all buildings erected on same" on the 1st May 1888 to the **KAPANGA GOLD MINING CO.** This company was formed on 9 March 1886.

1894: The 28 March was the day the first **K.G.M.Co** went into liquidation. The new **KAPANGA GOLD MINING CO LTD** was incorporated 3 October 1893. Our one acre section and buildings was transferred along with all other assets to the new KMG Co Ltd, by transfer of shares to the original company's shareholders. William Henry Argall (Mine Manager) acted on behalf of the new KMG Co Ltd.

1901: December 31 saw the new Kapanga Gold Mining Co go into liquidation. **HENRY BATTENS** was the Mine Manager at this time, and he bought the property off the collapsed company for 175 pounds.

1905: Henry Battens sold to **WALTER EDWARD SMITH**, a Butcher of Coromandel on 15 September 1905 for 300 pounds and the Land Transfer Act's Certificate of Title was produced 27 March 1906.
At this time W.E.Smith's neighbours were Joseph Bullen Rockliff, J.P. settler, and on the other side, Samuel James, an Ironmonger of Coromandel.

1908: JOHN THOMAS, retired Merchant of Ashburton, bought this property from W.E.Smith on 24 July 1908 and it remained in Thomas family hands for 29 years when sold to the Coromandel Hospital Board.
During the Thomas period, mail was addressed to Kapanga House, Rings Road, Coromandel.

1937: The COROMANDEL HOSPITAL BOARD which took control on 2 June 1937, used the property as their Resident Doctor's house.

1963: The Coromandel Hospital Board sold to Electrical Contractor **NOEL WILLIAM EDEN** and his wife **BETTY WINIFRED EDEN** on 20 October 1963. It is believed they did up the house, restoring it to its original condition.

1977: February 11 the present owners **LAWRENCE JOHN OLLIFF** and his wife **LOUISE MARGURETE OLLIFF** bought the property.
In Jan 1987 we found they have built the Coromandel Colonial Cottages, a motel complex behind the house on the land where once the fruit trees, extensive gardens and stables stood.

We show two photos of the house on page 98.

The older one was taken soon after John and Phebe arrival in 1908 and includes some of the members of their Thomas family.

The present owners allowed us to take the other photo on Jan 1987.

1908… JOHN & PHEBE's RETIREMENT HOME
From L to R… Roy, Elsie, Phebe, Syd, George, Charles and John.

JOHN & PHEBE's RETIREMENT HOME as in 1987.

The Olliff's advised us the additional room on the verandah outside the dining room, was added by a Doctor who used it as an interview room, and except for an updated kitchen and more rooms added at the rear, the layout of the original building remained the same after 111 years. The motel units on the back section do not intrude on the old house.

Mr McNeil could remember the large gardens out the back of the house where the Mine Managers used to entertain their visitors.

FRUIT… John appears to have had numerous fruit trees on the Coromandel property. Below is a photo from a magazine (believed to have been a Horticultural one from around 1915) of John in front of a well laden Osprey Improved Peach tree and proudly holding peaches which averaged nearly half a pound in weight each.

Grand-daughter Phyllis Rainbow confirms that John felt very highly of his peaches and took a great pride in them. In fact, Phyllis remembers that Elsie received three of these prized Peaches as her 21st Birthday present. She was expecting a watch … but it did not arrive.

JOHN THOMAS PROUDLY DISPLAYING HIS PEACHES

Grand-daughter Morva Fountain remembered that John would not let anyone touch his fruit trees, and that he used to leave a box of fruit at the front gate for the kids to take, (free) as they went past on their way to school.

George Herrick Thomas remembered visiting Coromandel and eating Passion Fruit his Grandfather John had grown there.

HOLIDAYS... John and Phebe often holidayed in Christchurch to keep in touch with the family, and generally stayed with son Syd. (HET)
Granddaughter Betty Thomas recalled her Grandfather John, on one of the trips south, teaching her to flick her wet hands at other people.

FRIENDS... Amongst their friends at Coromandel was a family named Applegate. We believe they had a farm and John and Phebe's grandchildren enjoyed visits there. Son Roy has a photo in one of his albums of the Applegate's horse.

FLOWERS... The old house photo shows that John and Phebe continued with and enjoyed their gardening.

Granddaughter Morva Fountain remembered Phebe tending to the flower garden and taking flowers for internal church decoration. When there was a good supply, she would distribute some to the sick at the hospital over the road.

FOOD... John's greatest weakness may have been his love for toast. Well, toast with a special preparation and it appears he would do this himself.
He took a slice of bread, buttered it on both sides and then toasted it in the oven. He never put jam or anything on it, just another coat of better on top and he ate it plain. He would never let Phyllis Rainbow have any.

CHURCH... The family were still practicing Methodists and attended the Church in Rings Road. Living next door were the Petleys and a young Ron McNeil lived next to them.
The family did not always go to Church with John and he would take granddaughter Phyllis Rainbow when she was there.
She said she *"was not thrilled with that part of her visits, because in latter years John was a bit deaf and he would sit in the front row. There everybody could see you and John sang so loud."*

The original
Coromandel Methodist Church
Built 1898

CIRCUIT STEWARD...
A booklet produced for the Coromandel Methodist Church's Golden Jubilee celebrations in 1948 lists the Circuit Stewards from 1899 to 1948.
These Include:-
1920 to 1928... J Cleave and J Thomas.
1937 to 1941... A.R.Thomas (son Roy).

JEWELLERY...
The photograph below shows one of Phebe's pieces of Jewellery now held by Trevor Price, which will stay in the family. This was given to him by Phyllis Rainbow who received it and the story of the broach, from her mother Edith.
.... It appears John used to wander off by himself at any time and usually only for a few hours or maybe a day or two.
Once, he was gone for nearly a month and the first Phebe knew of his whereabouts was a letter from the family in Christchurch, saying ... how nice it was to see Father again.
When John arrived back in Coromandel he gave Phebe this Broach .... possibly as a peace offering. (photo not actual size)

ADDRESS... Phyllis Rainbow has an old postcard which gives John and Phebe's postal address as ....Kapanga House, Coromandel.

The Nov **1908 Parliamentary Roll** for Coromandel seems to confirm this address as it shows registered were:-
#5967 THOMAS: John   KAPANGA HOUSE, SETTLER
#5968 THOMAS: PHEBE   KAPANGA HOUSE, MARRIED
#5969 THOMAS: PHEBE ELSIE KAPANGA HOUSE, SPINSTER

101

1914... LOANS:

While researching the land of John's property at Coromandel, we came across these two loans.

Sarah Margaret Morgans, wife of David Thomas Morgans borrowed 50 pounds off George Herbert Applegate a local Storekeeper on 30 July 1906 and paid the debt on 8 July 1909.

(The Applegates were close friends of John and Phebe.)

The same Sarah Margaret Morgans borrowed 300 pounds from John Thomas at 7 pounds 10/- interest per annum (that's 2 ½%) from 1st November 1913. The mortgage document No 235002 was recorded 14 April 1914.

1918... Phebe's mother **Mary Ann Woods** died in Auckland on the 16th November aged 85.

1922... John & Phebe's **Golden Wedding Anniversary** was celebrated and a brief notice appeared in the Ashburton Guardian on the 30 Dec 1922.

GOLDEN WEDDING
ANNOUNCEMENTS.

THOMAS—WOODS.—On Dec. 31st, 1872, at the Whau, Auckland, by Rev. David Hamilton, John Thomas, to Phebe Woods, late of Ashburton. Present address: Coromandel.

JOHN THOMAS' DIED:

DEATH

THOMAS.—On March 4, 1928, at Coromandel, John Thomas (formerly of Ashburton); suddenly.

**Ashburton Guardian
5 March 1928**

1928... His Grandchildren advise that John was a Lay-Preacher and on the 4th March 1928 after morning service he took ill in the Coromandel Methodist Church vestry. He died soon after of a heart attack, aged 76, and is buried at the Coromandel Cemetery beside a lot of his local Methodist friends.

Sylvia Ritani remembers her Grandmother Edie saying ..."He put his hand on his chest and said... 'I have a pain' and just dropped dead."

Morva Fountain recalls her grandmother Phebe telling her that John left home in an excited mood that day and really looking forward to singing in church. After leaving her at the gate he came back and asked her if he had kissed her goodbye. He died that day and Phebe often remarked that that day she got two kisses.

OBITUARY...

The 21 April 1928 issue of the NZ Methodist Times reports......
On March 4, a great gloom was cast over the township of Coromandel, when it became known that Mr Thomas had passed away suddenly, immediately after the morning service in the Methodist Church, the late Mr Thomas being a member of the choir, church steward and trustee.

He had sent his goods, on the previous day for the harvest festival, and saw the fruits of his labour on the stalls that morning and had a short practice for his part for the night's service, viz, "Sing to the Lord a New Song" etc.
He then walked into the vestry and collapsed. Mr Thomas was always interested in the welfare of the church and financially was the main support. He had, for some time, been troubled with a heart complaint and was seventy six years of age. He leaves a wife and grown-up family of 7 sons and daughters to mourn their loss. (FC.)
   "Sing to the Lord a new song" was used on John's headstone.

JOHN'S WILL...

On the first March 1915 John Thomas signed his Will.
He appointed wife Phebe and upon her death son George Bertram Thomas as Trustees of his estate.   In 1915 he still owned the property at 186 Havelock Street, Ashburton and it appears Thomas Bros rented it off him and paid the Rates on it.
      The conditions he laid down were:-
1.   The trustee was to hold this land and buildings for his three sons Alfred, Percy and George (the Thomas Bros team), providing they paid Phebe two pounds per week during her lifetime.
2.   He left George one hundred pounds "for the trouble of Executing his will" after Phebe died.
3.   The residue of his estate to be held while Phebe lived and afterwards to be divided equally between all his children, or their widow or grandchildren if a child predeceased him.
Burgess and Brooks were his Solicitors in 1915.

On the 9th March 1928 Phebe and George visited the Solicitor's office and legally signed papers accepting their roles as Trustees of John's Will.
The Coromandel house was occupied by Phebe and Elsie for the next six years until Phebe died and then George allowed Elsie to stay on for a further three years until June 1937 when she found another residence.

PHEBE'S WILL:
All of John's Insurance Policies, Houses, Lands and Financial dealings were at Phebe's death transferred to George as trustee for all his brothers and sister.

Phebe however had some money of her own and personal items and on the 15 April 1931 she signed all these over to her only living daughter Phoebe Elsie Thomas. Elsie signed acceptance as Trustee of Phebe's Will on the 19 July 1934.

When Elsie moved out of the house in 1937, George sold it to the Coromandel Hospital Board. However the Solicitors (now Brook and Tonkin) did not wind up the estate until 12 years later in June 1949... some 21 years after John died.
--oo0Ooo—

JOHN'S ESTATE:
The 1949 Statement from Brook and Tonkin, Solicitors (copy held by John Hunter Thomas) is an account of how John's final 1735 pounds 19 shillings & 11 pence was distributed to his eight living children or their descendants.

We do not know the full extent of John's financial and property holdings at the time of his death but the statement shows a Mortgage to Mr Woodhouse, Rent from Christensen Farm, Interest on Mortgage received from Davis, Rent from Gamble and the Sale of the Peachy property. John obviously kept his solicitors and his money busy working for him whilst he lived at Coromandel.

The Solicitors charged him 47 pounds to wind up the estate... and we all know solicitors don't come cheap... so that 1735 pounds left for the beneficiaries must have been quite a princely sum in those days. In fact if we assume that inflation has averaged 10% per annum over the 40 years since the 1735 pounds was distributed, then it would have a buying power in 1993 of nearly half a million dollars ....yes... a very impressive total.
--oo0Ooo—

1934... PHEBE DIED: Aged 79 on 23 June.
Phyllis Rainbow remembered her mother Edith Thomas, travelled to Coromandel to help nurse Phebe when she became ill.
She rests with John at Coromandel Cemetery.
Eight of their children survived them both, seven sons and daughter Elsie.

The PHOTO of the HEADSTONE reads ....

IN LOVING MEMORY
OF
JOHN
BELOVED HUSBAND OF
PHEBE THOMAS
WENT HOME 4TH MARCH
1928

I SING UNTO THE LORD A
NEW SONG
ALSO
PHEBE
HIS WIFE, WHO JOINED HIM
23RD JUNE 1934.

PHEBE AT COROMANDEL

THE LOWE AND WOODS FAMILIES:

1803... In Flintshire, Wales at the village of Ysceifiog, **EDWARD GRIFFITHS** married **JANE EVANS** on 14 May 1803.

They had 2 children, JOHN in 1803 and ANN in 1805.

ANN GRIFFITHS married **GRIFFITH LOWE** in Flintshire at Flint on December 6, 1830.

Our Griffith Lowe was born about 1805, maybe in Wales or England.

GRIFFITH and ANN LOWE:
They raised 5 children ... EDWARD born 1829 and JOSEPH 1831 were baptised at the Overton Church in Flintshire. Then three children baptised at the Extra Parochial Chapelry at Threapwood by Rev John Frederick Churton.

MARY	LOWE was baptised on 16 February	1833
JOSEPH	LOWE was baptised on 29 September	1833
WILLIAM	LOWE was baptised on 16 June	1839.

The Rev J F Churton took over the Threapwood Church in 1832 and his last official duty at Threapwood was a baptism on 29 September 1839. This gentleman came to New Zealand and later became the first Bishop of Auckland and a monument stands to his memory in Shortland Street. The ship's records show that our Lowe family *"were engaged on behalf of the New Zealand Company for emigration, by the Rev J F Churton"*, who was then aged 41 and travelled as a Cabin passenger along with his wife, 2 sons and 4 daughters.

> We believe our Lowe family and the Churtons left Threapwood at the same time… soon after 29 September as they sailed for New Zealand on the 19th November that year from Gravesend, London.

The New Zealand Company was formed in England in 1839 for the purpose of sending British settlers to New Zealand on a planned basis.

"The BOLTON" (a Clipper of 540 tons with John Percival Robinson as Captain) was the sixth emigrant ship to sail from London's Gravesend for New Zealand. She left at 10.30am on 19 November 1839.

The Bolton's "Register of Emigrant Labourers" who received free passage to NZ, details 156 Steerage Passengers and 33 Cabin Passengers including 56 males, 47 females and 86 children.

Among the Steerage passengers were ...

GRIFFITH	LOWE	age	36	Labourer
ANN	LOWE	age	35	Wife
EDWARD	LOWE	age	11	son
JOSEPH	LOWE	age	9	son
MARY	LOWE	age	7	daughter
JOHN	LOWE	age	5	son
WILLIAM	LOWE	age	1.5	son

It was a five month trip for the Lowe family. Three days after leaving Gravesend they were off the Isle of Wight and took just under one month to reach Santa Cruz, Tenerife. It berthed here on 12 December "to procure stock, severe losses by death amongst them having taken place during bad weather". They re-sailed on 15th and celebrated Christmas and New Year on board.
A couple of items of interest in the ship's records show that ….
178 dinners were served to passengers at the Captain's Table, mainly fresh meat and poultry, at a cost of two shillings per head … Also, three
children were born and seven passengers died during the 154 day voyage.

The Bolton berthed at Port Hardy (Nelson) on 12 April 1840 and re-sailed at 2pm the 18th April. Three days later (?) she arrived at Port Nicholson (Wellington) at 2 pm the 21st April 1840, 5 months after leaving Gravesend. The passengers seem to have stayed on board until unloading was nearing completion as the records show "all passengers were victualled for 176 days" and that our seven Lowes "disembarked on the 7th May 1840". All passengers were landed at Thornton Beach and the greater part of them lived in very primitive shanties, known as "Bolton Row" until they could build themselves something more substantial.

It would appear that although the seven members of our Lowe family survived the crossing, the marriage of Ann and Griffith did not.
Nine months after landing at Wellington Ann gave birth to George, who took his father's name of Morris. Ann and SAMUEL MORRIS had four children, George, Jane, Sarah and Henry. At the break-up of the marriage Griffith appears to have taken custody of the two eldest Edward & Joseph and stayed in Wellington, whilst Ann took her six youngest ... Mary Ann, John, William George, Jane and Henry and made her home in Auckland. No divorce from Griffith Lowe has been found and partner Samuel Morris went to the goldfields before 1849 and did not return. Mary Ann now aged 16.

GRIFFITH LOWE DIED: He died in Wellington aged 47 on 15 October 1852. Six years later and now aged 54, Ann married at her home in Victoria St, Auckland to MOSES CROCKER (a Tailor) on 28 October 1858.

ANN DIED: On 19 November 1869 aged 64 and buried at Grafton Cemetery.

Of **ANN'S NINE CHILDREN** we know ...

Nothing of **Edward & Joseph Lowe** who we think were raised in Wellington.

Mary Ann Lowe married John Woods (Seaman) and had 10 children.
>   One of these named **Phebe Woods married John Thom**as (Storekeeper) who we detail in Chapter 4.

John Lowe (Storekeeper) married Rebecca Taylor in Auckland, raised 3 girls.

William Morris was a lay preacher and remained single.

George WD Morris (Master Builder) married Agnes Turner, raised 7 children.

Jane Morris married George Thomas (Storekeeper) who we detail here in
>   Chapter 5. George was younger brother of John Thomas. (Star Mills).

Sarah Morris died aged 10 months.

Henry Morris died aged 5.

(Much more detail of these families in **"The WOODS family"** book)

PHOTO: Ivy Morrison, Jessie Gow, Jane Haslett & MARY ANN WOODS.
Ivy was daughter of Phebe's brother John. Jessie & Jane were Phebe's sisters. Taken at the Haslett house, Pah Road, Epsom, Auckland.

ANN LOWE FAMILY TREE

Ann married Griffith Lowe					Samuel Morris			
5 children					4 children			
Edward	Joseph	Mary Ann	John	William	George W. D.	Jane	Sarah	Henry
1828	1830	1833	1834	1837	1841	1842	1845	1847
?	?	M	M	S	M	M	X	X
		1853	1873		1865	1860		
		John Woods	Rebecca Taylor		Agnes Turner	George Thomas		
children		10	3		7	12		
		Martha	Alice		Henry	Selina		
		Phebe	Martha		Agnes	Eliza		
		Jessie	Eveline		Ada	Elizabeth		
		George			George	Mary		
		John			Arthur	John		
		Jane			Edith	William		
		Agnes			Mildred	George		
		William				Richard		
		Edward				Esther		
		Henry				Edward		
						Alfred		
						Hilda		

MARY ANN (LOWE) WOODS
Aged about 45 in 1877

COROMANDEL:

These two photos are from the Elsie Thomas
Collection, now in the care of Mary Thomas.
Elsie has written on the back of the photos…

"Coromandel under snow, red roofs now white … 1930"

JOHN THOMAS and PHEBE WOOD'S CHILDREN

MARY JANE THOMAS   First child
born 5 February 1874 at Whau (now Avondale), Auckland
died 30 November 1878   aged 4 years 10 months.
Buried at Anglican Cemetery, Papanui, Christchurch.

ARTHUR HAMILTON THOMAS   Second Child
born 17 January 1875 at Star Mills, Whau, Auckland
baptised 9 February 1875 by Rev Tinsley, Primitive Methodist Church.
died 19 April 1875 aged 3 months.
Buried at Auckland.

ALBERT JOHN THOMAS   Third child
born 2 January 1876 at Star Mills, Waterview, Auckland.
baptised 11 April 1876 by Rev Tinsley, Primitive Methodist Church.
died 13 October 1876 aged 9 ½ months at Waterview, Auckland.
Buried at Grafton, Auckland

JOHN WOODS THOMAS   Seventh child
born 7 October 1880 at Southbrook, Canterbury.
died 2 March 1881 aged 5 months,
at Southbrook. (Registered at Rangiora)
Buried at Anglican Cemetery, Papanui, Christchurch.

BERTHA MAUD THOMAS   Fourteenth child
born 14 May   1890 at Allerton, Ashburton.
Died 1 February 1891 aged 8 1/2 months,
Buried at Ashburton.

The birth and death information of these children have helped
us to follow our family's journey throughout New Zealand.

111

ALFRED EDWARD THOMAS

(1877-1947)

1877... Alfred was born 21 March 1877, the fourth child of John and Phebe Thomas, at the Whau in Auckland.

He was to become their eldest living child.

He reached the age of five while the family was living at Allerton. We presume he went to school somewhere nearby, probably in the Ashburton township.

Alfred must have started work at his father's Nursery at Allenton and he was there on the day the Shop opened in Ashburton in 1893.

It was Alfred, aged 16 years that delivered their first sale of one Bushel of Wheat by hand cart. We have a photo taken later at the front of the shop, during Thomas Bros days, showing Alfred seated behind a horse on a cart loaded with sacks of produce to be delivered. (see page 88)

Before he settled down in Ashburton, in employment with his father, Alfred worked among the Maoris for a few years. He returned to Ashburton about 1902 aged 25. (JHT)

1898... When aged 21 Alfred purchased a section, Lot 960 unimproved land, in Grey Street, Ashburton. The 1899 Rates were three shillings. He held this land for about 3 years then sold it in 1902 to his brother Percy.

1903... Wises N.Z.P.O. Directory lists Alfred (now 26) as "Storeman.... Ashburton" and although it does not say so we presume he was once again working with his Father in the Havelock St produce store.

PARTNERSHIP:
1905... Along with his 3 brothers Percy, George and Jack, Alfred went into business. Their partnership took over their Father's shop at 186 Havelock Street and renamed it Thomas Bros, a Seed, Grain and Produce store. Very soon Jack wanted out of the partnership and the other three worked together for the next 20 years, employing other members of the family including youngest brother Roy for a while.

1907... The page 112 photo was taken when Alfred was nearly aged 31.

MARRIAGE:
1908... Alfred aged 32 married **SARAH ANN CATES** aged 25, on 17 Sept 1908 at the Methodist Church in Ashburton.
Their wedding photo is shown on the next page.

Sarah was known by all as **Annie** and was born 3 February 1878,
A daughter of George Cates (a Storekeeper, born in London) and
Sarah Ann Jerrard Hunter (born Weymouth, Dorchester).
George and Sarah married in Oamaru NZ, on 21 Jan 1875.
Annie's brother Arthur Cates married Georgina Page, a sister
of Susan Page who married George Bertram Thomas.

Alfred and Annie had six children whom they named ....
Phoebe Elsie Thomas born 22 June   1909, known as Phoebe.
John Hunter Thomas born 8 January   1913, known as John.
Vivian Athol Thomas born 7 April   1914, known as Athol.
Ronald Claude Thomas born 12 May   1918, known as Ron.
Doris Ophir Thomas born 17 January 1919, known as Doris.
Wyvern Ian Thomas born 31 July   1920, known as Vern.

1925... In this year the Thomas Bros partnership split up.
George bought Percy and Alfred out and carried on the business himself
Percy went into partnership with brother Jack in a nursery and retail florist shop in Invercargill.

ALFRED & ANNIE THOMAS 17 September 1908

GROCERY BUSINESS:
1925...
> Alfred started his own Grocery Business in Ashburton, on the corner of Wakanui and Eton Streets in Ashburton East.

He named it "A.E. Thomas... Cash Supply Stores."
As well as the usual Grocery lines he handled Produce and Hardware. Tough trading times and bad health put paid to Alfred's desires to be successful on his own and the business went under in 1929. The Ashburton Guardian reports the business was sold to Alexander Reed on 9 April 1929 and that on 4 July 1929 Alfred was adjudged bankrupt. Alfred got another mention in the paper on 4 July 1930. Later the shop closed and the next buyer picked the building up, turned it around and placed it further back on the section, finally converting it into the house as we saw it in December 1988.

122 GREY STREET:
All of Alfred and Annie's children married and most of these would have left from their residence at 122 Grey Street, Ashburton.

114

ALFRED'S GROCERY SHOP.

The family moved to this 122 Grey Street house after the business was sold in 1929 and eldest daughter Phoebe was married from there in 1930.
This address was the Cates family home and Annie was able to look after her sick and ageing father more easily.

HEIRLOOMS:
Annie's **Food Ration Book**, dated October 1943, shows that she was still living at 122 Grey Street a year after Alfred died.
This book is now in the care of her granddaughter Beverley Keating.

Annie worked at the Ashburton Hospital and son John has a **partly filled diary** she kept during this time.

Daughter Phoebe has her **mother's hand bag** which she was using just before she died and it contained a 1909 Death Notice for Alice Mary Thomas... the daughter-in-law of William Thomas page 60 who was the brother of John Thomas 1851-1928.

This card proved very valuable in leading us into William's background.

OVAL PHOTOS:

Phoebe has two large oval shaped **Wedding photos** of Alfred and Annie, and son John has a set of large photos of Annie's parents George and Sarah Cates.

Son John recalls his father as a quiet man who never talked about him-self and who never raised his voice. He recalls Alfred as hard working, often at home planting for the shop until eleven o'clock at night.

"COCKY":

Alfred had a **white Parrot** and he and the bird talked to each other. Cocky sat on his shoulder especially when he was replanting plants. John advises that the parrot used to tell tales on the children, and they used to try to get on the good side of it, by giving it extra titbits of food ... but it always chatted away to Alfred. (JHT)

SEAMSTRESS:

Beverly Keating remembers her grandmother Annie, as being blessed with both beautiful handwriting and the ability of a quality seamstress.

It appears that twice a year she used to travel two hours by coach from Ashburton to Longbeach, to the Griggs Homestead. (In 1988 this took 20 minutes) She would stay there for six weeks and bring all their torn and buttonless clothing up to date. On one trip she made Bib-overalls for twins John and Gilbert Griggs. She enjoyed her visits there and loved the sewing room, as it overlooked the lake.

"TREVES"

Alfred enjoyed for a long time the companionship of a **Corgi dog** named "Treves". We do not know the origin of the dog's name but it was very faithful.

It loved its master so much that when Alfred went into hospital, Treves found his way there and was discovered sleeping under Alfred's bed. Poor old Treves missed Alfred so much that he died within weeks of Alfred's death. (JHT)

> Alfred never recovered to full health after the shop
> collapsed, and he died 2nd May 1942 aged 65.
> He is buried at Ashburton Cemetery, along with Annie
> Who joined him 13 October 1974 aged 96.

ANNIE & ALFRED's CHILDREN & SPOUSES
VERN, RON, R Love, W Ching, JOHN< ATHOL
Phyllis, Grace, DORIS, ANNIE, PHOEBE, Ivy, Peggy

The CATES family on 29 January 1930.
At rear GEORGE junior and ARTHUR
At front ANNIE, GEORGE & SARAH and JOCK.

ALFRED EDWARD THOMAS FAMILY TREE:

3rd Generation:

ALFRED EDWARD THOMAS.......married...........................SARAH ANN (ANNIE) CATES

b 21 March 1877	17 September 1908	b 3 February 1878
at Whau, Auckland.	at Ashburton.	at Ashburton.
d 2 May 1942 (65)		d 13 October 1974 (96)
Bur at Ashburton.		Bur at Ashburton.

Annie was daughter of GEORGE CATES and SARAH ANN JERRARD HUNTER.

Alfred and Annie had 6 children known as; Phoebe, John, Ronald, Athol, Doris & Vern.

++

4th Generation	5th Generation	6th Generation	7th Generation
PHOEBE ELSIE THOMAS	NORMAN DAVID CHING	GAYLE ALISON CHING	PETER JAMES ANDERSON
b 22 June 1909	b 7 December 1930	b 16 March 1956	b 23 August 1976
at Ashburton.	at Ashburton.	at Burwood, ChCh.	at Christchurch.
m 7 May 1930 =====	d 9 December 1976	m 23 April 1976===	
at Ashburton.	Bur at Christchurch.	at Christchurch.	
WILLIAM DAVID CHING	m 19 November 1955=	DAVID JOHN ANDERSON	RUTH JESSICA ANDERSON
b 30 August 1899	at Mangakino.	b 5 July 1956	b 28 March 1979
at Kaiapoi.	ELIZABETH ANN CORFIELD (Betty)	at Rakaia, ChCh	at Christchurch.
d 27 April 1972	b 14 June 1936		
Bur at Ashburton.	at Koutu, Nth Auckland.		
		SHARON ROSE CHING	RYAN JAMES GRANT
They had 8 children.	They had 8 children.	b 10 December 1957	b 19 January 1983
(He was the son of	(She was daughter of	at Leeston, ChCh.	at Nambour, Queensland
William Ching and	Vernon Albert Corfield	m 23 August 1980====	Australia.
Caroline Annie Margets)	and Emily Adelaide Russell)	at Christchurch.	
		ROBERT PATRICK GRANT (Bob)	ZETA ROSE GRANT
		b 5 November 1955	b 16 June 1985
		at Ashburton.	at Nambour, Queensland Australia.
			DAYNE PATRICK GRANT
			b 21 October 1987
			at Nambour, Queensland Australia.
		DONNA MARGARET CHING	JESSICA NANCY ROBERTSON
		b 8 September 1959	b 20 December 1979
		at Darfield.	at Christchurch.
		m 11 February 1984 ===	
		at Templeton, ChCh.	
		GRIERSON EDWARD ROBERTSON	NEIL DAVID ROBERTSON
		b 9 November 1948	b 26 June 1981
		at Christchurch.	at Lincoln, ChCh.

Alfred Thomas cont.

4th Generation	5th Generation	6th Generation	7th Generation
Phoebe continued.	Norman continued.	**DIANE PHEOBE CHING** b 19 September 1960 at Darfield. m 17 October 1986=== at Tauranga. **KENNETH JOHN McLEOD** b 16 June 1956 at Tauranga.	**JASON DAVID McLEOD** b 18 August 1978 at Lincoln, ChCh. **DANIEL JAMES McLEOD** b 5 March 1981 at Te Puke. **DONNA MARIE McLEOD** b 24 August 1983 at Tauranga.
		LINDA FAY CHING b 29 October 1961 at Lincoln, ChCh. m 9 February 1980 === at Taitapu, ChCh. **LAURIE KEMP** divorced 9 Feb 1985	**LORINDA KYM KEMP** b 18 June 1980 at Nambour, Q'land, Aust. **DARRYN VERN KEMP** b 23 January 1983 at Nambour, Queensland Australia.
		VERNON NORMAN CHING b 13 February 1963 at Christchurch.	
		FIONA MARIE CHING b 12 October 1964 at Lincoln, ChCh. m 23 December 1989 at Christchurch. **MARK STEPHEN FOURIE** b 14 May 1960 at Pretoria, South Africa.	
		WENDY DAWN CHING b 12 June 1968 at Christchurch.	
	EUNICE next page	GLYNN next page	

Alfred Thomas cont.

4th Generation	5th Generation	6th Generation	7th Generation
Phoebe continued.	**EUNICE MAY CHING** b 25 September 1932 at Ashburton. m 20 February 1954 === at Ashburton. **MALCOLM CHARLES FRYER** b 19 February 1923 at Timaru. d ( ) Bur at Ashburton. They had 6 children. (He was son of Charles Fryer and Elizabeth Potts)	**GLYNN CYRIL FRYER** b 6 November 1954 at Ashburton. m 20 September 1975 at Christchurch. **ROBYN LYNETTE WEST** b 15 February 1952 at Te Kuiti. **ALLAN MALCOLM FRYER** b 15 May 1956 at Ashburton. **KEITH CHARLES FRYER** b 7 September 1959 at Ashburton. **HELEN ELIZABETH ANNE FRYER** b 14 October 1960 at Ashburton. **RHONDA MAY FRYER** b 20 January 1966 at Ashburton. **MARIE JOYCE FRYER** b 22 April 1967 at Ashburton.	
	PHOEBE DAPHNE CHING b 8 November 1933 at Ashburton. m 17 November 1956== at Ashburton. **ARTHUR HENRY BYRON** b 13 January 1927 at Auckland. Divorced 13 Aug 1985 They had 4 children.	**BRUCE ARTHUR BYRON** b 19 November 1957 at Ashburton. **COLIN STUART BYRON** b 26 July 1959 at Ashburton. m 3 November 1979 == at Ashburton. **DEBORAH MARY LUCKING** b 25 November 1960	**JAMIE ALLAN BYRON** b 7 December 1980 at Ashburton. **SHANE STUART BYRON** b 13 September 1982 at Ashburton.

Alfred Thomas cont.

4th Generation	5th Generation	6th Generation	7th Generation
Phoebe continued	Daphne continued.	Deborah continued. at Oamaru.	**LISA JEAN BYRON** b 23 September 1985 at Ashburton.
		MARGARET ELSIE BYRON b 26 August 1960 at Ashburton. married first on 25 October 1977===== at Ashburton. **PHILLIP GEORGE WILLIAMS** b 7 November 1956 at Christchurch. : : : : : : : married second on 25 January 1986 at Ashburton.======= **RICHARD JOHN WARD** b 7 August 1957 at Ashburton.	**SARAH JANE WILLIAMS** b 5 January 1978 at Ashburton. **AMANDA DAPHNE WILLIAMS** (twin) b 11 January 1980 at Christchurch. **VICTORIA RUTH WILLIAMS** (twin) b 11 January 1980 at Christchurch. **SIMON GEORGE WILLIAMS** b 30 December 1983 at Oamaru. ----------------- **DOMINIQUE MARGARET WARD** b 13 June 1986 at Ashburton. **RYAN ANDREW MALCOLM EVANS** b 19 November 1990 at Christchurch.
		RACHEL BARBARA BYRON b 4 August 1963 at Ashburton. 1st m 23 March 1985 at Gore, Southland. **MERVYN RALPH ROBERTSON** b 30 April 1960 at Gore................ 2nd m 25 April 1992=== at Ashburton. **MURRAY DAVID AMYES** b 20 October 1954 at Leeston, ChCh.	**MICHAEL JAMES AMYES** b 25 September 1990 at Ashburton. **MELISSA FAYE AMYES** b 19 October 1992 at Ashburton.

121

Alfred Thomas cont.

4th Generation	5th Generation	6th Generation	7th Generation

Phoebe continued.

DORIS FAY CHING
b 15 July 1937
at Ashburton.
d 18 December 1984
Bur at Dunedin. (47)

LAWRENCE PERCIVAL CHING
b 12 December 1939
at Ashburton.

CYRIL EDWARD CHING
b 11 November 1942
at Ashburton.
d 17 August 1944
Bur at Ashburton.

A SON b 1947
has requested all
his family details
be withdrawn.
Sorry.

WILLIAM MURRAY CHING (Bill)
b 2 July 1950
at Ashburton.

JOHN HUNTER THOMAS
b 8 January 1913
at Ashburton.
m 25 June 1936=====
at Ashburton.
IVY LILLIAN ROBINSON
b 7 January 1912
at Christchurch.
d 5 November 1986
at Ashburton. (74)

They had 5 children.
(She was daughter of
John Robinson & Emma
Elizabeth Jackson.)

DESMOND JOHN THOMAS
b 12 June 1935
at Ashburton.
m 20 February 1960 ==
at Ashburton.
AVIS ELLA LILLIAN MUIR
b 15 March 1936
at Ashburton.

They had 5 children.
(She was daughter of
Thomas William Muir
and Hazel Ella Read.)

NEVILLE WILLIAM THOMAS
b 15 May 1962
at Ashburton.
m 28 November 1992
at Milford, Auckland.
RACHEL SUSAN ABOUD
b 22 November 1965
at Wellington.

SUSANNE KAY THOMAS
b 19 June 1963
at Ashburton.
m 28 October 1988===
at Ashburton.

KATE LAURA McNAB
b 5 July 1991
at Gore, Southland.

4th Generation	5th Generation	6th Generation	7th Generation
John & Ivy continued	Desmond & Avis cont.	Susanne married **ANDREW GRANT** **McNAB** b 21 April 1963 at Balclutha.	
		BRENT JOHN **THOMAS** b 26 August 1965 at Ashburton. m 27 February 1993 at Methven, Canterbury. **MICHELLE MARIE** **HAYES** b 10 June 1967 at Dunedin.	
		RICHARD JAMES **THOMAS** b 30 June 1969 at Ashburton.	
		ANDREA JANE **THOMAS** b 30 March 1971 at Ashburton.	
	MARION LOIS **THOMAS** (twin) b 15 February 1937 at Ashburton. m 24 May 1958===== at Ashburton. **TREVOR JAMES** **LOVE** b 28 January 1935 at Ashburton. They had 1 child. (He was son of Robert John Love who was to marry Marion's Aunt, Doris Ophir Thomas)	**GLENDA MARION** **LOVE** b 20 June 1959 at Ashburton. married first on 17 March 1979====== at Ashburton. **PAUL JOHNSTON** b 1 August 1956 at Ashburton. : : : : : married second on 8 July 1989 at Ashburton.======= **JOHN ROSS** **WALKER** 22 June 1948 at Dunedin.	**MEGAN MARION** **JOHNSTON** b 4 May 1980 at Christchurch. **JODI KATHLEEN** **JOHNSTON** b 12 August 1982 at Christchurch. **ANDRE PAUL** **JAMES JOHNSTON** b 12 September 1985 at Christchurch. **SHANNAN JOHN** **WALKER** b 31 March 1990 at Christchurch.

4th Generation	5th Generation	6th Generation	7th Generation
John continued.	Marion & Trevor cont.	**MALCOLM TREVOR LOVE** b 15 August 1961 at Ashburton. m 14 Nov 1981 at==== Geraldine, Canterbury. **CYNTHIA MARIE TOOMEY** b 10 November 1961 at Geraldine.	**MELISSA JANE LOVE** b 25 March 1990 at Christchurch.
		DONALD ROBERT LOVE b 14 July 1963 at Ashburton. m 17 Nov 1984 ====== at Methven. **KAY DAWN THOMAS** (no relation) b 13 October 1964 at Methven, Canterbury.	**ROBERT WILLIAM LOVE** b 13 May 1989 at Ashburton. **CAMERON DONALD LOVE** b 8 May 1991 at Ashburton.
		ANDREW JOHN LOVE b 8 April 1965 at Ashburton. m 30 June 1990 ===== at Rakaia, Canterbury. **SHERYL ANNE BRADY** b 22 February 1958 at Hamilton.	**NICHOLAS ANDREW LOVE** b 6 January 1992 at Christchurch. baby due October 1993 at Christchurch.
		ROGER STUART LOVE b 22 March 1978 at Carew, Canterbury.	
	BEVERLEY DAWN THOMAS (twin) b 15 February 1937 at Ashburton. m 27 September 1958== at Ashburton. **SAMUEL HASLETT KEATING** b 26 February 1933 at Ashburton. They had 4 children.	**SHARON ANNE KEATING** b 23 December 1959 at Ashburton.=======	**ALENA DAWN KEATING** b 15 March 1982 at Ashburton. **KYLE SAMUEL DONALD BLAMPIED** b 2 July 1986 at Ashburton. Shane next page...

124

Alfred Thomas cont.

4th Generation	5th Generation	6th Generation	7th Generation
John continued.	Beverley & Sam cont. (Samuel was son of Samuel Keating and Florence Haslett)	Sharon continued	**SHANE ANDRE BLAMPIED** b 30 October 1988 at Ashburton.
		DIANA BEVERLEY KEATING b 16 February 1962 at Ashburton. m 4 Sept 1982====== at Ashburton. **ALAN SMITH HARRISON** b 3 September 1957 at Ashburton.	**CHARLOTTE IVY HARRISON** b 20 September 1988 at Ashburton. **SAMUEL DUDLEY HARRISON** b 11 October 1990 at Ashburton. **EMMA-LOUISE HARRISON** b 23 July 1992 at Ashburton.
		DAVID SAMUEL JOHN KEATING b 22 March 1964 at Ashburton. **ROCHELLE ANGELA KEATING** b 17 January 1971 at Ashburton.	
	NEIL HUNTER THOMAS b 14 May 1938 at Ashburton. m 16 November 1963== at Ashburton. **SHIRLEY IRENE TELFER** b 22 June 1942 at Ashburton. They had 4 children, (She was daughter of John (Jack) Henry Telfer and Daisy Violet Coxon)	**VERNON NEIL THOMAS** b 27 September 1965 at Ashburton. **DEBORAH KAYE THOMAS**.........married b 3 May 1967 at Ashburton. **MAREE ANN THOMAS** b 11 March 1969 at Ashburton. **NICHOLA JANE THOMAS** b 30 December 1972 at Ashburton.	**KEN FREWER** on 6 March 1993 at Rossly Hill, Hampstead, England.

125

Alfred Thomas cont.

4th Generation	5th Generation	6th Generation	7th Generation
John continued.	**ENID LORRAINE THOMAS** b 28 February 1941 at Ashburton. m 9 March 1963 ===== at Ashburton. **JOHN ROBERT NEWLANDS** b 28 November 1938 at Ashburton. They had 3 children. (He was son of William Clement Newlands and Margaret Reid Oliver)	**ANNETTE LORRAINE NEWLANDS** b 26 September 1964 at Ashburton. m 16 Nov 1985 ===== at Ashburton. **ROGER DAVID BRASELL** b 20 January 1960 at Ashburton.	**JONATHON ROBERT BRASELL** b 2 October 1988 at Ashburton. **HAYLEY LORRAINE BRASELL** b 24 December 1990 at Ashburton. **MATTHEW LUKE BRASELL** b 19 September 1992 at Ashburton.
		DAVID WILLIAM NEWLANDS b 30 May 1968 at Ashburton. He has plans to marry in March 1994. **ROBERT JOHN NEWLANDS** b 23 June 1970 at Ashburton.	
RONALD CLAUDE THOMAS b 12 May 1918 at Ashburton. Married first on 1945===== at Ashburton. **VALERIE** (Bonny) **BRONWYNE GRICE** b 6 December 1927 at Ashburton. They had 3 children. (Bonny has remarried, and now Mrs McGarry) Ronald continued. : : : : : :	**RAELENE ANNETTE THOMAS** b February 1946 at Ashburton. d 11 March 1946 (3 wk) Bur at Ashburton. **RHONDA ANNE THOMAS** b 20 February 1947 at Ashburton. m 11 Nov 1967===== at Timaru. **PETER LESLIE MORGAN** b 16 August 1948 at Timaru. Reginald next page...	**DARRYL IAN MORGAN** b 26 March 1968 at Timaru. **NIGEL PAUL MORGAN** b 15 March 1969 at Timaru. Rachel next page...	

126

Alfred Thomas cont.

4th Generation	5th Generation	6th Generation	7th Generation
Ronald continued : : : : : : : : : : : : : : : : : :	**REGINALD JOHN** **THOMAS** b 8 April 1948 at Ashburton. m 3 Aug 1968 ===== at Timaru. **LORRAINE** **SMALLRIDGE** b at Timaru.	**RACHEL JOY** **THOMAS** b 3 December 1968 at Timaru. **WARREN JAMES** **THOMAS** b 18 March 1970 at Timaru. d 18 October 1972 Bur Timaru. **KARL BRENDON** **THOMAS** b 6 June 1974 at Timaru	
married second on 1957===== at Christchurch. **GRACE DOREEN** **ANNAND** b at Wellington. d 17 December 1983 Bur at Ashburton. They had 2 children.	**WARREN JAMES** **THOMAS** b at Ashburton. d 19 November 1957 Bur at Ashburton. **MURRAY BRUCE** **THOMAS** b December 1959 at Ashburton. d 7 February 1970 at Ashburton.		
VIVIAN ATHOL **SINCLAIR THOMAS** b 7 April 1914 at Ashburton. d 18 January 1992 Bur at Ashburton. m 10 March 1944===== at Ashburton. **MARGARET IRIS** **CALEB** (Peggy) b 6 May 1928 at Ashburton. (She was a daughter of Arthur Caleb and Mabel Annie Wakelin)	**JOCELYN** **MARGARET** **THOMAS** b 15 May 1948 at Christchurch. m 9 March 1968 ===== at Ashburton. **DAVID BENJAMIN** **TOPP** b 23 September 1944 at Rotherham, Canterbury. (He was son of Harry Topp and Rita Alma Norrish)	**TRACEY JAYNE** **TOPP** b 28 May 1969 at Ashburton. m 21 March 1992 at Christchurch. **GRANT RANGI** **KELLETT** b 22 March 1967 atTimaru. **DEBORAH MARIE** **TOPP** b 16 April 1970 at Christchurch.	

Alfred Thomas cont.

4th Generation	5th Generation	6th Generation	7th Generation
Athol & Peggy cont.	Jocelyn & David cont.	**BRENDON MICHAEL DAVID TOPP** b 8 April 1974 at Darfield, Canterbury.	

DORIS OPHIR THOMAS b 17 January 1919 at Ashburton. d 10 October 1972 Bur at Ashburton. (53) married first on 14 April 1939 ====== at Ashburton. **FRANCIS SAMUEL HETHERINGTON** b 23 August 1908 at Caversham, Dunedin. d 28 January 1958 Bur at Ashburton. (49) They had 3 children. (He was a son of Christopher Watson Hetherington and Elizabeth Martin who m 13 October 1897.)	**MALCOLM BRUCE HETHERINGTON** b 17 January 1941 at Ashburton. d 28 September 1992 at Tamar Valley, (51) Tasmania, Australia. m 17 Oct 1964====== at Ashburton. **CAROL ANN SMITH** b 7 March 1944 at Ashburton.	**SHARON ANN HETHERINGTON** b 7 December 1966 at Geraldine, Canterbury m 17 January 1989 at Georgetown, Tasmania, Australia. **JOHN ANTHONY FRENCH** b 17 September 1962 at Barnsley, Yorkshire, England. **GRANT ADRIAN HETHERINGTON** b 12 June 1969 at Ranfurly, Otago. m 1 September 1990 at Invercargill. **LISA JANE HOFFMAN** b 30 October 1970 at Gore, Southland.	
	NOELA LYNETTE HETHERINGTON b 26 December 1945 at Ashburton. m 21 May 1966===== at Timaru. **MALCOLM JOHN VINCENT** b 26 April 1945 at Temuka.	**CRAIG ALEXANDER VINCENT** b 5 July 1967 at Wellington. **BRENT JOHN VINCENT** b 1 April 1969 at Lower Hutt. **JARRAD FLETCHER VINCENT** b 6 December 1977 at Lower Hutt.	
	David next page...		

128

Alfred Thomas cont.

4th Generation	5th Generation	6th Generation	7th Generation
Doris & Francis cont. : : : : : : : married second on 22 December 1962 at Ashburton.======= **ROBERT JOHN LOVE** b 24 November 1908 at Ashburton.	**DAVID FRANCIS HETHERINGTON** b 2 October 1953 at Ashburton. m 8 April 1978 at Nelson. **SHELLEY KNAPP** b at **PETER JOHN LOVE** b 16 December 1963 at Geraldine, Canterbury		
WYVERN (Vern) IAN THOMAS b 31 July 1920 at Ashburton. married first on 14 July 1947 ======= **PHYLLIS HILDA GRAY** b 13 March 1926 at Ashburton. (She was daughter of Charlie Edward Gray and Lucy Jones) : : : married second on 22 December 1978 at Timaru. ======== **Mrs WILLIAMINA DOCKERILL (Ina)** b 12 October 1918 at Timaru. (She was daughter of William David Watson and Hannah Christian)	**IAN WAYNE THOMAS** b 2 July 1948 at Ashburton. m 21 Aug 1971 ===== at Timaru. **JANICE LYNETTE GRIEVE** b 19 November 1950 at Palmerston North. **GRAEME EDWARD THOMAS** b 20 January 1958 at Timaru. 1st m 12 April 1979 at St Albans, ChCh. **SUSAN LILLIAN HARPER** (no children.) : 2nd m 30 Sept 1989 at Christchurch. ===== **HELEN DOREEN RHODES** b 19 June 1960 at Akaroa, Canterbury.	**AMANDA MEGAN THOMAS** b 23 December 1974 at Christchurch. **STEFFAN MARK THOMAS** b 1 January 1977 at Christchurch. **REBECCA HELEN THOMAS** b 8 March 1991 at Christchurch.	

129

FREDERICK WILLIAM THOMAS (1878-1935)

1878.. Frederick was born the fifth child of John and Phebe Thomas, at Styx, to the north near Christchurch.

He was known as Fred and was to become their second eldest child.

He shifted with his family to Southbrook, Christchurch and would have arrived at Allenton aged about four, in 1882.

Frederick must have left for all his schooling from the Allenton Nursery, as he was 15 in 1893 when the family moved to the Grey Street house in Ashburton.

Son George advises that his father attended the Ashburton Borough School.

We do not know what Fred did when he left school. He may have also immediately joined his father at the J Thomas Grain & Produce store as did his brother Alfred.

1899... On 25 December Frederick aged 21 was bestman at the wedding of his first cousin John Coates Thomas to Alice Mary James, at Levin.
Fred noted his occupation as a labourer and that he lived in Levin.

Fred's first child George (born 1904) remembers his father working all his life in and around Ashburton, for a while on the Railways and for many years as a Carter on the delivery lorry for New Zealand Farmer's Co-op.

MARRIAGE:

1903... Frederick aged 25, married **MARGARET JANE PAGE** aged 28, on the 11 June 1903 at the Ashburton Church of St Stephen.
Fred gave his occupation as Labourer.

> Margaret was a daughter of Matthew Page and Isabella Hillis.
> She was born 28 February 1874 at Cork in Ireland. Her mother Isabella died giving birth to their third child. Matthew remarried to Agnes McKeen. Margaret's half-sister Susan, married Fred's brother George Bertram Thomas.   (Page family detail, page 169)

Fred's father-in-law Matthew Page, is remembered by Fred's niece Phyllis Rainbow as a man with a long grey beard who never allowed any talking during a meal. She recalls a story passed on to her by Kate and Jean Page when Jean was dyeing a blouse using a pink dye soap. Before dinner Matthew Page went out the back and washed his face using the new pink soap beside the basin. He sat down at the table and the others were beside themselves when they saw the pink beard and of course they were unable to say anything until after the meal.

Frederick and Margaret had four children whom they named:-
GEORGE HERRICK THOMAS   born 3 August 1904, known as George.
ARTHUR RAYMOND THOMAS born 30 March 1906, known as Ray.
FREDERICK JOHN THOMAS born 1 March 1909, but died aged 4 in 1913.
CLARENCE MATTHEW THOMAS born 3 March 1912, known as Clarry.

1907... Frederick's photo on page 130 was taken when he was aged 29.

1909... The birth certificate for son Frederick John Thomas states he was born at 1 Creek Rd, Allenton and his father was a Carter aged 29. (MST)

1917... This issue of NZ Post Office Directory lists Fred's occupation as Carter and states he lived then at 76 Creek Road, Ashburton.

FISHING: The family had a hut at the mouth of the Ashburton River at Hakatere. Fred had a trout licence and did occasional trout fishing and sea fishing at the mouth where he caught many Kawhai.
Sylvia remembered one occasion when Fred's wife Margaret offered trout to the folk at Hakatere Beach and after they had eaten it, she told them it was eel.

MARGARET and FRED on 11 June 1903

1910.. CLOCK:

Granddaughter Noeline and Ray Chappell have in their care the 83 year old clock that Fred bought Margaret to celebrate their 7th Wedding anniversary in 1910. Son George now treasures this item.

George also told us that he was supposed to have been christened Eric but when asked for his name, his mother said Eric with a cold afflicted voice, that sounded like Herrick, and that is what the man wrote down.

HOME BREWING:

1925... Fred was also widely known for his Home Brewing skill and son George remembers one particular day. His father used to work his brew in an 18 gallon barrel. This barrel normally was turned upside down when not in use and the cat would sleep on top. On one occasion Fred had just made a brew and put it in the barrel to work when Arthur Cates called at the house with his dog. The dog saw the cat and chased it, and the cat dropped on top of the barrel and fell into the scalding hot beer. Fred pulled it out but it was too far gone and had to be destroyed. However, they went ahead with the working of the brew. Son Ray remembers a lady neighbour who always seemed to pop in when Fred lifted a brew and she got the first sample of the 'cat' beer.

She reckoned it was the best brew that Fred had ever made and he says nobody ever told her the truth.

Arthur Gates thought it was a good story and produced this poem.

DEDICATED TO THE LATEST BREW.

1.'Twas on the 5th day of September
   In the year nineteen twenty-five
   As far as I remember
   Fred boiled his cat alive.

2. Now Fred had got a thirst up
   And he got his loving wife
   To help him make some beer up
   To end that thirsty life.

3. And she worked & watched all day
   At that boiling stuff sublime
   Says Fred "My darling wife
   Next week that will be fine."

4. Then Fred had got a cobber come
   With bottle good and true
   Says Fred "By gosh that's dash good stuff
   Next week I'll shout for you."

5. And they strolled around the garden
   To see what could be seen
   And the dog he spied a pussy cat
   A playing on the green.

6. A scream, a yell & Fred looked round
   To see what he did hear
   And there he saw his pussy cat
   A boiling in his beer.

7. Now Fred has got an invite out
   To friends both wide and near
   To call along at any time
   To try his new brand of beer!

Fred's son Clarry took a copy of this poem to the WW2 with him and says it brightened up many a quiet moment as he related the tale to his mates.

Phyllis remembered Fred and his home-brewing and recalled that for months after he was still generously offering it to all-comers, but now telling them that he had taken out the dead cat.

GARDENING:
Son George advises that Fred always had vegetables in his garden and that on the section were five apple, two apricot and a plum tree plus gooseberries and black & red currant bushes. There was also a row of raspberry canes... enough to make their own jam. As well as all this gardening and tree attending Fred had a couple of pigs which were used for bacon and enough fowls to keep them in eggs. The fowls were killed and boiled when they got too old for laying.
Granddaughter Shirley was told by her mother Sylvia that she thought Fred had a great sense of humour and was a good gardener. She says he used to cook the roast dinner every Sunday while the family went to Church. Son Clarry said that when their Aunty Elsie visited from Coromandel, all the brothers except Fred would go off to church that Sunday. Fred said he couldn't be a hypocrite.

CARDS: Clarry also remembers that Fred taught his father John to play 500, a pastime they both enjoyed for many years.

THREE GENERATIONS ... George, Phebe and Fred.

FREDERICK WILLIAM THOMAS

Fred died 31 July 1935. Margaret died 14 May 1938.
Both are buried at Ashburton.
We have an old photo of Fred, Margaret and the three boys outside an Auckland address, 8 Alderley Road, Mt Eden, the back of the card says, even though the numeral ? 6 is visible in the photo.
We wonder who they were visiting?

MATTHEW PAGE with his grandchildren
from left ... RAY, CLARRY and GEORGE

FREDERICK WILLIAM THOMAS FAMILY TREE:

3rd Generation:
FREDERICK WILLIAM THOMAS.......married.....................MARGARET JANE PAGE
b 13 May 1878   11 June 1903   b 28 February 1874
at Styx, Christchurch.   at Ashburton.   at Cork, Ireland.
d 31 July 1935 (57)   d 14 May 1938 (64)
Bur at Ashburton.   Bur at Ashburton.

Margaret was a daughter of Matthew Page and Isabella Hillis his first wife.
Frederick and Margaret had four children known as; George, Ray, Fred and Clarry.

++

4th Generation	5th Generation	6th Generation	7th Generation
GEORGE HERRICK THOMAS	SHIRLEY MARGARET THOMAS	PETER ROY GOSS	CHRISTOPHER JOHN GOSS
b 3 August 1904	b 19 July 1932	b 3 September 1960	b 6 October 1988
at Ashburton.	at Wanganui.	at Auckland.	at Wellington.
d 21 January 1989	m 23 April 1955=====	m 15 May 1988 =====	
Bur at Napier. (84)	at Napier.	at Wellington.	NICOLE JANE GOSS
m 30 April 1931=====	ALAN MONTGOMERY GOSS	MARYANNE PATRICIA BARRY	b 17 January 1991
at Christchurch.		b 24 March 1964	at Wellington.
SYLVIA MARTHA COX		at Wellington.	
b 16 March 1907	b 16 October 1922		
at Christchurch.	at Napier.		GOSS
d 9 July 1988 (81)			due August 1993
Bur at Napier.			at
		JOHN HERRICK GOSS	
They had 3 children.		b 26 August 1961	
(She was a daughter of Albert Henry Cox and Rhoda Mabel Voice.)		at Taihape.	
	MURIEL JOAN THOMAS	KAREN JANE HARVEY	EMMA JANE WEENINK
	b 26 November 1936	b 27 October 1963	b 29 December 1992
	at Hawera.	at Dannevirke.	at Wellington.
	m 2 January 1960===	m 20 Jan 1989 =====	
	at Napier.	at Wellington.	
	JOHN ELLIOT HARVEY	BRENT GERALD WEENINK	
	b 11 February 1935	b 30 December 1963	
	at Wairoa.	at Ashburton.	
		SHONA JOY HARVEY	
		b 30 August 1965	
		at Dannevirke.	
		m 13 May 1989	
		at Napier.	
		DAVID PATRICK MILLNER	
		b 28 August 1962	
		at Taihape.	

4th Generation	5th Generation	6th Generation	7th Generation
George continued.	**NOELINE ELIZABETH THOMAS** b 28 December 1939 at Hastings. m 19 August 1961 ==== at Napier. **RAYMOND JOHN CHAPPELL** b 6 February 1937 at Timaru.	**MARGARET LEE CHAPPELL** b 14 October 1963 at Gisborne. m 6 February 1993 at Lower Hutt. **ARTHUR RICHARD KITCHING** b 3 April 1964 at Hamilton. **JAMES THOMAS CHAPPELL** b 28 September 1965 at Gisborne. **LYNETTE RAE CHAPPELL** b 15 June 1976 at Bangkok.	
ARTHUR RAYMOND THOMAS (Ray) b 30 March 1906 at Ashburton. m 30 December 1931= at Ashburton. **EVA ISOBEL SOAL** b 25 November 1905 at Ashburton. They had 2 children. (She was a daughter of Frank Soal and Evangeline Edge.)	**PATRICIA MERLE THOMAS** b 13 August 1933 at Ashburton. m 12 November 1955== at Ashburton. **GEOFFREY ALAN FORD** b 22 November 1928 at Christchurch.	**ROBYN SHIRLEY FORD** b 30 June 1960 at Ashburton. m 26 July 1985 ===== at Ashburton. **PETER MATHEWS** b 6 October 1959 at Wellington. **HEATHER KAY FORD** b 26 September 1963 at Ashburton.	**SAMUEL THOMAS MATHEWS** b 17 May 1991at Wellington.
	IAN RUSSELL THOMAS b 10 March 1937 at Ashburton. m 6 January 1967===== at Invercargill. **KATHLEEN ELIZABETH DEANE** b 30 January 1944 at Bristol, England.	**PHILLIPA JANE THOMAS** b 14 February 1969 at Greymouth. **MICHAEL IAN THOMAS** b 22 January 1972 at Foxton.	

Frederick next page...

138

4th Generation	5th Generation	6th Generation	7th Generation
FREDERICK JOHN THOMAS b 1 March 1909 at Ashburton. d 1911 aged 2 years Bur at Ashburton.			
CLARENCE (Clarry) MATTHEW THOMAS b 3 March 1912 at Ashburton. m 5 October 1946==== at Ashburton. **MARGARET JENNY SWANN** b 14 March 1925 at Coventry, England. d 22 November 1986 Bur at Ashburton. They had 2 children.	**JILL ANNETTE THOMAS** b 9 October 1947 at Ashburton. m 7 Dec 1968 ====== at Ashburton. **RICHARD JOHN LYE** b 24 December 1942 at Ashburton.	**MICHAEL ANDREW LYE** b 25 May 1971 at Ashburton. **SIMON MATTHEW LYE** b 27 April 1973 at Ashburton. **DUNCAN GARETH LYE** b 19 January 1975 at Ashburton.	
	ROGER LEE THOMAS b 2 June 1950 at Ashburton. m 29 June 1974====== at Christchurch. **RAEWYN SOPHIA HUBBARD** b 12 June 1951 at Rangiora, Canterbury.	**EMMA LOUISE THOMAS** b 2 March 1977 at Christchurch. **JANE KATE THOMAS** b 18 April 1978 at Ashburton.	

JESSIE ELIZABETH THOMAS

ESSIE

JESSIE ELIZABETH THOMAS *as a healthy young woman*

Jessie Elizabeth Thomas was born 23 June 1879 at Southbrook, north west of Christchurch, and her birth was registered at nearby Rangiora.

She remained single and seems to have battled poor health all her life.

Jessie suffered for many months from Lung and Intestinal illnesses.

The above photo is thought to have been taken in Christchurch, in honour of her 21st birthday. She died aged 28 on 6th September 1907 at her parent's home in Grey Street, Ashburton. The Rev H E Bellhouse of the Wesleyan Church supervised her burial at Ashburton Cemetery.

Jessie, photographed
about middle 1907,
near the end of her life.

The Headstone on Jessie's
Ashburton gravesite.

In
Loving + Memory
of
JESSIE ELIZABETH
DAUGHTER OF
JOHN & PHEBE THOMAS,
WHO DIED SEPT. 6th 1907
AGED 28
"THY WILL BE DONE"

WALTER PERCIVAL THOMAS

(1881 – 1966)

1881... Walter Percival Thomas was born 17th November 1881, the eighth child of John and Phebe Thomas at Barbados St, Christchurch.
(ex birth certificate)
He was known as Percy.

Wises NZ Directory shows nobody named Thomas owning land in Barbados St and no hospital or nursing home but there was a Mrs Nichol .... Midwife, listed between Chester & Armagh St on the right side from the North. Percy's children, Hector and Lillian, always thought he was born at Styx, near Christchurch, as was his brother Frederick.
The family could have lived at Styx for a while at about this time.

1882... Before Percy's first birthday his family moved to Ashburton and his father and Uncle William started their nursery business at Allenton.
We assume Percy also went to the Ashburton Borough School as did his brothers and sisters, while they were all living at the Allenton Nursery.

1893... When Percy was 12 years old the family (now 10 children alive) moved into Ashburton township to live at 64 Grey Street. Father John had sold the Nursery and started his... 'J Thomas Grain and Produce Store' at 186 Havelock Street.
We believe Percy went to work at his father's shop when he left school.

1902... Percy, aged 21, bought his first piece of unimproved land in 1902 from his brother Alfred. Lot 960 in Grey Street, which he held until 1907.

PARTNERSHIP:
1905... Thomas Bros Ltd was formed by four Brothers. Alfred (28), Percy (24), Jack (21) and George (23). The 1906 edition of NZ Post Office Directory first lists Thomas Bros Grain and Produce Store. They carried on the Havelock business that their father had started. Very soon Jack wanted out but the other three worked together for the next 20 years.

George was the one with managerial skill, Alfred did a lot of the deliveries, so this left Percy with the shop customers to satisfy. We know that younger brother Roy worked for them for a while and that there were other employees too. Over the following years Thomas Bros slowly purchased the two sections containing the Shop and House and also the section containing the Stable, from their father John.

1907... The photo on page 142 was taken when Percy was aged 25.

1907/8... Percy sold unimproved Lot 960 and bought Lot 901 with a dwelling on it, over the road in Grey Street.

GREY STREET LOT 901 ASHBURTON on 26 January 1911.

PERCY and ELSIE 9 November 1908

MARRIAGE:

1908... Percy aged 26, married **ELSIE MAUD STEVENS** aged 22 on 9th November 1908 at the Waterton Methodist Church. (Ashburton District) Wedding witnesses were Elsie's father William Stevens and Percy's brother George Bertram Thomas.

Elsie was a sales girl in a near-door bakery when Percy met her.
She was born 13 May 1886 at Ashton, to Jemima & William Stevens.
William was a farmer at Ashton in the Ashburton farm district.

Elsie was the 7th child of 13. Jemima's maiden name was Johns and both she and William Stevens came to New Zealand after they married, from Loddiswell in Devonshire, England.

Brief details of the Stevens and Johns families are shown here on page 153-155 ... but more information is available from our .... 'The STEVEN'S family' book.

144

Percy and Elsie had three children whom they named ...

Hector Percival Thomas   born 21 June   1909, known as Hec.
Lillian Elsie Thomas   born 3 August   1912, known as Lillian.
Leslie Walter Thomas   born 23 January 1915, known as Les.

1909... Thomas Bros bought Lot 184 together with the building used for the shop at 186 Havelock St, Ashburton.

1911/12... Lillian was told that the family visited Percy's parents in Coromandel, on holiday during December 1911 / January 1912 but she has no recall of it as she was only "on-the-way".

PROPERTY:
1912... Percy bought lots 898/9 in Grey St on the 14th May 1912 from his father and had a house built there.

Son Hec was born in the first house on Lot 901, now known as 108 Grey St and Lillian and Leslie were born two doors away in the new house (below) on Lot 899, now in 1996 known as 78 Grey St. Elsie did not fancy nursing homes.

The 78 Grey Street, Ashburton house

At this time Percy also sold the property on Lot 901 to William & Daisy Hockings. Daisy was Elsie's sister and their daughters, Jessie & Lillian, became strong friends for the rest of their lives.

1915... Father John, now living in Coromandel was still selling off his Ashburton properties and Percy, together with brothers Alfred and George bought Lot 886 in Aitken St. This was an unimproved paddock next to the Shop's Stables that Thomas Bros bought from John in 1913.

1924... Brother Jack returned to Ashburton and persuaded Percy to join him in a partnership to buy out J Lennie and Sons, nursery, in Invercargill. Thomas Brothers of Ashburton was wound up. Alfred went into a Grocery business, whilst George stayed on at the Grain and Produce store having bought his brother's shares.

1925... This issue of NZ Post Office Directory lists Percy at 100 Grey St, Alfred at 82 Eton St and George at 64 Grey St, Ashburton.

1925 PERCY, Lillian, Leslie, Hector and ELSIE THOMAS
Taken just before they left Ashburton for Invercargill.

1925... Thomas Bros Ashburton, sold Lot 864 with a dwelling, in Aitken St to Percy presumably as part payment for his shares. A look through the Rates records shows that Percy first paid rates in 1925 and that Thomas Bros bought it in 1920. Percy still owned the property in 1933/34 rates year when it was rented to R Stephenson until 1936/7 when Mr G Daikee paid the rates. In 1937/8 Percy's name was not listed so we presume he sold it in 1935/6.

This must have been a nice investment for the 12 years Percy owned it. When we viewed the property in 1989 it looked all of its 70 year age.

INVERCARGILL:

1925... Percy and Elsie and their three children left Ashburton on the 20th January to live in Invercargill.

Their 100 Grey St (Lots 898/9), Ashburton home was transferred to William Stewart Kerr, an Ashburton Grocer on 17 February 1925.

They initially lived in a working men's cottage at the Nursery until they shifted into their permanent home on 3rd April 1925, also at the Nursery at Great North Road, Waikiwi, Invercargill.

Partner Jack had a house at 166 Leet Street, Invercargill.

Their Invercargill nursery's first advertisement is on Page 148.

Generally, Jack organised the Dee Street shop and the finances, and Percy managed the Nursery.

Lennies had a Florist shop in Esk St and Jack sold this shop with Tearooms over, three days after buying it, at a good profit.

They leased a shop in Briscoe's Building at 106 Dee St for their retail Florist Shop.

By 1926 the Nursery had grown from 10 to 14 acres.

Son Hector became an employee at the Nursery, whist Lillian and Leslie went to school near the Nursery at Waikiwi, Invercargill. (more detail p 310)

1930... Jack and Percy were of different personalities and the partnership was strained for some time and eventually Jack bought Percy out. Percy stayed awhile working at the Nursery for wages.

1935... Daughter Lillian married Nelson Price on 18 November.

These are the author's parents and further information
on Nelson's PRICE family is contained in the book
"MORGAN PRICE and Family"

THOMAS BROS. INVERCARGILL advertisement ... JUNE 1925

THOMAS BROS, Invercargill Delivery Truck

1936… Son Leslie was killed on the evening 9th October 1936 when aged 21. He was an apprenticed Electrician at Parkinson's Electrical shop in Dee St Invercargill, and was travelling home by bicycle on a dark wet night when he was hit by a car from behind.

Elsie also lost a brother named Leslie aged 22, in the First World War and after her son's death asked her family not to use the name Leslie again.

LESLIE THOMAS and his bicycle

HECTOR THOMAS at
Invercargill Nursery with
Floral bouquet.

LILLIAN, LESLIE,
HECTOR, PERCY &
ELSIE THOMAS
Outside their Invercargill
nursery home's front door.

HECTOR in old Army uniform, PERCY and ELSIE and LESLIE.
Taken Christmas 1927. Lillian took the photo.

1935... Son **Hector married Ruby Margaret Crawford** (a Taranaki girl) on the 19th December and in 1940 moved from Invercargill to New Plymouth.

They had 3 children, Lois, Kevin and Grahame. (details page 156)
Horticulture was Hector's business for most of his life but later he worked as storeman for Winstones Ltd, New Plymouth.

HOBBIES: Percy had two main hobbies, photography and painting.
He not only enjoyed taking photos but also developing and printing them, in the bathroom of their home.

He also enjoyed oil painting and Lillian still has one landscape depicting Mitre Peak. He did pen painting on glass jugs and a cracked sample of his work still exists, as does the metal paint box he used.

WEST PLAINS SHOP:

1935… On 4th December Percy, Elsie, Hector and Leslie moved to nearby West Plains, close to the railway line. Percy had bought the West Plains Grocery Cash Store and Ironmongery. There was a separate house behind the shop, where they lived.

RETIREMENT:

1940… Percy and Elsie sold the West Plains shop in January 1940, to a Mr Marshall and took in part payment Mr Marshall's house at 34 Huia St, Waikiwi. Percy retired at Huia St aged 58 on his Doctor's advice. He had heart trouble over previous years and had just had a stronger attack.

At Huia St they had large vegetable and flower gardens and many fruit trees. There was also a large chicken run. Elsie kept a budgie called Billy, a pet that her mother Jemima also used to enjoy. Elsie was clever with her hands and many samples of her crochet work still exist. In his retirement Percy took up Bowls and became Caretaker for the Waikiwi Bowling Club just across the Domain from his home.

1965… With Percy's health worsening they moved closer to daughter Lillian, to 414 Herbert St, on 9 June. Percy died on 4 January 1966 aged 84 and is buried at St John's Waikiwi Cemetery. Elsie joined him 26 April 1975 aged 88.

Elsie stayed on at 414 Herbert St until April 1972, when she moved over the road into Lillian and Nelson's home at 420 Herbert St where she lived for the next three years.

ELSIE's Brooch and Pendants.

The JOHNS family of South Devon.

NICHOLAS JOHNS b c1779 at Plymouth, Devon.... A Militiaman
    Had two marriages .... and died 6 April 1845 aged 66.

1st Married 13 January 1814 at Loddiswell.
    SUSANNA SOUTHERN b 21 August 1781 daughter of Thomas
    Southern and Susanna Moore of Loddiswell. Susanna was the
    daughter of John Moore and Susanna Kennard.
    Wife Susanna died 1834 aged 52.

2nd Married 23 February 1835 at Loddiswell.
    JOANNA TOLCHARD b 1786 at Stokenham, the daughter of
    Richard and Elizabeth Tolchard.

Nicholas and Susanna had three children baptised at Loddiswell named
    THOMAS, WILLIAM and GRACE.

    WILLIAM JOHNS
    b 24 May 1818 m 23 June 1839
    At Loddiswell
    ELIZABETH TOLCHARD.
    b 11 May 1817 at Stokenham.
Elizabeth's mother (Joanna) married William's father (Nicholas)
four years earlier. William and Elizabeth raised 8 children...
two of Elizabeths and six of theirs. The children were named:-
**JANE, PHILLIP, MARY-ANN, SUSANNA, ELIZABETH, JEMIMA,
THOMAS, EMMA.** William Johns died 11 November 1873 (55)
        Elizabeth remarried 22 Dec 1878 to Richard Lane.

    JEMIMA JOHNS
    Born 10 August 1853 and baptised 25 September 1853
    at Woodleigh in South Devon.
    Married in the June Quarter of 1877 at Totnes, Devon to
    WILLIAM STEVENS and came to New Zealand.
Should more detail be desired about this family please refer to the book ....
    'The STEVENS family' of Devon & New Zealand.

The STEVENS FAMILY

JOHN STEVENS (Agricultural Labourer) born c1796 at Devonport, Devon, England, married c1819 ELIZABETH PEARSE born c 1796 Kingsbridge, in Devon. They raised 10 children named ...... ANN, ELIZABETH, WILLIAM born & died 1824, **WILLIAM,** GRACE, CHARLOTTE, MARY HARRIET, JANE, SARAH and JOHN.

WILLIAM STEVENS born 25 June 1825, baptised 9 October 1825 at
    Halwell, Devon. A Farm Labourer, he married 27 Dec 1848 at
    Woodleigh to MARY EVANS baptised 1828 at Woodleigh, the
    daughter of John & Mary Evans (buried at Woodleigh).
    John's parents were William and Margaret Evans.

William and Mary Stevens had 12 children named ...twins MARY-JANE and ANN, JOHN, **WILLIAM,** ELIZABETH EVANS, EDWARD, SILVANUS, LOUISA, JAMES EVANS, NICHOLAS, AMOS and CHARLOTTE AMELIA.

WILLIAM STEVENS bapt. 2 April 1853 at Woodleigh, Farm Labourer.
    Married 20 June 1877 at Brixham, Devon to
    JEMIMA JOHNS born 10 August 1853 a daughter of William
    Johns and Elizabeth Tolchard.

    William Stevens aged 22 first arrived in New Zealand on the "Rangitiki" which left England on 4 Dec 1875 and arrived at Lyttleton 14 Feb 1876. He found work with Mr John Grigg at Longbeach in Canterbury and then returned to Devon to collect his family.

    William and Jemima Stevens with daughter Emily, using the assumed name of Evens, left Loddiswell on 30 Oct 1877. As assisted immigrants on board the "Carnactic" they left Graves End, England on 5 November 1877 and arrived at Lyttleton NZ, on 1 February 1878.

    They had a family of 13 named ... EMILY, JESSIE, MARY, WILLIAM, LOUISE, JESSIE, **ELSIE,** DAISY, ALBERT, STANLEY, NIGEL, LESLIE and IVANHOE.

    (Daughter ELSIE MAUD STEVENS
    Married PERCIVAL WALTER THOMAS)

About 1885 the family settled to farm 166 acres on the seaward side of the junction of Lower Beach Rd and Terrace Rd at Ashton, on the Canterbury coast, south-east of Ashburton and here their last seven children were born.

William and Jemima retired in 1920 to 42 Stewart St in Christchurch.

William died on
23 Sept 1930 (77)
and Jemima died on
8 June 1936 (82)
Both are buried at Ashburton.

Photos of
WILLIAM STEVENS

and

**JEMIMA STEVENS
nee JOHNS**

For more detail of this family see .... "The STEVENS family" book.

WALTER PERCIVAL THOMAS FAMILY TREE

3rd Generation

WALTER PERCIVAL THOMAS ... married .... ELSIE MAUD STEVENS

b 17 November 1881 (Percy)	9 November 1908	b 13 May 1886
at Christchurch.	at Waterton, Canterbury.	at Ashton, Canterbury.
d 4 January 1966 (84)		d 26 April 1975 (89)
bur Waikiwi, Invercargill.		bur at Waikiwi, Invercargill.

Elsie was the daughter of WILLIAM STEVENS and JEMIMA JOHNS.

Percy and Elsie had 3 children known as Hector, Lillian and Leslie.

+++

4th Generation	5th Generation	6th Generation	7th Generation
HECTOR PERCIVAL THOMAS	LOIS MARGARET THOMAS	TRACEY GRETA SCOTT	KATE LOUISE MOONEY
b 21 June 1909	b 20 April 1938	b 9 October 1962	b 2 July 1987
at Ashburton.	at Invercargill.	at New Plymouth	at Hastings.
d 27 April 1987 (77)	m 14 May 1960 =======	m 28 March 1987 =======	
bur New Plymouth	at New Plymouth.	at Okato, Taranaki	CONNOR JAMES
m 19 Dec 1935	RONALD LESLIE	TIMOTHY JOHN	MOONEY
at Hawera ============	SCOTT	MOONEY	b 18 July 1989
RUBY MARGARET	b 14 September 1937	b 27 August 1959	at Stratford.
CRAWFORD	at Wellington.	at Kaikoura.	
b 28 March 1910			TYLER MATHEW
at Hawera.	(He was son of Harold		MOONEY
	Leslie Scott and Grace		b 3 February 1991
(she was daughter of	Florence Knight)		at Stratford.
Oswald Crawford and			
Sarah Hicks)	They had 3 children		COURTNEY SCOTT
	Tracey, Lianne, Lisa		MOONEY
They had 3 children			b 20 January 1994
Lois. Kevin & Grahame			at Stratford
		LIANNE MARGARET SCOTT	THOMAS SCOTT McELROY
		b 31 January 1965	b 29 January 1993
		at New Plymouth.	at New Plymouth.
		m 8 April 1989 =========	
		at New Plymouth.	
		JUSTIN McLEOD	LUCY RACHEL
		McELROY	McELROY
		b 20 February 1963	b 14 July 1996
		at Stratford.	at New Plymouth.
		LISA SARAH SCOTT	DAMON CURTIS
		b 21 November 1967	RADFORD SCOTT
		at New Plymouth =======	b 24 April 1988
		CRAIG RADFORD	at New Plymouth.
		continued... next page	

156

4th Generation	5th Generation	6th Generation	7th Generation
Hector & Ruby cont.	Lois & Ronald cont.	CRAIG RADFORD b 29 March 1966 at Opunake.	ZOEY ALANA JESSIE RADFORD SCOTT b 26 October 1992 at New Plymouth.
	KEVIN LEES THOMAS b 2 March 1940 at Invercargill. married first 1963 at New Plymouth LYNETTE CADDY : married second on 8 March 1975 at New Plymouth. HEATHER PHOEBE STAPLES b 8 March at New Plymouth.		
	GRAHAME HECTOR THOMAS b 20 November 1943 at Hawera. m 4 April 1964 ======== at Waitera, NZ. DOROTHY JEANETTE POWELL b 21 January 1944 at Hawera. 3 Children .. (She was daughter of Arthur Albert Powell and Elvina Maud Alvis)	DEAN GRAHAME THOMAS b 18 April 1965 at New Plymouth d 18 June 1981 (16) bur New Plymouth GAVIN WAYNE THOMAS b 13 April 1967 at New Plymouth. DARRIN KARL THOMAS b 22 June 1970 at New Plymouth.	
LILLIAN ELSIE THOMAS b 3 August 1912 at Ashburton. d 2 January 1999 (86) at Invercargill. m 18 November 1935 ====	TREVOR NELSON PRICE b 24 March 1937 at Invercargill. m 8 October 1960 ===== at Invercargill. Jill next page	JEFFREY NELSON PRICE b 18 January 1964 at Takapuna, Auckland m 30 June 1988 ======= at Glenfield, Auckland. Pauline next page	TERESA ANN PRICE b 19 January 1991 at Takapuna, Auckland. MELISSA RACHEL PRICE

157

Percy & Elsie continue

4th Generation	5th Generation	6th Generation	7th Generation
Lillian married .. at Waikiwi, Invercargill NELSON PRICE b 6 December 1910 at Athol, Southland. d 25 June 1993 (82) at Invercargill. (Nelson was a son of James McDonald Price and Hannah Soper) They had 3 children Trevor, Marlene and Christopher	Trevor married .. JILL VIOLET SOMERVILLE b 31 August 1941 at Gisbourne. (She was daughter of James Morrison Somerville and Edna Margaret Bell)	Jaffrey married .. PAULINE CATHERINE GEMBITSKY b 6 May 1961 at Takapuna, Auckland. (She was daughter of Felix Gembitsky and Kathleen Veronica O'Driscoll)	Melissa continues ... b 18 June 1992 at Takapuna, Auckland. KEVIN JAMES PRICE b 15 December 1994 at Takapuna. Auckland. JASON MARTIN PRICE b 4 June 1996 at Takapuna, Auckland.
		TONY JAMES PRICE b 11 October 1965 at Takapuna, Auckland. m 14 November 1992 === at Northcote, Auckland. KIRI ELIZABETH ATTREE b 14 January 1968 at Timaru. NZ. (She was daughter of Malcolm Stuart Attree and Christine Janet Mary Rogers)	ZANE MORGAN PRICE b 12 January 1999 at Auckland. XANTHE ROSINA PRICE b 16 September 2002 at Takapuna, Auckland. SEAN MALCOLM PRICE b 23 July 2004 at Takapuna, Auckland.
		JANENE CAROL PRICE b 2 October 1969 at Takapuna, Auckland. m 27 February 2008 ==== at Blackball, NZ NICHOLAS (Nick) STANLEY OSBORNE b 18 December 1965 at Hitchin, England. (he was son of Enid Gray & William Stanley Osborne)	EMMA GRACE OSBORNE b 9 March 2009 at Takapuna, Auckland.

	MARLENE JOY PRICE
	b 17 April 1939
	at Invercargill.
	d 10 Sept 1988 (49)
	bur Christchurch.
	m 3 March 1960 =======
	at Invercargill.
	
	cont. next page ..
		RAEWYN JOY GORRIE
		b 2 November 1960
		at Roxburgh, Otago.
		m 1 February 1980 =====
		at Invercargill
		MURRAY DAVID
		WOODGATE
		
		cont. next page ..
			KELLY ANNE
			WOODGATE
			b 1 April 1984
			at Perth, Australia.
			  1 child 8th Gen
			  GEORGINA JOY
			  GORRIE ARNOLD
			  b 7 August 2020

Percy & Elsie continue

4th Generation	5th Generation	6th Generation	7th Generation
Nelson & Lillian cont..	Marlene married NOEL HERBERT GORRIE b 20 September 1938 at Invercargill. d 19 July 2021 bur Christchurch.	Murray continued b 14 May 1958 at Christchurch. d 22 April 1992 (33) at Christchurch. (2 children ... Kelly & Tom)	THOMAS ANDREW GORRIE (Tom) b 11 May 1989 at Christchurch
	(he was son of Herbert James Gorrie and Anne McIntosh) they had 4 children, Raewyn. Lianne, Ritchie & Kyla.	LIANNE GORRIE b 26 July 1962 at Invercargill. m 19 Sept 1987 ======== at Sandnes, Norway. PER HENNING QVALE b 8 February 1962 at Norway.	LISA MARLENE QVALE b 23 April 1992 at Sandnes, Norway. CHRISTINA ANN QVALE b 25 November 1994 at Sandnes, Norway.
		RITCHIE NOEL GORRIE b 24 January 1966 at Invercargill. m 9 February 1991 ===== at Christchurch. KIM VERONICA OSKAM b 17 December 1967 at Dunedin.	JESSICA ROSE GORRIE b 30 October 1996 at Christchurch.
		KYLA MARLENE GORRIE b 5 October 1971 at Invercargill m 23 October 1999 ===== at Tai Tapu, ChCh. Dr PETER MILES DAVIES b 23 March 1967 at Stockport, England. (Peter was son of Alun Davies and Anna Lynette Miles)	HANNAH MARLENE DAVIES b 15 August 2000 at Christchurch. SAMUEL NELSON DAVIES b 14 November 2003 at Christchurch.
	Noel remarried, widow MARGARET RAE HUDDLESTON b 5 June 1942 at Waikari, Canterbury.		

159

Percy & Elsie continue

4th Generation	5th Generation	6th Generation	7th Generation
Nelson & Lillian cont...	CHRISTOPHER THOMAS JAMES PRICE b 29 October 1951 at Invercargill. m 2 October 1976 ==== at Invercargill. ESTHER ANNE BRYAN b 21 August 1958 at Invercargill. (The daughter of Earl Bryan and Ruth Evans) They had 3 children, Matthew, Jonathan and Hannah.	MATTHEW THOMAS PRICE b 26 June 1982 at Invercargill. m 31 March 2012 ====== at Invercargill. SHELLY ANNE WEIR b 12 March 1987 at Invercargill.	MILLIE ANNE PRICE b 9 May 2013 at Invercargill. LIZZIE ROSE PRICE b 26 Augusr 2015 at Invercargill. THOMAS STEWART PRICE b 8 December 2017 at Invercargill.
		JONATHAN JAMES WALTER PRICE b 18 September 1983 at Invercargill. m 13 September 2013. in U.S.A. KIRSTEN MICHAEL LATTANZIO b 12 October 1976 in U.S.A.	ALARIC MICHAEL ALLEN b 16 Oct 1999 USA HANNAH JANES DOBBS b 6 Oct 2004 USA MORGAN ALTHEA DOBBS b 26 July 2007 USA
		HANNAH RUTH PRICE b 23 August 1985 at Invercargill partner ========== CHEYNE HARRY THOMAS MANN CARDOSO b 8 September 1981	ANASTA LILLIAN PRICE b 28 April 2007 at Invercargill. MANAIA CHRIS PAULO CARDOSO b 27 April 2016 at Invercargill. THIAGO HARRY NELSON CARDOSO b 14 December 2017 at Invercargill. Manaaki next page

4th Generation	5th Generation	6th Generation	7th Generation
Nelson & Lillian cont...	Chris & Esther cont ..	Hannah continues ..	MANAAKI ANTONIO BENJAMIN CARDOSO b 29 July 2021 at Invercargill.
			JEROME SOE HAKI BUCKLEY-FA'ATOIA b 19 July 2005
			BAILEE - ROSE JACQUELINE CARDOSO b 23 April 2007
LESLIE WALTER THOMAS b 23 January 1915 at Ashburton d 9 October 1936 (21) bur Waikiwi, Invercargill.			

Three
Surviving
photos
taken and
processed
by Percy
Thomas.

A hobby
he enjoyed.

Views of
The Domain,
Ashburton

GEORGE BERTRAM THOMAS (1882-1946)

1882... George was born 21st Dec 1882, the ninth child of John and Phebe Thomas and the first of their children to be born at the Allenton Nursery, in Ashburton.

He was to become their fourth eldest surviving child.

We presume that he too was educated at the Ashburton Borough School and as soon as he could he joined his father at the J Thomas Grain and Produce Store.

1904... George spent his entire working days at 186 Havelock Street, rising from general roust'-about in his father's shop, then to a third partnership with brothers Alfred and Percy.

The name of the business changed to Thomas Bros... Seed, Grain and Produce Store.

1925... In 1925 the partnership broke up and George bought Alfred and Percy out and became the full owner of the business.

During this later period George's children took part with son Allan being prepared to take over the family business while daughter Betty did the books.

Betty recalls her father grew many plants in the glasshouse at their home, for sale in the shop. More than 300 boxes of plants and annuals were sold each year. Farmers used to bring their surplus eggs in to the shop and these were taken to Christchurch each week.

Bananas did not arrive ripe and had to be ripened in a special room insulated with sawdust to maintain an even temperature, and a gas jet was kept going day and night to help ripen them. In those days bananas were sold, not by weight but by numbers, 8, 10, 12 according to size.

Betty advises that George hoped to be in the business for 50 years, but ill health forced him to give up six months short of his goal. (HET)

1905... George at the age of 23 bought from his father unoccupied section Lot 961 in Grey Street and paid rates of 3/- that year. By 1909 the rates had climbed to 7/-, then in 1909 George had a house built on the land and in 1910 the Rates jumped to one pound nine shillings and nine pence. George did not pay the Rates on the property in 1914 because about the end of 1913 he, his wife Susan and son Allan now aged three, shifted to their Creek Road home.

1907... Photo page 162 was taken when George was aged 24.

1908... Parents John and Phebe moved to retire at Coromandel.

1909... WEDDING
Jean Page, GEORGE & SUSAN, Elsie Thomas and William Page.

MARRIAGE:

1909... George aged 26, married **SUSAN PAGE** aged 22, on 17th March 1909 at St Stephen's Church in Ashburton.

Susan was born 26 March 1887 at Ashburton, a daughter of Matthew Page and Agnes McKeen. Agnes was born in Belfast and was Matthew's second wife. His first wife died after the birth of their third child. Susan was a half-sister to Margaret Page who married George's brother Frederick. PAGE family detail on page 169.

George and Susan had seven children whom were named:-

Allan Bertram Thomas   born 4 November 1910, known as Allan.
Audrey Jean Thomas   born 20 November 1914, known as Audrey.
Hope Elizabeth Thomas born 16 February 1917, known as Betty.
George Morris Thomas   born 29 January   1918, known as Morris.
Elsie May Thomas   born 20 October   1919, known as Elsie.
Dorothy Amelia Thomas born 17 March   1921, known as Dorothy.
Valmai Agnes Thomas   born 25 March   1923, known as Valmai.

JOHN and PHEBE THOMAS' house, when GEORGE & SUSAN were living there. The Cates residence is on the right. Pre 1936.

Daughter Betty advises that when George and Susan first married they lived opposite brother Percy in Grey St (on Lot 961) and this is where Allan was born. They shifted to Creek Rd where Audrey, Betty, Morris and Elsie were born, then George bought the previous Grey St home of John and Phebe and here Dorothy and Valmai were born.

George bought this house on 17 July 1920 and on 23 July 1946 the Public Trust took control. We have found only one photo of the 64 Grey St house, taken while George owned it and while it was covered in snow, on page 158.

There was a good fall of snow on 14 July 1945 in Ashburton and this could be the date of the photograph. The house finally left Thomas hands and was demolished in 1978 to make way for a block of 4 flats.

1917... This issue of the NZ Post Office Directory lists George Bertram Thomas (aged 35) as residing at Creek Road, Allenton, Ashburton and lists his occupation as Produce Merchant.

PROPERTY:

1920... George and family came back to Grey Street in 1920 with the purchase of John and Phebe's Lot 880/1 and unimproved section behind 880. (Lot 869)

Over the years the postal numbers have changed in Grey St. John's house where George grew up was No 126 (now 64) and next door where George, Susan and family and now (1992) daughters Betty & Valmai live, was No 128 (now 54). George made some alterations to number 64, adding two glass houses to the section, one to the rear and one to the west side of the house. George sold a lot of Flower plants at his shop and grew them here. The house received attention too. A sunporch was added to the west wall, two bedrooms were made on the North wall by dividing one large room, the kitchen was altered from Scullery and Kitchen to one big Kitchen. The Toilet and Washhouse were outside until in later years George converted one of the north bedrooms into a washhouse.

1923... George bought unimproved Lots 882/3/4 and these two houses and four empty sections were still in his hands in the 1928/9 rates year, however after paying the rates he sold these three Lots to John Nicol.

After paying the rates on Lot 869 he sold it in the 1929/30 year to Francis Lennon. George continued to own Lots 880/1 until he died in 1946.

GEORGE and SUSAN THOMAS.

GEORGE... the man.

Included in George's non business activities were fishing, rabbiting and cards. In his youth he was a keen footballer and in one game he was tossed into the air. After that he received the knick-name "Tossie" and this stuck with him the rest of his life.

George was a member of the Ancient Order of Druids and for a few years he was a member of the Fanciers Society and bred and showed birds whenever possible.

George attended the Ashburton Anglican Church but supported both Anglican and Methodist Churches financially. He was also most generous with donations to many other organisations. (HET)

3 generations: SUSAN, MORRIS & MICHAEL THOMAS.

SUSAN... the woman.   Before she married, Susan was an apprentice dressmaker at Heffords in Ashburton. She was a very reserved person. She loved children and whenever any child arrived on her doorstep, out would come the sweet tin or biscuit tin.

Susan knitted a lot during the war years, plus many pairs of sox for the Plunket Society and crocheted Afghan patterns for rugs for the crippled Children's Society. This pastime continued right up to the last few years of her life.

A good cook was Susan. She made wonderful Bread & Butter pudding and in the eyes of her family, no one could beat her. Also, her Rice Pudding "Was out of this world". Every day when her children came home from school there would always be hot scones, or pikelets or a cream sponge for them to consume.

Susan was always busy about the house and seldom left it. Her elder children did the shopping. On one occasion Susan and Alfred's wife Annie, went into town and when they had finished shopping, they called in at the shop to get a ride home. George was down the back of the shop and came up to serve them and it was not until he was very close that he recognised his own wife.

Susan enjoyed Poetry and telling stories and often recited to her children whilst they huddled around the fire at night. They would each have a special request. Some were very sad and would leave the children crying. Some of the favourites were "Don't teach the old man, boys"… "Little Bessie lay asleep"…. and… "The Prisoner."

In her younger days Susan belonged to the Band of Hope League. (HET)

DEATH:
George died 25th February 1946 aged 64 and is buried at Ashburton Cemetery. His wife Susan joined him on 3rd January 1966 aged 78.

During her latter years Susan was very ill and was constantly looked after and nursed by Betty and Valmai. (MST)

Today, Betty and Valmai regularly attend George and Susan's grave and while there they keep an eye on Jessie Elizabeth Thomas's grave also.

--ooO0oo--

PEGGE—PAGE FAMILY TREE

MATTHEW PEGGE was born 1843 Ireland & died 1921 in Ashburton,
NZ and was first married **to ISABELLA HILLIS.**
The spelling of the name Pegge changed upon entry
To New Zealand….. to Page.
Matthew Page 11, born in Ireland but died young.
Margaret Jane Page born 1874 in Ireland married Frederick
William Thomas at Ashburton NZ… refer page 130.
Annie Page married Stephen Charles Gregg and stayed in Ireland.
They had two daughters, Rachel and Annie.
Isabella died giving birth to her third child.

MATTHEW PAGE then married **AGNES McKEEN nee McMillan** in
Ireland, a widow with one daughter named Hannah who married
James Mathers and stayed in Ireland. Hannah had 13 children and
the eldest Alexander, when 15 came to NZ, settling in Ashburton.
Three sisters and a brother of his, settled in Syracuse, N.Y. USA.

Matthew and Agnes had two children in Ireland, then travelled to NZ where 6
more children were born

Elizabeth Page   (known as Auntie Kate)
Georgina Page born March 1881 in Belfast, married Arthur Cates,
the brother of **Annie Cates who married Alfred Edward
Thomas** on page 110.
Matthew Page (the third),was born July 1883 in New Zealand, 6 weeks
after the family arrived here.
William Page married Harriett Elizabeth Stock.
Susan Page married George Bertram Thomas ….page 164.
Robert Alexander Page married twice, Mary Elizabeth Crawford,
then Amy Adelaide Weston.
Harry Page died young.
Amelia Jane (Jean) Page

A photo of Matthew Page (senior) appears on page 136.

Information on this page supplied by Michael Stanley Thomas, a grandson of
Susan Page and George Bertram Thomas.

GEORGE BERTRAM THOMAS FAMILY TREE:

3rd Generation:
GEORGE BERTRAM THOMAS.............married.........................SUSAN PAGE.
b 21 December 1882   17 March 1909   b 26 March 1887
at Allenton, Ashburton.   at Ashburton.   at Ashburton.
d 25 February 1946 (63)   d 3 January 1966 (78)
Bur at Ashburton.   Bur at Ashburton.
Susan was a daughter of MATTHEW PAGE & second wife Mrs AGNES McKEEN nee McMillian.
George and Susan had 7 children known as; Allan, Audrey, Betty, Morris, Elsie, Dorothy & Valmai.
+++

4th Generation	5th Generation	6th Generation	7th Generation
ALLAN BERTRAM THOMAS b 4 November 1910 at Ashburton. d 29 March 1948 (37) Bur at Ashburton. m 20 Nov 1933 ===== at Ashburton. JEAN ROWENA SUTHERLAND b 26 February 1912 at Fairton, Canterbury. (She was a daughter of David St Clair Sutherland and Mary Ross Shand) Thay had 3 children.	KARENE JEANETTA THOMAS b 15 February 1939 at Ashburton. m 8 Oct 1960 ===== at Christchurch. BARRY FRANCIS LAWRENCE b 3 November 1937 at Christchurch. (Son of Robert Francis Lawrence born 1902 , died 1962 and Olive Mary Holmes b 31 Oct 1911, died 15 July 1961)	CHRISTOPHER CHARLES LAWRENCE b 29 November 1961 at Christchurch. m 14 April 1990===== at Wellington. NOATIA ALEFAIO b at <hr>CHIQUITA OLIVE LAWRENCE b 21 July 1965 at Christchurch. m 26 Dec 1989 ===== at Palmerston North. RICHARD CHARLES HANSEN b 3 June 1960 at Christchurch. <hr>VERONICA JEAN LAWRENCE b 3 November 1967 at Christchurch.	HELENA JEAN LAWRENCE b 4 November 1992 at Wellington. <hr>ALISON AROHA HANSEN b 16 January 1990 at Palmerston North. ASHLEY NGUHUIA HANSEN b 6 September 1991 at Palmerston North.
	SUZANNE MARY THOMAS b 7 May 1940 at Ashburton. m 29 July 1961 ===== at Ashburton. ALBERT RAYMOND HAYWOOD b 25 October 1938 at Riverton, Southland. continued...	DAVID RAYMOND HAYWOOD b 13 March 1963 at Riverton, Southland. m 25 June 1983 ===== at Dipton, Southland. DEBORAH JUNE BRICK b 24 June 1966 at Cromwell, Otago. continued...	KEVIN DAVID HAYWOOD b 26 December 1983 at Invercargill. RAYMOND PATRICK HAYWOOD b 17 May 1985 at Invercargill. Jason next page...

George Thomas cont.

4th Generation	5th Generation	6th Generation	7th Generation
Allan and Jean cont.	Suzanne and Ray cont. RAYMOND was son of Herbert James Haywood and Ethel Grace Bye)	David & Deborah Ccont.	**JASON CHRISTOPHER HAYWOOD** b 19 December 1986 at Invercargill. **?** **HAYWOOD** b November 1989 at Invercargill.
		SANDRA ANNE HAYWOOD b 18 July 1964 at Riverton, Southland. m 15 July 1983 ===== at Riverton. **DAVID FRANCIS SMITH** b 12 December 1955 at Gore, Southland.	**MECAELA DIANNE SMITH** b 26 December 1986 at Invercargill.
		DIANNE MARY HAYWOOD b 9 April 1967 at Invercargill. m 20 February 1988=== at Riverton. **GRAEME ALBERT KENNEDY** b 1 April 1961 at Riverton.	**CHANTELLE MARIE KENNEDY** b 14 August 1988 at Invercargill. d 24 August 1992 at Invercargill. **APRIL LEE KENNEDY** b 12 February 1990 at Invercargill. **KENNEDY** b June 1993 at Invercargill.
	DAVID BERTRAM THOMAS b 14 January 1943 at Ashburton. d 20 September 1981 Bur at Ashburton. (36)		

Audrey next page...   Allan next page...   Mark next page...

George Thomas cont.

4th Generation	5th Generation	6th Generation	7th Generation
AUDREY JEAN THOMAS b 20 November 1914 at Ashburton. d 4 June 1988 (73) at Christchurch. m 29 June 1936 ===== at Ashburton. **FRANCIS HENRY BAYLISS** b 28 February 1912 at Christchurch. (Son of Francis Henry Bayliss senior and Elva Gladys Brunt.) They had 3 children.	**ALLAN MORRIS BERTRAM BAYLISS** b 21 November 1936 at Ashburton. m 23 Sept 1961 ===== at Christchurch. **JUDITH KATHLEEN HENDERSON** b 30 April 1940 at Sunderland, County Durham, England.	**MARK ALLAN BAYLISS** b 19 November 1962 at Ashburton. **JOANNE MARY BAYLISS** b 30 September 1964 at Ashburton.	
	BARRY ALBERT BAYLISS b 29 May 1940 at Ashburton. m 23 October 1965==== at Ashburton. **SHIRLEY PATRICIA SKUDDER** b 13 May 1945 at Timaru.	**DAVID VAUGHAN BAYLISS** b 26 December 1972 at Christchurch. m 12 October 1991==== at Takaka, Golden Bay. **LEANNE MAUREEN DODGE** b 15 October 1972 at Christchurch. **KATRINA JOY BAYLISS** b 15 March 1976 at Oamaru.	**JAMIE ZANE BAYLISS** b 4 March 1993 at Nelson.
	GEOFFREY FRANCIS BAYLISS b 4 December 1948 at Ashburton. married first on 1st June 1977 ===== at Ashburton. **SHIRLEY DIANNE DOBBS** b 30 August 1952 at Christchurch. : : married second on 26 June 1986 ======= at Christchurch. **SUZANNE JULIE GIBBONS** b 20 December 1964 at Temuka, Canterbury.	**BRONWYN DIANNE BAYLISS** b 30 May 1975 at Ashburton. **GEORGINA FRANCES BAYLISS** b 5 December 1977 at Ashburton . **ANDREW SHANE BAYLISS** b 24 November 1987 at Christchurch. **REBECCA ANNE BAYLISS** b 12 October 1988 at Christchurch.	

172

4th Generation	5th Generation	6th Generation	7th Generation

HOPE ELIZABETH THOMAS (BETTY)
b 16 February 1917
at Ashburton.

GEORGE MORRIS THOMAS
b 29 January 1918
at Ashburton.
m 2 Aug 1941=====
at Ashburton.
WINIFRED JOAN BARRETT
b 16 February 1917
at Hororata.
d 27 August 1980 (63)
Bur at Ashburton.

(She was daughter of
Frederick Stanley Barrett
and Ina Alison Little)

They had 2 children.

MICHAEL STANLEY THOMAS
b 9 July 1942
at Ashburton.
d 31 October 1991 (49)
Cremated Wellington.

GARY ROYDON THOMAS
b 13 December 1945
at Ashburton.
m 7 Dec 1974======
at Dunedin.
SARAH-JANE WALDEN MUNRO
b 22 January 1949
at Dunedin.

REBEKAH- JANE THOMAS
b 14 July 1978
at Ashburton.

NATHAN DAVID THOMAS
b 25 December 1979
at Ashburton.

ELSIE MAY THOMAS
b 20 October 1919
at Ashburton.
m 14 Sept 1949 =====
at Ashburton.
VAL ERIC JAMES JORGENSEN
b 16 July 1923
at Wellington.
(He was the son of
Thomas Hans Jorgensen
and Margaret Dickson)
They had 1 child.

SUSAN MARGARET JORGENSEN
b 10 February 1954
at Ashburton.
m 20 Jan 1973 ======
at Ashburton.
ROBERT WESTLY EVANS
b 1 September 1942
at Harrow, England.

MICHAEL THOMAS WESTLY EVANS
b 7 December 1974
at Suva, Fiji.

TIMOTHY CRAIG EVANS
b 8 December 1976
at Invercargill.

DAVID ROBERT EVANS
b 30 March 1981
at Invercargill.

DOROTHY AMELIA THOMAS
b 17 March 1921
at Ashburton.
m 10 May 1944=====
at Ashburton.
JAMES SHAND SUTHERLAND

MALCOLM JAMES SUTHERLAND
b 18 October 1944
at Ashburton.
d 13 April 1985 (40)
Bur at Ashburton.

173

George Thomas cont.

4th Generation	5th Generation	6th Generation	7th Generation
Dorothy and James cont. JAMES continued... b 24 April 1910 at Fairton, Canterbury. d 1987 (77) Bur Ashburton. (He was son of David St Clair Sutherland and Mary Ross Shand) They had 6 children.	**MARY ELIZABETH SUTHERLAND** b 30 September 1945 at Ashburton. d 29 December 1975 at Hamilton. (30) m 10 January 1967=== at Frankton, Hamilton. **COLIN WILLIAM FRASER** b 7 October 1935 at Christchurch, son of James Muir Fraser and Estelle Gertrude Mavis Robertson) : 2nd m 12 Sept 1982 at Karratha, N/W Aust. **ANDREA MAY BUSH** b 12 March 1959 at Hamilton. (5th daughter William Henry Bush and June Winifred Conchie)	**DARREN CRAIG FRASER** b 11 December 1967 at Frankton, Hamilton. **JUANITA CHERIE FRASER** b 2 June 1970 at Frankton, Hamilton.	
	TREVOR GEORGE SUTHERLAND b 17 November 1947 at Ashburton. m 22 February 1969 == at Ashburton. **RAYLENE GLADYS GLOVER** b 28 August 1949 at Ashburton.	**KYLIE ELIZABETH SUTHERLAND** b 1 November 1976 at Ashburton. **MARK JAMES SUTHERLAND** b 28 September 1978 at Ashburton.	
	HELEN DOROTHY SUTHERLAND b 6 April 1949 at Ashburton. m 23 February 1967 === at Ashburton. **ROBERT ERNEST LEATH** b 6 January 1946 at Fairton, Canterbury. They had 4 children. continued...	**JANE SUE LEATH** b 23 August 1967 at Ashburton. m February 19 at Ashburton. **CRAIG ROBERT STREET** b at Tony next page...	

174

George Thomas cont.

4th Generation	5th Generation	6th Generation	7th Generation
Dorothy and James cont.	ROBERT cont.. (Son of Leslie Leath and Annie Alexander Johnston Young)	**TONY ERNEST LEATH** b 12 February 1969 at Ashburton.	
		KAREN ANNE LEATH b 9 May 1972 at Ashburton. m 10 July 1992 ===== at Ashburton. **WAYNE JOHN CHRISTIE** b 17 November 1968 at Clyde, Central Otago.	**HANNAH LOUISE CHRISTIE** b 11 September 1992 at Christchurch.
		CAROL DAWN LEATH b 18 December 1973 at Ashburton.	
	CYRIL IAN SUTHERLAND b 16 March 1953 at Ashburton.		
	BARBARA ANN SUTHERLAND b 4 February 1959 at Ashburton. m 13 May 1985 at London, England. **PHILIP HARRIS** b 21 August 1953 at London, England.		
VALMAI AGNES THOMAS b 25 March 1923 at Ashburton.			

SUSAN THOMAS

175

JAMES <u>SYDNEY</u> THOMAS

1884.. James Sydney Thomas was born 14 October 1884, the 10th child of John and Phoebe Thomas at Allenton.

He was known as Syd and was to become their 5th eldest surviving child.

He would have started school from the Allenton Nursery and finished it from the Grey St home. We presume he too went to the Ashburton Borough School.
He was nine years old when the family moved into the Ashburton township.

When he finished school he worked as a clerk for a firm of accountants, Bullock & Cow, for 5 shillings a week.

Later he worked for Kernihan Grocery and also for Fletchers for a while.

1907... The photo above was taken in 1907 when Syd was aged 22.

GROCER:
1907... Syd (22) became a Grocer about 1907. He went into business with a partner and traded under the name of "Buxton and Thomas Ltd".
They operated a "Triangle" grocery agency. The shop was situated at the corner of Cass and Victoria Streets, Ashburton and faced Victoria St, which in Syd's days was called Wakanui Road.

SYD's GROCER SHOP in Ashburton... 1907-1926

The above photograph is of the shop in the early days...possibly even 1907 and below is the same building in November 1989.

New window frames and entrance replace Syds, but it is the same building.

His grocer shop expanded over the years to take in the drapers shop next door.

In the original photo there are four men standing outside, thought to be the total staff at this time:- Fred Buxton, an unknown man, Syd's brother Charles Thomas aged 18, and Syd.

1908... Syd's parents John & Phoebe Thomas moved to Coromandel.

MARRIAGE:
1911... Syd aged 26, married **MURIEL MILES SEGERS** aged 23, on 6th April 1911 at the Methodist Church in Baring Square, Ashburton.

They were attended by Sybil Segers (Muriel's elder sister) as Bridesmaid and Syd's brother Jack Thomas was Bestman. Also in the wedding party were Enid Segers and Charles Segers.

SYD and MURIEL's WEDDING DAY 1911.

The SEGERS family

Muriel was born 21st December 1888 at Ashburton,
to Henry Constable Segers and his wife Louisa Margaret Tulley.
H. C. Segers came out from England as a young man.
Both his parents had died of TB and his Aunt who brought him
up, fearing the same fate for him if he stayed in England they,
encouraged him to emigrate after training at Marshall
Snelgroves, in London.

He seems to have worked in Christchurch first, for here he met
and married Louisa Margaret Tulley. It must have been after this
they moved to Ashburton where he opened a business of his own
a department Store in East Street.

Henry and Louisa Seger had a family of 6 ....
Sybil, Charles, Miles, Muriel, Hedley and Enid.
Muriel was left her parent's home at 9 West Street, Ashburton.

Syd and Muriel Thomas had a family of two whom they named:-
Morva Sybil Thomas born 11 May 1912, was known as Morva.
Una Miles Thomas   born 13 July 1916, was known as Una.

The Ashburton Guardian announced Morva's birth in the 14th May
1912 edition and Una's in the 15th July 1916 isue.

PROPERTY:

1916... Syd and Muriel first lived in Walnut Avenue, Ashburton after their
marriage, and both Morva and Una were born there.
Sometime soon after the end of World War One in 1918 they moved to number
201 Cameron Street, just around the corner from Syd's shop.

1921/2... The first time Syd appears in the Ashburton Borough Council
Ratepayer's book was in 1922. We would assume from this that he purchased
two adjacent part sections (Lots 696/7) known as number 201 in Cameron Street,
in 1921.
The number of the house was later changed to 249 Cameron.

1922... Syd was in business from 1907 to 1926.
The Rates records of the Ashburton Borough Council shows the following facts
about the shop property Lot 727 Victoria Street.

179

1906/7: Property owned by Thomas Bullock the Land Agent and he paid the rates that year.

1907/8: Buxton & Thomas now owners and occupiers of Shop and Dwelling then known as Lot 726 Whakanui Road. The property was valued at 40 pounds and they paid rates of 3 pounds 10 shillings that year.

1913/14: House and shop section was redesignated as Lot 727.

1914/15: Whakanui Road renamed…. Victoria Street.

1918/19: The partnership bought Lot 754 in Victoria St which was diagonally over the road from their Grocery / China Shop.

1919: Mr Buxton left the partnership and started a Produce Business.

1920/1: Buxton & Thomas Ltd now only has "Lot 727 Stores" with a value of 73 pounds and Rates paid were 6 pounds 7 shillings & 9 pence.

Fred Buxton now owned Lot 754.. a store in Victoria St, plus Lot 507 a Factory in Willis St and Lots 715/6 a dwelling in William St, Ashburton.

1924… This issue of the NZPO Directory lists:-
"Sydney Thomas, 201 Cameron Street, Ashburton… Grocer."

SHOP ADVERTISEMENTS:

We have found 5 days when advertisements were put in the Ashburton Guardian, mostly of 1 column by 5 lines. The family has full copies of these, but items mentioned include, Tea at 1 shilling & 3 pence per pound (1/3) on 17 February 1914; Quick set jellies, 3 packets for 1 shilling.

Shaving mugs for 2/6, 30 different patterns of Jam & Butter Dishes, a beautiful line of Children's Tea sets at 10/6, Fancy Porridge Plates at 1/3, etc, in separate adverts on page one of 1st February 1920 edition. English white and gold Breakfast Cups & Saucers at 6 shilling a half dozen, etc, on 2nd January 1925.

The earliest advert we could find, 4 February 1907 was 1 column by 2 inches (25mm) deep and proclaimed that Buxton and Thomas had now procured a horse and trap and could deliver all orders at the shortest notice and asked for a trial run.

We noticed the Guardian was eight pages long and on 17 February 1914 cost the buyer one penny, and on 2 January 1925 it was still eight pages long but now cost one and a half pennies to buy.

The 2 January 1925 paper held the largest advert of 1 column by 6 inches which mentioned possible New Year Presents of Jugs, Salad sets, Children's Knives, Forks and Spoon sets and general comment of the imported China available and the wide range of Confectionery held by Buxton and Thomas,

'Triangle Stores', Phone 20, Ashburton. No advert gave a Street address. He must have been well known in the town by then.

Over the twenty years or so in the Grocery business, Syd increased his product range and when he put his business up for sale, we can see from the advertisement that it included a very large China department specialising in Moorcroft, Irish Beleek, Royal Dalton and Kookaburra wares.

Quality products from around the world. If there was any one part of the business Syd enjoyed more than the others, then it was his China department. He was especially interested in the Moorcroft.

He kept some in his own home and these have been passed on to daughter Morva. He probably didn't realise it then, but today in 1989 Moorcroft has become quite valuable and earlier this year a buyer from overseas was asking for Moorcroft in our daily papers.

SHOP SOLD:

1926... In October, at the age of 42 Syd sold his business and retired at the end of that month. The Ashburton Guardian records the sale as follows....

> *"Mr S J Thomas, trading as Buxton & Thomas, grocery, crockery and hardware merchants, Triangle, has disposed of the business to Mr George Currie, formerly of the firm of Manchester Brothers. Mr Currie will take over the business at the beginning of November."*

The business had a good name and George Currie carried on using the Buxton & Thomas title. We noticed an advertisement on page 1 in the Ashburton Guardian for Buxton and Thomas, Crock Shop on 2 January 1930. Although Syd was no longer involved it was nice to find the business still operating some four years after he sold.

Syd's Doctors in Ashburton & Christchurch had advised him he was terminally ill. He sold the business as he wished to leave Muriel unconcerned with business worries and to see that she was financially secure. It was discovered during his operation that the problem was not as bad as first thought and after a full year of recovery, he went on to live a further 46 years.

From November 1st 1926 and after recovering from the operation, Syd's sporting, gardening & religious activities continued to occupy him.

--ooo0ooo--

SPORT:

Throughout his life he was always interested in sport, all sport.

He played Rugby for an Ashburton team and later acted as a referee. He played Tennis for many years and Golf for many more years…winning tournaments and travelling away with local teams.

In the Ashburton Guardian we found two records of Syd's tennis activities in 1910 for the St Andrews Lawn Tennis Club.

A.   On 28 January he beat C E Manchester 6-5 in the Men's Singles.
Syd and W S McGibbon beat Manchester & W H Higgins 6-2 in the Men's Doubles, and with Miss E M Stewart, Syd lost to Miss A Dixon and Manchester 5-6 in the combined Doubles. The St Andrews Club beat the Baring Square Tennis Club that day.

B.   On 25 February Syd beat S Culverhouse 6-2 in the Singles and with EC Naylor he beat Culverhouse and G McKenzie in the Men's Doubles 6-3. Syd did not play in the Combined Doubles and even though he was victorious, his St Andrews Club was beaten this time by the Tinwald Tennis Club.

He was a very good shot and for many years went annually to Mt Algidus Station in the upper Rakaia region, Deer stalking. The manager of Mt Algidus, Ron Anderson and his wife Mona were lifelong personal friends and always called at the Thomas house when they came to Christchurch. (Mona was the authoress of many books about the high country, e.g. "A River Rules My Life." etc) Syd shot one of the finest heads ever to come out of the Rakaia Basin, a 27-pointer considered by many to be one of the original stags released in that area. The mounted head adorned one of the walls at 1 Rochdale St, until his death.

Syd was always interested in young people in sport and living opposite Christchurch Boys High School he was a regular spectator at all their games. He was given a complimentary ticket to all games by the Chch Boy's High authorities and his proudest moments were watching his own grandson, Ross Fountain, play for Christ's College 1st XV against Boy's High for three years.

WEST STREET:

Daughter Morva married in 1935 and soon after this Syd, Muriel and Una moved to 9 West St, where Muriel's parents had left her their lovely home in spacious grounds. That home is now called "Westside Manor" and is a Bed & Breakfast house. Since Syd sold it various owners have put in a road and cut off several sections, leaving the original house on a very small section.

ROCHDALE ST:

1937... The family shifted to live at number 1 Rochdale St, Fendalton, Christchurch. On many visits south John (and Phebe when she came) would stay at Syd and Muriel's home. It was on a corner site with Straven Rd. They had a double section and kept a most attractive garden. Syd (now 53) did not go back into business in Christchurch but spent much time in his garden and doing voluntary work mentioned below. Syd was always willing to help his friends by pruning their trees and roses etc.

ALBUM:

Mary Thomas (Syd's brother Roy's daughter-in –law) has in her care an album believed to be Syd's or sent from Syd to his sister Elsie. The album contains photos of a trip to Stewart Island, described as ...

"Isle of beauty ..Fare thee well", and put together by photographer C.H.M. Segers of Ashburton ... Muriel's brother Charles.

1924/5... During World War Two, Syd continued helping others by doing much voluntary work, such as packing many overseas parcels etc.

Syd had a wide circle of friends and was admired and respected by all. Although a convinced Christian, he did not parade his faith, but by a life of consistent work, friendship and sound advice helped many young men facing the turmoil of growing up in a difficult world. Although worshipping with the Open Brethren in Christchurch, he was a truly ecumenical spirit and had many friends in many Churches and helped wherever he could.

> Muriel died aged 66, on 11 January 1955.
> Syd   died aged 87, on 28 January 1972.
> Una   died aged 63, on 20 July   1978.

All three died at their 1 Rochdale Road home, with Una spending many hours nursing Syd and Muriel. They are all interred in the same plot at Ruru Lawn Cemetery in Christchurch.

> We thank Morva and husband Russell Fountain
> for much of the above detail and memories.

--oo0Ooo--

JAMES SYDNEY THOMAS FAMILY TREE:

3rd Generation:

JAMES SYDNEY THOMAS............married....................MURIEL MILES SEGERS

b 14 October 1884	6 April 1911	b 21 December 1888
at Ashburton.	at Ashburton.	at Ashburton.
d 28 January 1972 (87)		d 11 January 1955 (66)
Bur at Christchurch.		Bur at Christchurch.

Muriel was a daughter of HENRY CONSTABLE SEGERS and LOUISA MARGARET TULLEY.

Sydney and Muriel had two children known as Morva and Una.

++

4th Generation	5th Generation	6th Generation	7th Generation
MORVA SYBIL THOMAS	HELEN MARGARET FOUNTAIN	ELIZABETH ANN PARRY-JENNINGS	MATTHEW SETH RUSSELL MEEK
b 11 May 1912	b 17 February 1936	b 28 October 1965	b 18 August 1988
at Ashburton.	at Wellington.	at Folkstone, England.	at Christchurch.
m 14 May 1935 =====	m 21 November 1964==	m 4 March 1988 ====	
at Ashburton.	at Hove, England.	at Christchurch.	
HAVELOCK RUSSELL FOUNTAIN	Rev CHRISTOPHER WILLIAM PARRY-JENNINGS	BRADLEY SETH MEEK	
b 19 August 1908	b 21 December 1935	b 29 October 1962 at Watford, Herts, England.	
at Akaroa, Canterbury.	at Blackheath in Kent,		
d 19 April 1993 (84)	England.		
Bur Christchurch.		JONATHAN MARK PARRY-JENNINGS	
	(He was son of Eric	b 24 January 1968	
(He was son of Kenneth	Parry-Jennings and	at Christchurch.	
Howell Fountain and	Enid Gwynne Davies)		
Bertha Dearsly)			
They had 2 children.	JOHN ALLAN ROSS FOUNTAIN	JOANNA MARY FOUNTAIN	
	b 7 September 1938	b 26 June 1968	
	at Christchurch.	at Bristol, England.	
	m 17 March 1967====		
	at Christchurch.	KATHARINE JANE THOMAS FOUNTAIN	
	ANNE THOMAS	b 3 July 1970 (Katie)	
	b 14 December 1938	at Lincoln, Christchurch.	
	at Purley, Surrey,	New Zealand.	
	England.		
		SARAH ANNE FOUNTAIN	
	(Daughter of George	b 22 October 1972	
	Harry Thomas and	at Lincoln, ChCh, NZ.	
	Audrey Brookes Spratt)		

UNA MILES THOMAS
b 13 July 1916
at Ashburton.
d 20 July 1979 (63)
at Christchurch.

PHOEBE ELSIE THOMAS

1886... Phoebe Elsie Thomas was born 11 January 1886, the eleventh child of John & Phoebe Thomas at Allenton, Ashburton. She was known as Elsie and was to become the only surviving girl with eight brothers.

We presume she attended the Ashburton Borough School and the Wesleyan Methodist Sunday School and Church.

She was seven years old when her father sold the Allenton Nursery and started his J Thomas, Grain & Produce store in Ashburton.

We do not know if she ever went out for employment in Ashburton or if she stayed home, assisting her mother Phebe to wash, feed and generally housekeep for the nine men in the family.

We do not know if there ever was a romantic man in her life, but she remained unmarried for her 85 years.

1907... The photo above was taken when Elsie was aged 21.

1908... Her parents retired from active business life and Elsie, then 22, travelled to Coromandel to live with them and her brothers Charles and Roy.

In Coromandel she made a life for herself, working first in a Fabric Shop and becoming involved with the Coromandel Methodist Church, teaching Sunday School and regularly attending Church services. We have learnt that when called upon she was a capable Lay-Preacher as well and often fitted in especially when the Minister was out of town.

There is a picture of Elsie at the Coromandel Museum with her Sunday School Class. One of those who attended her classes told us he really enjoyed them, as Elsie would illustrate the stories with pictures on a felt board. Mr Ron McNeil in 1988, still remembered her as "a quiet and saintly person."

The 1908 Parliamentary Rolls have her listed to vote in that year's election.

CHARLES, PHEBE, ROY and ELSIE on a picnic.

1937... The family's big house in Coromandel was sold to the Hospital Board and used by them as a Doctor's Residence. Ideal because it was diagonally opposite the entrance to the hospital.
The Hospital added the room on the porch that can be seen in the 1988 photos and the Doctors used it as an emergency surgery.
Elsie now 51, used to housekeep for the Doctor for a while. (HET)

186

ELSIE's HABERDASHERY SHOP in Coromandel

We have no dates but about this time Elsie's closest friend a Miss Thompson died. She used to have a Haberdashery and Stationary Shop with accommodation behind it. When she died, she left the lot to Elsie and this became Elsie's main occupation and residence before she moved back to Christchurch. Betty Thomas (niece) remembers visiting Coromandel with her father George in 1935 and Miss Thompson still had the shop then. She also states that Elsie was generous to her customers and if someone could not pay at the time she would never press for payment. (This building in 1989 was a Doctors Surgery.)

Betty felt Elsie had a wonderful sense of humour.

We have learnt that Elsie often popped down to Ashburton and Christchurch for visits and that her brothers usually went to Church that Sunday. Fred was the only abstainer and generally none of her brothers were "into religion" as deeply as Elsie and her parents and Roy. We are told that it was easier for most of them to just go, as Elsie was a determined lady.

Niece Betty recalls that her Auntie Elsie did beautiful needlework and crochet just like her mother Phebe.

ELSIE......
sitting in
the lounge
of the
Coromandel
house.

1955... When Jane Haslett died in 1955, she left Elsie 500 pounds. Jane, nee Woods, was Phebe's sister and Elsie's Aunt.

PLATE... Late in her life Elsie passed onto her niece Phyllis Rainbow a plate measuring about 20cm in diameter that had been in the family for many generations. Elsie told her that it used to belong to NZ 4th Generation Phyllis's (5) Great Great Great Great Great Grandmother. We have not reached back that far in our research, so do not have any names for that lady, but allowing say 25 years for each generation, this would date the plate to 1730-50. The back of the plate has nothing on it at all. Photo page 197. We believe it could either be a Thomas or Woods family heirloom, but it is impossible to know which.

ELSIE's
Coromandel friend
Miss Thompson

Mary Thomas, (Roy's daughter-in-law) has one of Elsie's photograph albums and we have copied a lot of these photos for use in this book.

1969... Elsie left Coromandel and shifted to Christchurch to be nearer to her brothers. She lived for a while at 101 Retreat Road with brother Roy and Margaret. She lived her final days in a Home and Lillian (Percy's daughter) recalls a story that even in these days she continued with her religion and her wish to help others. There was an elderly Catholic lady in the home with her, who could no longer manage the Rosary and Elsie learned it off and said it with the frail old lady.

1971... Elsie died 10 February 1971 aged 85 and rests at the RURU Lawn Cemetery in Christchurch.

> In her will Elsie left all her Great Nephews and Nieces a copy of
> The New Testament, (The New English Bible...Popular Edition)
> Many who received these told us in 1989 that they still had them.
> The writer still has his copy.

189

JOHN HENRY THOMAS (JACK) (1887-1939)

1887.. John Henry was born on the 5 August 1887, the 12th child of John and Phebe and was John Thomas IX. He was known as **JACK** and became their seventh surviving child.

When Jack was six, the family moved from the Allenton Nursery into their Grey St, Ashburton home.
Jack would have gone to the Ashburton Borough School.

For a while, later on in life he received the nick-name of "Adolphus" from a close friend ... Fredrica Johnstone (known as Dick) .
Someone signing "Violets" sent a postcard from Milton on 4 October 1911 to him addressed to "Adolphus" Thomas. This nickname does not appear to have been in wide use.

1905... Havelock Street Shop:
Along with brothers Alfred, Percy and George, Jack (then 18) formed a partnership called Thomas Bros, that took over their father's Grain & Produce Store at 186 Havelock Street in Ashburton.
However, Jack soon decided this was not for him and arranged for the others to buy him out. The other three carried on the business until 1925.

1907... The photo above was taken when Jack was aged 20.

1908... Jack's parents moved to Coromandel.

1908... About this time Jack went south to try his luck.

It seems for some time he was employed by the Singer Sewing Machine Company. He was sent to help out their branches, build up the sales and moved on to another branch. We have postcards which indicate that he lived and worked for a while at Dunedin, Leeston, Riverton and Otautau and of course Timaru.

It was while working at Timaru he met Edie, who was then employed as Demonstrator of the Singer Sewing Machines, and she too travelled from branch to branch. A postcard that reached Jack at Otautau was dated 4 October 1911, only a couple of months before he married Edie, so we assume that they first lived here.

1911... Jack was Best Man at his brother Syd's wedding to Muriel Segars at Ashburton on 6 April 1911.

MARRIAGE:
1911... Jack aged 24, married **EDITH ELIZABETH MARTIN** aged 21, at the Methodist Church, Invercargill on 20th December 1911.

Edith was mostly known as Edie.

The MARTIN FAMILY: Edie was born 9th May 1890 at Riverton, Southland, to George McVeigh Martin and his wife Margaret Raines. George and Margaret had 5 sons and 3 daughters including Edie. Her father died before 1911 and the story goes that he was shipwrecked three times coming out to New Zealand from Northern Ireland.

Jack and Edie had one child whom they named ......
Phyllis Eva Thomas born 7 November 1912 and known as Phyllis.

OTAUTAU:

At Otautau Jack went into partnership with J Wesney and they operated a retail Cycle shop. It soon became clear to Jack that the Motorcar was going to become the machine to own and the main use for transport, so he sold his share of the Bicycle business and went into a joint venture Motor Garage with Eardley Bell at Otautau. He knew nothing about cars, could not drive one and said he did not want to.

One day a farmer's car, somewhere up country would not go, so Eardley persuaded Jack to go with him for a ride. Eardley found the car had to be bought back to Otautau to the Garage and he made temporary repairs to enable that. He then advised Jack that he would drive the farmer's car into town but that he would have to drive the one they came in. After this Jack could not be kept out of a car.

After a few years Jack bought Eardley Bell out of the business and our photo of the Otautau Motor Garage proudly proclaims:-
"J. H. Thomas ... Proprietor".

We also have a photo of the Otautau home of Jack and Edie and of some prize-winning marrows grown there by Jack.

Jack was called up for the First World War while he had the Garage at Otautau but it ended before he had a chance to serve.

After some time he sold the Garage and the family travelled for about a year throughout New Zealand living in Hotels.

INVERCARGILL:

1925... Jack returned to Ashburton and persuaded his brother Percy into joining him in a partnership to buy out J Lennies Nursery in Invercargill.

Thomas Bros Ltd of Ashburton was wound up. Alfred went into a Grocery business, whilst George stayed on at the Grain and Produce Store having bought the other's shares.

June 1925 was the date of the first advertisement for Thomas Bros Nurseries and Florist Shop at Invercargill. Lennies had a nursery on the Great North Road at Waikiwi and a retail shop in Esk St in Invercargill. Jack sold the Esk St Shop (with tea rooms overhead) three days after they took ownership and made a good profit. They rented a shop in the 106 Dee St 'Briscoes Building' for their Florist Shop (we have a photo) and by 1926 the nursery had grown from 10 to 14 acres.

Percy and his family lived on the nursery and Jack's family lived at 166 Leet St Invercargill. Generally Percy ran the Nursery and Jack ran the Shop and managed the finances. Later on Jack built and moved into a house a couple of sections from the corner of North and Bainfield Roads ... opposite St Stephen's Church, at Waikiwi.

Some years later the partnership broke up and Jack bought Percy out. For a while Percy stayed on working for wages then bought the West Plains Grocery store. Jack appointed Mr Sexton as manager of the nursery and the business continued after Jack died. Jack had been slowly selling off the business by selling shares to the staff at the nursery and the shop and planned to shift to Australia but he died in 1939 aged 52.

Edie still had some shares in the Invercargill nursery when interviewed by M S Thomas on 1st May 1971.

PHYLLIS and her mother EDIE THOMAS in 1929

Early in the 1950's a second shop was opened in Kelvin St, Invercargill, specialising in grain, seeds and shrubs, managed by Bob Boyen.

SPORT:

Jack was an active man and sporting person. He was good golfer, a member of the Invercargill Golf Club and won many trophies. He did a lot of fishing. Was a Committeeman and member of the Southland Acclimatization Society and in the early years was a member of the Southern Gun Club. Photographs show that he enjoyed boating and fishing for Salmon.

Daughter Phyllis recalls her mother occasionally asked her father if they could go for a drive. He usually agreed but they always seemed to end up searching for new places for Mai Mais or new fishing holes to try one day.

Here we display a mention Jack received in a book of cartoons, a limited edition called…
   "New Zealanders As We See 'Em".

No one ever thought Jack would die in bed and everyone who knew him well, said he would die with his boots on. He had so many near escapes being too daring for his own good.

J.H.T. " IT WAS AS LONG AS THAT, & WEIGHED THIRTY NINE POUNDS "
AUDIENCE "SOME FISH, MR THOMAS."
J.H.T "WHO'S TALKING ABOUT FISH ? I'M REFERRING TO MY LAST YEAR'S PRIZE TURNIP."

THOMAS, JOHN HENRY.

Mgr. Thomas Bros., Seedsmen, Nurserymen & Florists, Dee St., Invercargill. C'tteeman Acclimatisation Socy., Southland. Member Invercargill Golf and Southern Clubs. Recreations: Fishing, Shooting and Golf. In past: Tennis and Football.

195

Phyllis recalls one of the adventures when he and his friend Ben Dixon left Te Anau and went down the Waiau River in a rowboat to the mouth a few years before Zane Grey and Bob Carey attempted a similar feat but did not go all the way. Phyllis went part of the way once with her father between Te Anau and Manapouri before the river was dammed) but swore never to do so again, not having the same desire for hair raising exploits as her father.

1939… JACK DIED 8th August 1939 aged 52 and is buried at Invercargill's Eastern Cemetery. He died at Kew Hospital where he had survived a Hernia operation. Unfortunately, a fire occurred and patients were evacuated onto the lawn and he caught pneumonia from which he died.

1988... EDITH DIED and joined Jack some 49 years later on the 2nd August 1988 aged 98.

GREYSTONES: Michael Thomas had the privilege to interview Edie and this record of Jack is mostly from notes he took, and the memories of daughter Phyllis. After his death Phyllis worked for Jack's business until it was sold.
Soon Edith sold the Waikiwi house, and they built a lovely large home at Riverton Rocks which they named "Greystones". A doll's house was built for the Red Cross during World War two and won in a raffle by a young girl who wanted to sell it, so Edie bought it for her granddaughter Sylvia and had it erected at "Greystones".

FAMILY HEIRLOOMS: Phyllis had many Thomas family photographs and postcards, most having messages written on them from the sender, as well as numerous items of Phebe's needlework.
Jill & Trevor Price are proud that she chose to allow us to hold for future Thomas descendants a 30cm Tray Cloth depicting a Lyre bird and also a Brooch of Phebe's and a lot of her surplus family photos.

Phyllis had two items that predated John & Phebe by a number of years.
One is a Thomas or Woods plate measuring 8 inches and believed to have been in the family for 150 years and handed down to her from Elsie Thomas.

Also received from Hilda Turner was a 7inch tall vase that used to belong to one of the Turner family predecessors. William Robert Turner was Martha Wood's husband and Martha was the elder sister of Phebe Thomas. These are now being cared for by daughter Sylvia Ritani.

JOHN (JACK) HENRY THOMAS FAMILY TREE:

3rd Generation:
JOHN (JACK) HENRY THOMAS....married..........................EDITH ELIZABETH MARTIN

b 5 August 1887	20 December 1911	b 9 May 1890
at Ashburton.	at Invercargill.	at Riverton.
d 8 August 1939 (52)		d 2 August 1988 (98)
Bur at Invercargill.		Bur at Invercargill.

Edith was a daughter of GEORGE McVEIGH MARTIN and MARGARET RAINES.
Jack and Edith had one child whom they named Phyllis.

++

4th Generation	5th Generation	6th Generation	7th Generation
PHYLLIS EVA THOMAS	SYLVIA MARGARET RAINBOW	GABRIELLE JOCELYN WHYTE	
b 7 November 1912	b 30 November 1943	b 3 March 1967	
at Invercargill.	at Invercargill.	at Lincoln, Canterbury.	
d 18 Sept 1990 (77)	married first on		
Bur at Springston,	7 April 1966 ========		
Canterbury, NZ..	at Christchurch.	LUCYNDA MAREE	
m 25 June 1941=====	RIWHI WHYTE	WHYTE	
at Invercargill.	b 18 October 1938	b 10 September 1970	
EDWIN FREDERICK	at Kawa Kawa.	at Christchurch.	
RAINBOW	d 14 October 1985 (47)	m 17 April 1992	
b 27 January 1902	Bur at Springston,	at Christchurch.	
at Christchurch.	Canterbury, NZ.	PAUL IAN HADLEY	
d 8 Sept 1980 (78)	(Son of Rangi Whyte	b 6 June 1968	
Ashes scattered at Sea,	and Peta Kupa)	at Christchurch.	
near Chatham Islands.	:		
	:		
(He was the son of	:		
Samuel Rainbow and	married second on		
Amelia Goodwin.)	7 December 1986		
	at Christchurch.		
They had 1 child.	WALLACE LEE RITANI		
	b 2 October 1929		
	at Taumaranui.		
	(He was son of Thomas		
	Edward Ritani and		
	Ngarewai Mere Ngatai)		

197

CHARLES ERNEST THOMAS: (1888-1916)

1888.. Charles Ernest Thomas was born 14 November 1888, the 13th child of John and Phebe Thomas at Allerton, Ashburton. He was referred to by sister Elsie and fiancé Ivy Woods in Postcards we have ….. as Charl.

He probably did not start School until after the family had moved to 54 Grey Street, Ashburton. He would also have attended the Ashburton Borough School.

1906/7… photo of Buxton and Thomas Ltd, Grocers of Ashburton (see page 175) shows Charles in working apron, standing in front of the shop with the owners ... his brother Sydney and Fred Buxton. We assume he was employed here for up to two years before moving to Coromandel.

1907… The photo above was taken when Charles was aged 18.

1908… His parents shifted to retire at Coromandel and Charles now aged 20, his sister Elsie aged 22 and 7 year old Roy went with them.

1909… Charles played rugby for the Northern Football Club. We have a photo of his 1909 team after winning the Coromandel Rugby Union Cup

CHARLES JOHN WOODS and fiancé IVY WOODS.

1910...About this time Charles met his cousin Ivy May Woods. Ivy was the daughter of John Woods, a brother of Phebe, who lived at Mt Albert in Auckland. Charles and Ivy became engaged, however, they did not marry as the First World War intervened. (Ivy later married Alexander Morrison a farmer of Eltham, near New Plymouth).

1916… CHARLES DIED aged 27 on the 12 November 1916 …
(two days before his 28ᵗʰ birthday) … of wounds received in World War One.
His Memorial Card mentions he …"closed a beautiful life, fighting for
His King and Country, in France."

Mary Thomas (Daughter-in-law of Roy, Charles's brother) has numerous items
of Charles's War memorabilia.
Included is his Soldier's PAY BOOK which shows the date he joined up, his next
of kin and the dates and places of training, as follows:-

Date of Attestation 8 March 1916. Aged 27.

New Zealand Infantry.

Next of Kin…father…John Thomas of Coromandel.

Person to whom allotment is payable… Miss Ivy Woods.

7 March … 1 April 1916 at Trentham.

2 April … 27 May 1916 at Featherston.

28 May … 20 June 1916 at Trentham.

21 June … 1916 … Off overseas.

Died of wounds … 12 November 1916.

Mary Thomas
has a large
copper coloured
medallion, (The
Death Penny) and
the War Medal
awarded to
Charles.
She also has a
letter from
Buckingham
Palace signed by
King George
and a Commem-
orative Scroll
and letter from
the NZ Minister
of Defence.

200

A POSTCARD signed ... 'Ivy' states ... "Charl goes off to Trentham next Tuesday. I shall miss him. It is hoped the war will be over before he gets there. A line to thank you for the cigars, Father and Charl enjoyed them immensely."

1 May 1916… CHARLES in World War One NZ uniform.
The photograph on page 200 mentions his grave in France and states:-
> NZ Expeditionary Force.
> Thomas 14505.   Rifleman C.E.
> Regiment…… NZ Rifle Brigade.
> Position of Grave…Y Farm..Mil Cem 5.
> Charles's name appears on the Coromandel Memorial to those who lost their lives in the Great War 1914-18.

ALEXANDER ROY THOMAS
(1901-1972)

1901... Alexander Roy Thomas was born 28 September 1901,
The 15th child of John & Phebe Thomas at Ashburton, probably at 54 Grey Street where the family was then living.
He was known as Roy and was to become their eighth surviving child.

At the time of his birth, his eldest brother Alfred was 24 years old.

Roy would have had two years of education at Ashburton Borough School before his parents shifted from Ashburton.

1908... His parents moved to retire at Coromandel when Roy was 7 years old. With them went his brother Charles (20) and sister Elsie (22).

We assume Roy did his remaining schooling at the Coromandel School. He must have been heavily involved with the Methodist Church and Sunday School activities of his parents and sister, because he was later to become a Minister of Religion.

There were always visits to Coromandel by his other brothers but because they were so much older they bought their wives and children.

One day Jack, Edith & daughter Phyllis came to visit. Phyllis was Roy's niece and eleven years younger than him. It appears that Roy made a set of Bow & Arrows and one day he challenged Phyllis to shoot an arrow over the house. Well, you will have guessed who was on the receiving end of the arrow ... yes,

His father John. She remembers Roy being severely spoken to and saw the bow and arrows confiscated. As long as she can remember, they stood in a corner of the kitchen. Roy made another set, but they did not play with these anywhere near the house.

We are not sure what Roy did between 1915 & 1925 but he has been identified in a photo in front of Thomas Bros Ashburton shop in working clothes, with his brothers Percy & Alfred. I think we must assume that for some time he was employed here before feeling the call to serve God.

1925... Now 24, Religion began to play a very large part in Roy's life. He entered the Home Mission work of the Methodist Church, serving first at Helensville and had two happy years at Richmond in the Nelson district. Then came a stint at Ohura in the King Country.

In his own words he records for the Outlook 16 August 1969 issue....
"There was no one to meet me at Ohura, but knowing I was expected to bach in the Church Vestry I proceeded there. I was not encouraged by what I found. The Vestry, a room about 12 foot by 8 foot, was furnished with a bed minus all bed clothes, a table, two hard chairs, a primus stove and an open fire place. I can tell you I sat down and surveyed my surroundings with something like despair".
A gentleman soon arrived, apologised for being late and took him home and fed him.

Roy continues... *"The next morning I visited the farm where the circuit horse, Jerry, was grazing. I am afraid he immediately sensed I was a new chum as far as horses were concerned and he proved very stubborn on many of my trips. I did have a bicycle, but as many of the roads were hilly and unmetalled, cycling was often not possible."*

Roy recalls 3 incidents that occurred at Ohura in the "Outlook" article.
We detail these so that we may appreciate the conditions of those times.

"One of my preaching places was in a valley about six miles from the centre. In this valley four families lived and all attended the services, so we usually had eight adults, two teenagers and about a dozen children. While I was there this day the rain fell in torrents and as about three miles of the road was metalled, I expected to be invited to stay the night. However the invitation was not forthcoming, so I set out on my bicycle. It soon proved impossible to ride it, however, owing to the mud and it soon

became impossible to push it, so there was nothing for it but to shoulder the bike and stumble my way through the mud until after what seemed like an eternity I reached metal, was able to scrape the mud from the wheels and proceed through the rain to my vestry abode.

Cold and miserable I was too tired to even make myself a cup of tea but removed my wet clothes and tumbled into bed."

In the second of Roy's stories, he *"set out on horse back for another preaching place about 12 miles away on a road of which only about six miles were metalled. Once again the rain started and the mud churned up to such an extent that Jerry was floundering up to his knees in it. Taking pity on the poor steed I got off and led it through the mud for at least two miles. I arrived just in time for the service, but hardly in a state to do myself justice. The fact that my notes had got wet and were almost illegible did not add to my peace of mind."…*

Roads of Clay and mud or stone metalled are a long way from todays 1993 tar sealed surfaces…. thank goodness.

He also writes, *"I was in bed one night when there was a knock at the door and when I opened it there stood three men carrying a large bundle. This proved to be an elderly man who, going home drunk, had fallen into a creek and drowned himself. His helpers wondered if I would mind sharing my abode with him for the night. He was wrapped in a tarpaulin, so I asked them to lay him in the Church. The next morning (Sunday) when the body was removed, I discovered blood had seeped through to the floor and I had quite a job cleaning the Church for the morning service."*

Roy advises us that *"Ohura, was at that time supposedly a dry area but of the 10 shops, seven were sly grog shops where liquor could be readily obtained. I ate my evening meal at the local boarding house. My other diners at first seemed to go out of their way to tell risqué stories and use indecent language. However, as I tried to take little notice, they soon stopped, in fact several commenced coming to Church on occasions."*

MARRIAGE:
1930… Roy aged 29, married **MARGARET ROSE BROWN** aged 24, on the 9th April 1930 at Ohura in New Zealand.

Margaret was born 8th August 1906 at Taumaranui, the daughter of transport foreman Francis Thomas Brown and his wife Margaret Hamilton Brown. (no relation to husband).

Roy and Margaret had two children who they named:-
>   **Mervyn Roy Thomas**   born   7 May   1931.
>   **Margaret Elsie Thomas** born   1 August   1933.

3 Generations...ROY & MARGARET, with PHEBE and MERVYN

1937... Roy was appointed a Circuit Steward for the Coromandel Methodist Church, a duty he performed until he joined the Presbyterian Church in 1941.

1941... Roy served at Hauraki Plains and at Apiti. During the NZ Depression years he engaged in other occupations, but in 1941 he was accepted as a Home

Missionary by the Presbyterian Church. He was appointed to Pio Pio and afterwards served at Katikati, at Rongotea and as Moderator of the Turua Parish, on the Hauraki Plains near Thames.

1956... A large group of parishioners and fellow Ministers from nearby towns gathered at the Church, when Roy was ordained to the full ministry of the Church. These included the Rev Colin McKenzie from Cambridge, the Rev R. Lapsley of Waihi, the Rev S.W. Webber from Thames, the Rev S.W. Perry of Tirau and the Rev D Glennie of Te Aroha.

1966... His last charge was Kamo at Whangarei where he spent over eight years before retiring in 1966.

Son MERVYN and MARY THOMAS' WEDDING Feb 1961

L to R...Mervyn's sister Margaret, MARGARET and ROY,
MARY and MERVYN, and Roy's sister ELSIE THOMAS.

1960... The photo on page 202 was taken when Roy was aged 58.

We have not used the 1907 photo for Roy, as we did for his brothers and sisters, as he was only aged between 5 and 6 at that time.

1966... RETIREMENT:

Roy and Margaret bought a house on 23rd February 1966, to retire in at 101 Retreat Road, Christchurch.

His sister Elsie lived with the family for some time before she died.

1970... Thomas Family Bible.

When John and Phebe died their Family Bible was cared for by Elsie.

She bought it to Roy's home when she came to live. About this time Michael Stanley Thomas visited the family and from the Bible he copied all the Birthdates, Names and other detail it contained which he used for the start of his 1970 Thomas Family Tree.

Then Roy died, Margaret took sick and was cared for by a Home, Elsie died and in 1979 son Mervyn died.

During these eight or nine troubled years, the Bible vanished.

It is believed that somebody outside the family may have it.

> **1972... ROY DIED** at the age of 71, on 2 November 1972
> and his wife MARGARET DIED aged 78, on 23 August 1984.
> Both are resting at Ruru Lawn Cemetery, at Christchurch.

--ooo0ooo--

ALEXANDER ROY THOMAS FAMILY TREE:

3rd Generation:

ALEXANDER ROY THOMAS..........married.............................MARGARET ROSE BROWN

b 28 September 1901	9 April 1930	b 8 August 1906
at Ashburton.	at Ohura, NZ.	at Taumaranui.
d 2 November 1972 (71)		d 23 August 1984 (78)
Bur at Christchurch.		Bur at Christchurch.

Margaret was the daughter of Francis Thomas Brown and Margaret Hamilton Brown.
Roy and Margaret had two children whom they named Mervyn and Margaret.

+++

4th Generation	5th Generation	6th Generation	7th Generation
MERVYN ROY THOMAS b 7 May 1931 at Fielding. d 21 August 1979 (48) Bur at Christchurch. m 11 February 1961 === at Mt Albert, Auckland. BEATRICE MARY FINLAY b 2 April 1937 at Auckland. (She was the daughter of James Finlay and Livinia Gladys Irene Vos) They had three children.	KARYN MARY THOMAS b 5 July 1962 at Christchurch. m 31 October 1981==== at Christchurch. PHILIP ANDREW COOPER b 24 January 1958 at Darfield, Canterbury. (Son of Raymond George Cooper & Myra Pearl Marcelle Tooley)	ANDREW MERVYN RAY COOPER b 22 June 1982 at Timaru. EMMA LOUISE COOPER b 28 February 1985 at Timaru.	
	JAN MARGARET THOMAS b 28 January 1964 at Christchurch.		
	SHANE FRANCIS THOMAS b 28 April 1965 at Christchurch. m 7 November 1987 == at Bishopdale, ChCh. DIANNE JOAN BOWDEN b 24 October 1968 at Christchurch. (Daughter of Richard Henry Norman Bowden and Coleen Ruth Ching.)	AYNSLIE RUTH THOMAS b 30 May 1988 at Christchurch. JARED NORMAN RAY THOMAS b 21 August 1989 at Christchurch.	
MARGARET ELSIE THOMAS b 1 August 1933 at Auckland. d 8 October 1984 (51) Bur at Christchurch.			

1837 GEORGE THOMAS FAMILY TREE

1st Generation
      1700 **WILLIAM THOMAS** & HESTER   see page 11

2nd   1730 **JOHN** **THOMAS** & **ELIZABETH**   see page 12

3rd   1766 **CHARLES THOMAS** & ANNE   see page 14

4th   1797 **WILLIAM THOMAS** & **ELIZABETH**   see page 17

5th   1837 **GEORGE THOMAS**......married.........**JANE MORRIS** (Polly)
&   born 21 August 1837   b 7 July 1860 born 2 October 1842
1st   at Bradwell Mill, West Down. at Auckland. at Wellington. NZ.
NZ   Baptised 10 September 1837   died 28 August 1911
       at C of E, West Down, Devon.   Bur St Judes, Avondale
       died 5 October 1902 (64)
       Bur St Judes, Avondale, Auckland.   Their story follows.......

George and Polly had 12 children :-

6th & 2nd NZ	Eliza Selina	Elizabeth	Mary John	William	Richard George	Ernest Esther	Hilda Alfred
		X			X		Trevor

| 7th & 3rd NZ | Ada Elsie Ruby | Harold Ivy Albert Hilda Florence Bertha Allan | Linda Muriel Myrtle Olive Algar Doris George | Rita Mabel Leila Norman | Ernest Albert George Victor Stanley Ernest Victoria | Gordan Dora Frances Norman | Dulcie Muriel Allan Jean | Neville Maurice |
| | p232 | p234 | p235 | p246 | p252 | p262 | p292 | p294 | p299 |

210

5th Generation.

GEORGE THOMAS and JANE.

1st Generation NZ.

1837... BIRTH:
GEORGE THOMAS, was the fifth child of William Thomas (a Mason) and Elizabeth Lewis. He was born at Bradwell Mill, West Down on 21 August 1837 and was baptised on 10 September 1837 in the Church of England at West Down in Devon, England.

1841... CENSUS:
He lived all his childhood years at the family home known as Bradwell Mill in the Parish of West Down, 7 miles south of Ilfracombe. He would have attended the School and Church in the West Down township.
In 1841 during the Devonshire Census he was aged 3 and is shown living with his parents and 5 brothers and sisters at Bradwell Mill.

1851... CENSUS:
During this census George was 13 years of age and the only child left at home. His occupation is recorded as "Miller" so he was learning the trade and working for his father, operating their own flour mill.

1855... MIGRATION:
George's elder brother John was the first to come to New Zealand and arrived in Feb 1854. He obviously found work, liked the country and got word back to Devon, because George aged 17 years, came to NZ accompanying John's wife Jane and her children William (6) and John (4).
George arrived at Wellington on the "Sea Snake" on 25th May 1855. Their arrival is recorded in the newspaper "The NZ Spectator & Cook's Strait Guardian" (more detail on pages 40, 41 in brother John's chapter).

George's early days in NZ were entwined with those of his older brothers. We have not duplicated the relevant passages but note here that George is mentioned quite often in John's Chapter Three. The first 4 Generations are identical to both brothers... so, Chapters One and Two could have been printed here too. A summary of George's Family Tree is opposite, and your branch will be shown, with details following later.

WELLINGTON:

We have not been able to determine how long George stayed in Wellington. The writer believes he came to Auckland with Jane and the boys and worked in the district. In 1860, five years after arriving in New Zealand, he married at Whau (now Avondale) in Auckland.

AUCKLAND:

Fortunately for us, George, or wife Polly, liked to have their life's activities recorded. From the Electoral Rolls and the Wises Post Office Directories we have been able to divide this George Thomas's working life into:-

1855-1860	Flour Miller.
1861-1865	Baker, Miller, Grocer.
1865-1874	Flour miller.
1874-1876	Flour Mill Owner.
1877-1881	Postmaster.
1881-1902	Baker/ Grocer/ Storekeeper.

Polly was first mentioned in the Eden Electoral Rolls in 1897 as……. Jane Thomas of Avondale…. Domestic Duties.

1855 to 1860:

Before he married George seems definitely to have worked at a Flour Mill. Albert B Thomas told his daughter Doreen on numerous occasions that his 'Grandfather had a Flour Mill at the Wade', on the Weiti River between the main Road and the Wade Hotel at Silverdale, and Albert's nephew Ron Thomas remembers, as a child, being told the same story when his family stayed at Albert's place at Snells Beach.

We have spent many hours in search of evidence but regret being unable to obtain land documents or written record of George, or any flour mill, at this place.

George was occupied and earning money somewhere during these five years and it could have been at the **WADE** or at his brother's Flour Mill at the **WHAU**. There is not much difference between these two names and the writer believes some innocent misunderstanding has come into the story when retold over the past 130 years via the past four generations.

Wherever he was employed he managed to save a fair amount of money, as he purchased his first piece of land at the age of 22, some four months before he married.

NAPIER St runs from left to right across the centre of the photo.

GEORGE & POLLY's HOME and BUSINESS AT NAPIER ST.

"Auckland Public Library"
Photo #A3779 May 1966

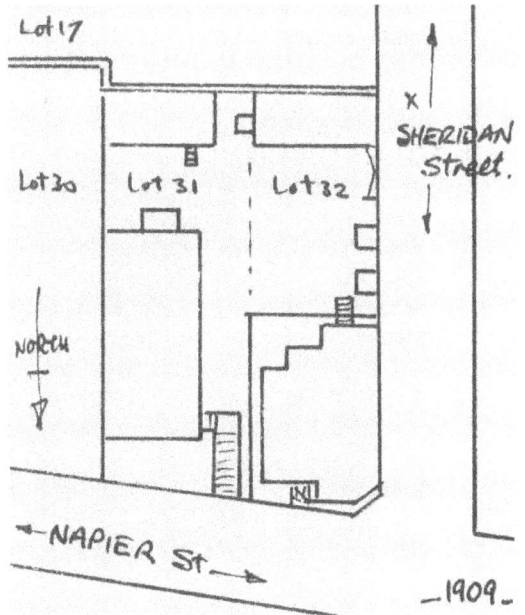

This outline sketch of the two single story buildings show the house on Lot 31 and a house-shop on Lot 32.
This was taken from Auckland City Council "Map F 10" dated 1909.

The aerial photo above shows them as they were in May 1966.

Another photo at the Library Dated 1905 shows a veranda over the doorway of the corner building.

213

SUMMARY OF 8 PROPERTY PURCHASES:

Due to the volume of property purchases, we felt this summary would help to prevent confusion when the details are read later.

1860 NAPIER St, Auckland. Bought 10 March	Sold 18 June 1870.
1864 SHERIDAN St, Auckland (A) Bought 31 Aug.	Sold 26 Nov.1864.
1864 SHERIDAN St, Auckland (B) Bought	Sold
1867 WHAU, TOWNSHIP. Bought 9 December	Sold 20 May 1889.
1871 TAUPAKI FARMLAND. Bought 17 October	Sold 3 July 1889.
1874 STAR FLOUR MILL. Bought 26 September	Sold 25 Mar 1876.
1882 HIGHBURY St, Avondale. Bought 5 July	Sold 13 Mar 1903.
1883 ROSEBANK Rd, Avondale. Bought 25 May	Sold 4 May 1889.

NAPIER ST, Auckland PROPERTY:

10 March 1860 ... Deed 8D:873 #16252

Richard Ridings, Solicitor and Hugh Coolahan, a Baker, sold to George Thomas, a Miller, Lots 31 and 32 facing Napier Street in the City of Auckland, for 100 pounds 4 shillings and 7 pence. Photo page 213.

There were 2 buildings on this property. One was obviously a residence and another photo taken in 1905, shows that the building on Lot 32 on the corner of Napier & Sheridan Streets, Freemans Bay, was a shop with a veranda over the footpath. No acreage was given but the oblong shaped land measured 101 feet by 67 ft 10 inches. (30.8 meters X 20.70m)

1860... WEDDING:

George Thomas, 23, married JANE (POLLY) MORRIS, nearly 18, on the 7 July 1860 in the house of Moses Crocker, Elliot St, Auckland.

(Polly's mother, Anne Lowe / Morris married Moses Crocker in 1858)

The Rev Mr Joseph Long of the Primitive Methodist Church officiated.

The wedding certificate shows that witnesses to the wedding were John Woods (who married Polly's half-sister Mary Anne Lowe) and Sarah Moore, a Dressmaker of Coburg St, Auckland who was not a family member.

Polly was born 2 October 1842 at Wellington in New Zealand,
A daughter of Ann Lowe and Samuel Morris.
She had two brothers and four half-brothers and a half-sister.

Refer pages 104 to 107 for the **LOWE** and **MORRIS** Family details.

214

THOMAS BIBLE:

The following list is contained in George and Polly's Family Bible which is now in the care of their Great Great Grandson Kevin George Thomas.

There were twelve Thomas children named:-

SELINA ANN	born 9 Apr 1861:	died 30 Apr 1932 (71)
ELIZA JANE	born 15 Sep 1862:	died 7 Jan 1878 (16)
ELIZABETH	born 10 May 1864:	died 6 Feb 1951 (86)
MARY ANN	born 12 Mar 1866:	died 24 May 1915 (49)
JOHN (Jack)	born 13 Aug 1867:	died 3 Sep 1943 (76)
WILLIAM	born 23 Jul 1869:	died 10 Aug 1945 (76)
GEORGE	born 2 Sep 1871:	died 26 Aug 1958 (87)
RICHARD HENESY	born 13 Jul 1873:	died __April 1875 (2)
HESTER	born 2 Oct 1875:	died 14 Feb 1943 (67)
EDWARD ERNEST	born 9 Aug 1877:	died 21 Apr 1953 (75)
ALFRED SAMUEL	born 7 Jun 1880:	died 4 Jan 1942 (62)
HILDA JANE	born 28 Feb 1883:	died 7 Sep 1958 (75)

NB: Some of these details differ from official records.

Each of these children's marriage details and descendant's lists follow in their Family Tree at the end of this Chapter.

PHOTO: We have not found any photo of George and Polly Thomas.

FAMILY BIBLE of GEORGE & POLLY THOMAS

1863...WAIKATO WARS:

While in Devon in 1990 the writer viewed letters from NZ to living descendants there and one from 1837 George's great-grandson, also named George, states that his great-grandfather "set up a Mill & Bakery at the junction of the Waikato & Waipa Rivers at Ngaruawahia to bake bread for the Red Coat soldiers and the Maoris they were fighting. When peace was restored, he returned to Auckland and established another mill on the Oakley Creek and a bakery at Avondale two miles distant".

Our research shows that the Waikato War occurred 1863/4.

A book by John Featon mentions that *"in July 1863 the Red Coats were paid, Sergeants 7/6, Corporals 6/6 and Troopers 5 shillings per day, and had to find their own rations"*. Later he states *"large supplies of flour, potatoes and kumeras were sent down the Waikato River to where there were situated several flour mills "*and *"The Waipa Primary School has four surviving Mill Stones from the old flour mills which used to operate in the immediate vicinity, but there is no recorded history of them."*

So, there could be some fact in young George's story, but no proof has been found to date. Maybe George, after he had married in 1860, went down to the Waikato to take advantage of the flour milling needed there. Who would have looked after his business at Napier Street?

Maybe George was called up to serve in the Militia as was his elder brother John. Maybe the Militia had them both Milling and baking bread in the Waikato.

SHERIDAN ST, Auckland (A):

31 Aug 1864 ... Deed 16D:556 #27745

John Benjamin Russel, Solicitor and Hugh Coolahan, a Baker, sold to George Thomas, a Miller, Lot 17 of subdivision of Allotments 24,25,26 & others of Section 44 in Sheridan Street, Auckland City for 54 pounds.

George paid Russell 5 shillings and Coolahan 53 pounds 15 shillings.

There was a house on this property in 1909. We have a sketch plan of it, but we do not know if it was there in 1864 when George owned it.

> (Sheridan St in Freemans Bay has been removed but was
> approximately sited where Gwilliam St is in 1993.)

SHERIDAN ST, Auckland (A continued):

26 NOV 1864 ... Deed 16D:558 #27746 George Thomas sold Lot 17 with part pieces of Lots 31 and 32 for 81 pounds, to six gentlemen named Thomas Booth, Benjamin Filgate, James Simpson, John Seabrook, Armstrong Newburn and Edward Tremain.

Booth and friends raised a mortgage that day and received it with a condition that the building be insured for at least 100 pounds.

1865... George's brother John died suddenly in 1865 aged 36, at his Oakley Creek flour mill. We do not know exactly what happened at the mill or who took managerial control during the next 5 years until June 1870.

John's two sons and some other men seem to have been running the Mill on George's instructions. He was probably appointed "Manager", because of his greater milling knowledge. **(Advert with his name dated 14 August 1867, see page 309)** In 1865 he was one of three people to sign a Bond document as security for the administration of his brother's estate. In the estate's 1870 legal papers payment of 45 pound was made under the heading "George Thomas and workmen's wages".

It seems certain that George had no financial investment in the Star Mill until 1874 but he gave his "place of abode" in the 1865 Bond document and in the 1869 Electoral records as "the Star Mill".

This implies George, wife Polly and 3 children, joined Jane and her 3 children in the Mill-house from mid 1865 until Jane remarried in August 1867. It was probably at this time that Polly received her nickname, as two Jane Thomas's living in the same house would be rather confusing. The property in Napier Street was not registered as sold until mid 1870 so, George must have had a shop manager, or leased the house and shop, between 1865 and 1870.

NAPIER ST, Auckland:

18 June 1870 ...Deed 23D:491 # 41589

George Thomas sold Lots 31 & 32 for 50 pounds, to Gustav Van Der Heyde, a Merchant. George had reduced the size of the sections a bit, adding them to lot 17 next door, which he owned for a brief time.

Further owner / occupiers of the house and shop on Lot 31 & 32 were .....

1871 George Rattray McNabb....Storeman.

1885 Thomas Veale....Grocer.

1887 John Buchanan....Merchant.

1891 J Buchanan went into Bankruptcy and both lots were sold to
John Blair Whyte a Gentleman and John Thomas Irvin...Grocer.

1918 – 1925 James Irwin a Grocer owned the property.

Mr Coolahan, who sold the property to George, was a baker and George may have baked here too.

We believe this continuation of Grocers and shop personal as owners of Lot 32 proves conclusively that a business was operated here at this time. Although George kept mentioning his occupation as Miller we do not think that he actually milled at this address but that he probably was a General Grocer or maybe a Produce Dealer and retailed wheat, corn, flour, mash etc, milled at his brother's Oakley Creek Mill.

SHERIDAN St, Auckland (B)

George is also thought to have had an interest for a time in Lots 38 to 44 inclusive, on Sheridan St, Auckland but his name has not yet been found on any of their titles. These lots were mentioned as his property in the 1865 to 1874 Electoral Rolls.

WHAU TOWNSHIP:

9 Dec 1867 ... Deed 22D:488 #36738

James Harris sold to George Thomas, a Miller, of the Whau near Auckland, Part 4 of Allotment 64 of Titirangi Parish containing about 7.65 acres... say 8 acres.

Lots 17, 18, 23, 24, 25, 26, 31 & 32 ... each 1 acre.

George paid 230 pounds for the land and all the buildings.

10 Dec 1867 Part 4, Mortage Deed 13M:130 #36739

George borrowed all of the 230 pounds from the seller J Harris and agreed to pay 10% PA interest. Mr Harris wrote his Will 31D:429 in April 1875 and left money to the Primitive Methodist Church in Edwards St, Auckland.

So George and James Harris would have attended the same Church especially over the preceding 7 years when the family lived in Napier St.

23 March 1882 Part 4, Deed C2:468 # 74825

George's friend J Harris has died by this date and the Mortgage was discharged.

23 March 1882 Part 4, Deed C2:469 # 74826

George was still described as a miller, when he took out a new Mortgage with the Auckland Savings Bank for 400 pounds at 9% interest.

17 June 1884 Part 4,

With the approval of the ASB, George leased out a quarter acre piece of Lot 24 fronting the Great North Road with a house on it, to Abraham Patterson a carpenter.

The Lease was for 10 years from 26 May 1884 at 10 pounds rental per year and Patterson had to pay rates , taxes and other outgoings.

3 April 1886 Part 4, Deed R17:645 # 98969

Mortgage paid off.

George became the land's owner once again.

3 April 1886 Part 4, Deed R17:645 # 98969

George, now described as Miller of Avondale, took a Mortgage from the NZ Land Mortgage Co of ... 700 pounds, interest 10% PA payable quarterly.

23 Feb 1887 Part 4, Deed R24:271 #102679

George (now described as a Storekeeper) took another Mortgage, with John Buchanan a Merchant, of 254 pounds at 10% PA.

20 May 1889 Part 4, Deed R29:956 # 111993

Unfortunately for George, Mr Buchanan died and George was adjudged bankrupt on 4 Jan 1889 and over ensuing months George broke his Mortgage requirements. The Power of Sale was exercised and the property was sold by the Official Assignee at Auction on 20 May 1889 for 640 pounds to Hermann Brown and others. When reregistered 12 Nov 1889, this property no longer contained the George Thomas name.

This 8 acre Avondale block of land, once owned by George Thomas, is in 1993 divided in half by Geddes St.   See page 220.

In the 1882 book "Freeholders of NZ" this was "valued at 700 pounds".

We believe that the Dec 1867 purchase detailed above was these 8 acres mentioned in the Rolls and that George & Jane and family lived here until they moved to Highbury St and then leased out the house on Lot 24.

--ooo0oo--

**LOCATION
of 8 ACRES
IN WHAU
TOWNSHIP.**

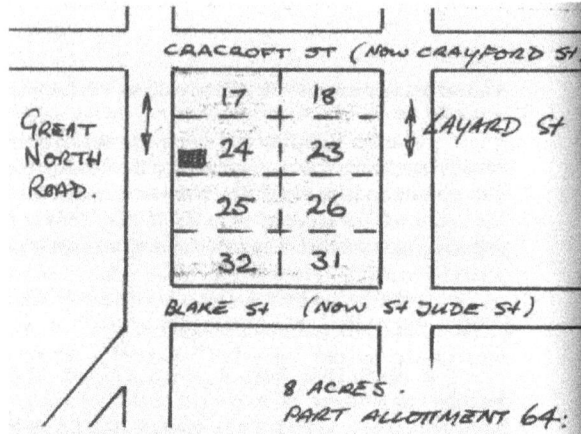

1870... TRUSTEE:
Auckland Provincial Government Gazette, 29 Oct 1870.

> George Thomas was elected a Trustee for the Whau Highway
> Board.... District 414, together with J H Hanson, John Bollard,
> Thomas Barraclough and John Buchanan.

Mr T Barraclough was an Oakley Creek Storekeeper, who registered the birth of
Elizabeth Thomas to John & Jane Thomas in March 1859 and became a one third
shareholder in the Star Flour Mill with William & John Thomas (George's
nephews) earlier in 1870 after George's brother John's death.

One page of the Minutes of the Highway Committee meeting dated 30 January
1871 have survived and shows that George Thomas was in attendance but
nothing else of interest was recorded for us on that page.

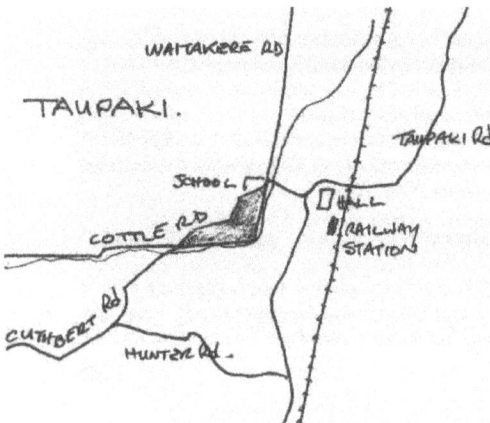

**TAUPAKI FARM:
17 OCT 1871**
Deed 24D/646   #44533.

Josiah Dell of Shortland
in the Province of
Auckland, sold Lot 30
Taupaki in the district of
Kaipara, of 20 acres, 1
Rood, 21 perchases, to
George Thomas, a
Miller, for 5 pounds.

220

It appears this land was registered to Josiah's wife, Amelia Ann Dell and when she died, she left it to her son John James Dell.

Father Josiah sold the land to George and contracted for his son John to officially sign it over to George when he attained the age of 21.
This deed has George's signature entered on 12 January 1872.

Taupaki is described in Wises 1979 as "… near the northern boundary of Waitakere and Rodney County, 4km NE from Waitakere and 6 km from Kumeu and 35 km from Auckland City. There is a Railway Station nearby, on the Auckland / Opua line".

12 Oct 1876 Deed 31D:535 #55225 This records the completion of transfer of the land from John Dell to George Thomas.

3 July 1889 Deed R31:386 #11189
This states George Thomas, Avondale Storekeeper, went Bankrupt.
The Official Assignee John Lawson sold this property to John Lake for 11 pounds, 4 shillings and 3 pence. Sale dated 9 August 1889.

STAR FLOUR MILL:
26 SEPT 1874 Deed 29D:76 # 50323 George Wm Binney, John Thomas and Thomas Barraclough sold all that was called "Star Mill" to George Thomas of the Whau, a miller. He was John's uncle.

George agreed to pay 1300 pounds for:-
"Part of Lot 18A and part Lots 31,32,33 together with the Mill and all else, plus scheduled items and including other debts due by John Thomas or Thomas Barraclough or the firm of Thomas and Barraclough of the Whau, Millers, known as The Star Mills".

Scheduled Items: Brown Mare.. "Gipsy"; Brown Mare.. "Darkey", Chestnut Horse.. "Duke"; one heavy Dray; one Spring Cart; 2 sets Leaving Harness; 1 set Shaft harness; 1 set Trap harness:

Barraclough Parlour….1 dining table square, 1 do round, 1 sofa, 1 chiffonier, 6 chairs, 1 iron sofa bedstead, 1 colonial sofa, 1 hall clock, picture and ornaments.

Barraclough Kitchen… 1 table, 3 chairs, 1 dresser, 2 forms, 1 Safe, 1 sideboard, Delf and glassware value 7 pounds, 6 candelsticks, Cooking utensils value 5 pounds, 2 tea caddies.

Barraclough Bedroom… 1 Kauri double bedstead & featherbed. 1 washstand, 1 dressing table, looking glass, 4 large clothes boxes.

221

Barraclough Dairy…. 1 chrome & 6 milk dishes, 1 large salter, 1 small do, cream pan, weights & scales, small safe.

John Thomas Parlour… 1 Dining table, 1 chiffonier, 4 chairs, 1 couch, 1 hearthrug, 1 Kerosene lamp.

Thomas Kitchen…. 1 square table, 2 chairs, 1 dresser, kitchen utensils value 5 pounds, 2 milk pans.

Thomas Bedroom…. 1 iron bedstead, 1 pair paliasses, 1 feather bed, chest drawers, 1 dressing table, swing looking glass, 2 "Sarvles" double barrel guns, 1 single do, 2 flasks & shot pouches etc.

Also items in and about the mill including 1 weighing machine, 1 chaff cutting machine, jacks, trucks, Mill picks, grindstone, and pint basalt. One yellow cow and Mill proof.

26 Sept 1874 Deed 20D:10 # 50324 Also recorded on day of purchase is a Mortgage from G W Binney to George Thomas, miller and owner of Star Mills near Whau, of 1200 pounds at 12% PA calculated on the monthly balance. (It would appear George put down 100 pounds cash for the purchase.) The deed also states he must insure the Mill and buildings for at least 600 pounds.

25 March 1876 Deed 29D:944 # 53770 This is a "Conveyance of Equity of Redemption" where …"George Thomas agreed to the absolute
sale to GW Binney at the price of 5 pounds upon condition G W B pay off the mortgage debts to David Nathan, being #41576 and #46624 of 550 pounds plus interest and that George be released from debt to G W Binney of mortgage # 50324." (We interpret this to mean George sold the lot for about 1800 pounds, however it was all owed… so George would have seen none of it.)

27 March 1876 Deed # 53771
David Nathan consigning the property and scheduled items to G W Binney.

Seventeen years earlier George's brother John Thomas started this Flour Mill. When he died in 1865 aged 36 his two sons and Barraclough took over and it was from them that George purchased the Mill.

In March 1876 the Star Flour Mill left Thomas family ownership.

Section 18a's three acres were subdivided in 1949 for housing.
The Part Lots 31, 32, 33 were added to the other part of their Lot and became land occupied in 1993 by the Auckland Psychiatric Hospital and the Carrington Technical Institute.

1877... POSTMASTER:

The electoral Rolls advised us of this different activity for George when he listed his occupation for the 1878 & 1880 elections. The PO Directory for 1872 records the Post Office as titled "Whau Bridge".

Enquires to New Zealand Post Archives and the Postal History Society, confirms that George Thomas was employed as Postmaster on two occasions, totalling over 5 years service.

Firstly, on 1 April 1871 he followed S McCallum and nearly 10 months later, on 20 January 1872, he handed the job over to William Morris. (Possibly William Lowe/Morris, wife Polly's half-brother.)

Five years later on 1 April 1877 W Morris handed it back to George and four and a half years later he resigned from 1 September 1881.

They advise that the Whau Bridge Post Office was a sub-office, and it is quite possible it was conducted from a private residence or from a local store. People called and collected their mail in those days, as it was not delivered.

Following George in 1881 the Postmaster was Mr J Leach, then 1884 HF Howard, 1885 H Bell and 1899 A Eyes. The Post Office was situated at the Avondale Railway Station from 1881 until at least 1899. It was sited at the Avondale Hotel in 1924 at the junction of five roads, where today's large roundabout is.

1878... Eliza Jane Thomas, George and Polly's second child, died 7 January aged 16. The family advise she died after being kicked on the head by a horse. She is buried at St Judes, with her Mother and Father.

1880...WHAU / AVONDALE GROCER:

From the directories and electoral Rolls we find the first entry in 1880 of "George Thomas ...Grocer...Whau Township." The word Grocer is also stated in 1893, 1894 and 1897 Rolls. All other entries from 1880 to 1902 are "Avondale Storekeeper."

We have not found any legal document or newspaper item which mentions the name of or location of George's grocery shop...except .. 'Avondale.'

He must have rented shop space there, as there does not appear to be any business property registered to him.

HIGHBURY St, Whau: (Avondale)

1882 ... This property purchase became the site and home of George and Polly for the next 20 years. Farm land was cut up for a housing subdivision and George bought Lot 20 at an Auction held at noon Wednesday 5 July 1882 by B Tonks & Co. Acting solicitors were Whittle, Russell & Buddle. For sale was all the land within the triangle formed by Rosebank Rd, Victor St (then Victoria St) and the Great North Road.

5 JULY 1882   Vol28/207   Purchased by Auction from John Murray and George Patrick Pierce, Lot 20 of 2 roods 5 perches, on plan 177 Subdivision of Allotments 6, 7, 14 & 15.
Transfer #4089 dated 1 August 1882 shows that George paid 16 pounds and described himself as "Whau Settler." Plan 177 shows this property on the East side of High St... now Highbury St. George and Jane were still living here when he died in 1902. The sale was registered 14 August 1882 and became Vol 30/18.

After this purchase George had to raise finance and have a home erected on the land. We believe the family moved out of their house on the 8 acres and into their new home probably in late 1883. We saw earlier where George had found a suitable tenant (Mr Patterson) for the '8 Acre' house and leased it out for 10 years from May 1884.

> During the late months of 1883 all 12 children had been born, 10 of them were still alive, and only Elizabeth was married by then.

This still left a possible total of 9 children to house, ranging from Selina aged 22 to Hilda aged about 6 months.
So, in 1882, now aged 45 George has found a home and a job that will see him through the rest of his life.   For exact location see map page 42.

29 Aug 1882 Vol 30/18 George mortgaged Lot 20 to William Ernest Bollard of Worchester, England...Gentleman, on 29 Aug 1882.
Document #2982 details destroyed. (sum stated at 70 pounds in 1889)
Mortgage discharged 7 June 1895 when section sold.

4 May 1889 ... Transmission #524.
The Official Assignee, John Lawson, filed for the Bankruptcy of George Thomas, Avondale Storekeeper, on 4 May 1889 on Lot 20. Bankruptcy was granted 11 June and registered against the properties 9 Aug 1889.

3 May 1895 Lot 20, Quote....
"The official Assignee in the Bankruptcy of George Thomas, sold
the property to the said George Thomas."
Transfer #16839 shows George agreed to pay seven pounds for
the return of his home to his ownership.
It would appear that W E Bollard has given George time to get through his bad
luck and extended the life of his August 1882 Mortgage.
We do not think George and his family were asked to leave the property during
this six year period. Repurchase was registered 7 June 1895.

7 June 1895 Lot 20, George raised a Mortgage with Robert McDonald.
Document #11429 was discharged 4 June 1897.

4 June 1897 Lot 20, George raised a Mortgage with Joseph William Gibbs.
Document #13288 was discharged 18 May 1901 but details have again been
destroyed.

18 May 1901 Lot 20, George raised a Mortgage with William Monaghan.
Unfortunately George Thomas died 5th October 1902 and Mr Monaghan had to
exercise his Mortgagor's Right of Sale.
Document #17706 was discharged 29 July 1903.

13 March 1903 Lot 20, Transfer #31494 records ....
"...default having been made in payment of the sum of 60 pounds
and also in payment of interest secured by Mortgage #17706..."
Mr Monaghan sold Lot 20 to Alfred Harris for 70 pounds on 29 July 1903. This
was registered 6 August 1903.

We do not know where wife Polly lived after George died...maybe she stayed
on at the Highbury address for a while and rented off Mr Harris..
Or maybe she lived with one of her children.
She died 9 years later "at her residence in Mt Albert." At the time George died,
all her children were married except for Hilda who was aged 19.

This property has had many changes in size and boundaries and the Ash St
extension has cut Highbury St in two but the old lot 20 sat where numbers 11 &
11a are today in 1993. See sketches on the next page.
We wonder how old is the large Date Palm in the front yard ?
Did it sit on George and Jane's front lawn 100 years ago?

225

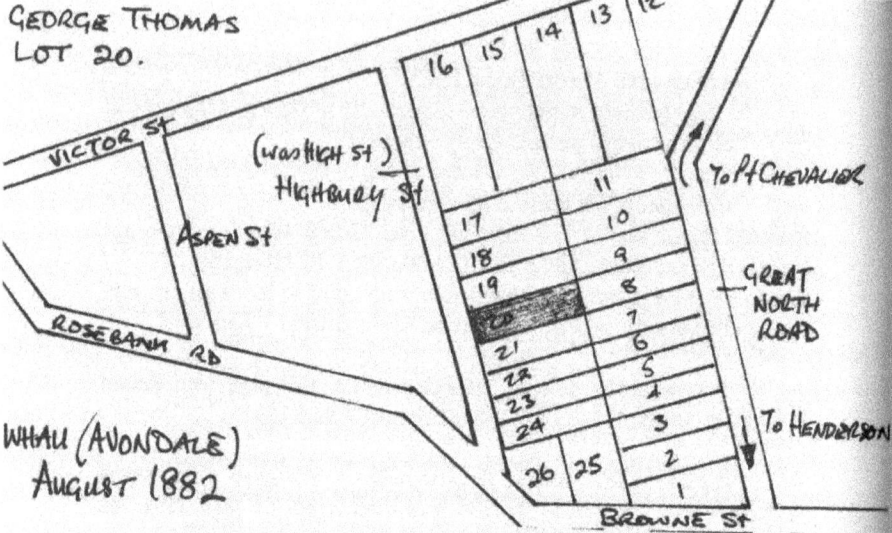

GEORGE THOMAS
LOT 20.

VICTOR St

(was HIGH St)
HIGHBURY St

ASPEN St

ROSEBANK RD

WHAU (AVONDALE)
AUGUST 1882

16 15 14 13 12

11

To PT CHEVALIER

17   10
18   9
19   8   GREAT
20   7   NORTH
21   6   ROAD
22   5
23   4
24   3   To HENDERSON
26 25 2
        1

BROWNE St

1882 HIGHBURY St and 1993 HIGHBURY St.

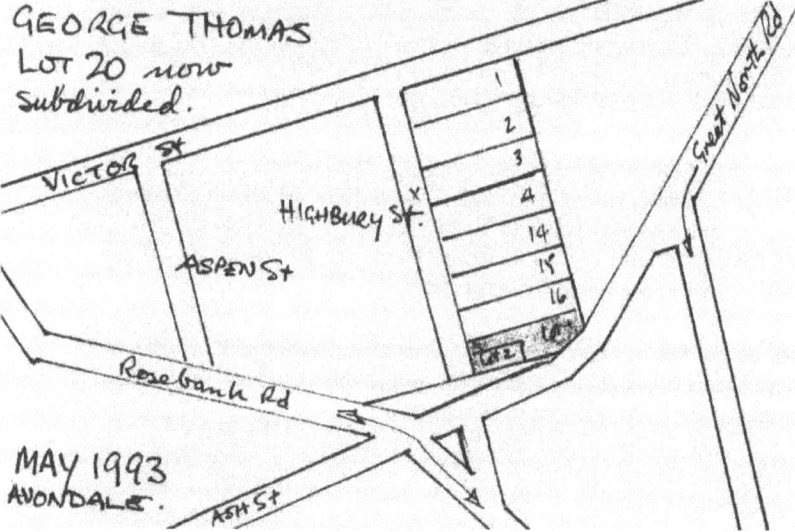

GEORGE THOMAS
LOT 20 now
subdivided.

VICTOR St

HIGHBURY St.

ASPEN St

Rosebank Rd

MAY 1993
AVONDALE.

ASH St

Great North Rd

1
2
3
4
14
15
16

1882…"FREEHOLDERS of NZ"

This book was printed in October and page 13 section T shows:-
GEORGE THOMAS…. STOREKEEPER at AVONDALE.
In Eden County, owns 8 acres at value 700 pounds.
In Waitemata County, owns 20 acres at value 20 pounds.

1882… Daughter **HILDA JANE THOMAS,** their 12th child was born and became their 10th living child. George and Polly had a dog named Bruce and it was Hilda's pleasant duty to see it fit and fed.

1883… It is probable that George and Polly moved into their new home on Lot 20 in Highbury St, Avondale, late this year.

ROSEBANK Rd, AVONDALE:

25 MAY 1883 Vol 30/157 Purchased from Thomas Aicken Lot 25 of 1 rood ex Allotment 9+10 subdivision on plan 207, Rosebank Rd. Transfer #5392 (which was originally dated November 1882) shows George paid 8 pounds 15 shillings and recorded his occupation as "Avondale Postmaster." Registration was on 17 December 1883 and became Vol 33/181.

4 MAY 1889 Vol 33/181 Lot 25, The estate and interest of George Thomas, a Bankrupt, was taken over by the Official Assignee. Both this Lot 25 and Lot 20 mentioned earlier, were listed together on the same Bankruptcy Transmission document #524 Registered on 9 August 1889.

We have traced this property to the position of 288 Rosebank Rd in 1993. We believe this plot of land and the 20 acres at Taupaki are what George's great-grandson George mentions in a 1984 letter to Devon as …
"a block of land used for farming to support his small family of 12."
George may also have grown items here for sale in his shop.

1884… The Whau name was changed between the elections of 1884 and 1887 to Avondale, but the district remained an independent borough until amalgamation with Auckland City in 1927.

1889… BANKRUPTCY:

George found himself with too many debts and not enough income and assets to cover them, so he took drastic steps on 4 May 1889.

A notice on page 1 of the NZ Herald on 6 May advises everyone that on the 4th May, George Thomas…"filed a petition to be adjudged bankrupt."

The notice also called for a Meeting of Creditors for Saturday 11 May.

Monday 13th, the paper reports the following in attendance at the Creditors Meeting:- Hesketh & Richmond, Solicitors for George, Mr John
Lawson the Official Assignee held the chair, & creditors, Messrs Hobart for the BNZ, Smith senior & junior, Dowden, Otto, and J & W Thomas.
Mr Lawson explained that negotiations had been going on for some days for a compromise, but the principal creditor insisted on 6 shillings in the pound being guaranteed, George, however, said he could not comply with this demand and Mr Lawson had to order assets to be sold.

(The 'J Thomas' in attendance was probably not William's brother John, as no debt was claimed in his name. We believe William was accompanied by his son John Coates Thomas who was then aged 22)

The Mercantile & Bankruptcy Gazette, 11 May 1889, p 141
lists George's Liabilities and Assets.
894 pounds represented three Secured Liabilities.
Two Mortgages on the 8 acre block in Whau Township and the Mortgage on his home property Lot 20 in Highbury St.
The unsecured Liabilities included small sums to SH Worth, JR Smith senior and junior, W Dowden, Gee & Porter, Hammond & Co, T Wilson, Roller Mills Co, Binstead Bros, A Martin, Runson & Martin, W Thomas, Wilson & Horton and J OTTs all of Auckland and in Sydney a W Morris.
Also in the Auckland list was an amazing sum of 400 pounds Unsecured Debt to the Bank of NZ. Next highest Auckland debtor was George's nephew William Thomas with 11 pounds.
Total unsecured debt was 530 pounds 5 shillings and 6 pence.
From this detail we presume most of these unsecured debts are from his business... the Avondale Grocery Shop he was operating from 1880.

George's assets were listed as:- Stock-in-trade 100 pounds and book debts of 150 pounds, horses, carts, cows etc, 46 pounds: property 41 pounds and furniture 40 pounds... total officially recorded as 357 pounds. (actually adds up to 377 pounds...?)

George must have found friends in the Official Assignee and his home mortgager the Rev W E Bollard, as he was not totally destroyed by the bankruptcy. It seems...

(a) Three of George's properties the 8 acre block, Rosebank section and the Taupaki farmland, were sold to realise money to pay off debtors.

(b) that George was allowed to stay in his home in Highbury St as he repurchased this 6 years later. And

(c) his shop was continuously trading, probably for a while under the financial control of Mr Lawson.

George was still a Grocer when he died 13 years later.

1889...DISCHARGE:

The Mercantile & Bankruptcy Gazette, 7 December, page 381 says:-

> DISCHARGES GRANTED at AUCKLAND
> George Thomas, of Avondale, Storekeeper.

That must have been a happy day for George and Polly.

METHODIST CHURCH:

The Waterview Methodist Church saw a lot of George and Polly and children. In their earlier days they attended the Primitive Methodist organisation in Edwards Street, Auckland. (now Airedale St) Formed in 1849, the Lowe, Woods and Morris families were early members.

The Primitive's records show George and Polly attended and seven of their children were christened into the faith. The Latter children were probably christened at Waterview but that branch's earlier records are no longer available. Initially the church sent preachers out to the Whau district from the Church in Auckland City.

The section on Fir St corner with Great North Rd, (Where the Methodist Church stands in 1993) seems to have always been involved with the Methodist religion. A house on this site was where the Whau Methodists met for their services which started out there about 1875.

Daughter Hilda's son Maurice advises that Hilda used to play the organ at that church (from about 1900) and that her father, George, insisted that all the family attend twice a day on Sundays.

1902... GEORGE DIED:

> On 5 October 1902 George Thomas died aged 65,
> at his residence in Highbury St, Avondale
> and was buried at St Jude's Anglican Cemetery,
> Rosebank Road, Avondale.

We have been unable to locate a copy of George and Polly's Wills.

GEORGE'S OBITUARY:

The NZ Methodist Times carried an Obituary for George Thomas, written by his minister the Rev W. S. Potter. In part he wrote...

"He served the district in many ways over the past 40 years, especially on the Roads and School Boards. Mrs Thomas has been a consistent member of our Church for years and Miss Thomas (Hilda) renders valuable aid as organist.

For more than 30 years our departed brother has worshipped amongst our people at Waterview and when the present (1902) Church was built, he became a Trustee.... on the finance committee he has rendered valuable aid... perhaps he most distinguished himself for his regular and punctual attendance at the means of grace.

Although he had a long way to walk, his place, no matter what the weather, was never empty. On Sunday evening October 5th, I conducted the service at Waterview. The night was densely dark, the roads in a most dirty condition and occasionally heavy showers of rain fell. There were only 16 persons present but brother Thomas was one of them and he appeared to take a real interest in the sermon.

At about 20 minutes to 8pm we bade each other a pleasant good night at the Church door. He was then apparently in the best of health and spirits, and we never dreamed it was our last meeting. He walked home without apparent fatigue, sat down and in a few minutes sighed and passed away."

On 6 October a news item in the NZ Herald on page 5 read....

"SUDDEN DEATH" A very sudden death occurred at Avondale Last night. Mr George Thomas, storekeeper, was sitting near the fire between eight and nine o'clock, talking to his wife, when he suddenly fell back dead. Mr Thomas, who was well known in the district, had reached the age of 65.

On 7 October the NZ Herald ran a death notice on page 1.

THOMAS "on October 5 (suddenly) at Avondale, George dearly beloved husband of Jane Thomas in his 65th year. The funeral will leave his late residence at 3pm today (Tuesday) for the Anglican Cemetery. Friends please accept this intimation."

On 8 October the NZ Herald reported on page 6 an **"INQUEST"**

"Yesterday afternoon an inquest was held on the body of George Thomas, who died suddenly, at his residence at Avondale on Sunday last. Dr Tracy Inglis, who made the Post-Mortem examination, stated that death was due to failure of the heart's action, and a verdict was returned in accordance with the medical evidence. Deceased was 65 years of age."

George's Death Certificate states under "Cause of Death"...
"Verdict of Jury ... Heart failure."

The headstone on George's grave carries the message:-
"Deeply regretted...Forever with the Lord.   Amen."

1911... POLLY DIED:

George's wife Jane (Polly) died on 28 August 1911 aged 68. The NZ Herald of 30 August advises she died "at her residence in Mt Albert."
She was buried by the Rev Harris of the Methodist Church, with George at the Anglican St Jude Cemetery, Rosebank Road, Avondale on the 31st.
Under her name on the headstone is written:-
"Gone…. but not forgotten."

4 GENERATIONS

Left to right….
George Albert Thomas born 1923

George Thomas born 1871

Albert Britton Thomas born 1895

and in front….
Kevin George Thomas born 1945.

SELINA ANN THOMAS:

1861… Selina was the first child of George and Jane Thomas, born 9th April while her parents were living in Napier St, Auckland Central.

She received the name Ann from her grand-mother Ann Lowe.

Her birth certificate records her birth on 25th April. (the 9th was written in the family Bible) She was born in Auckland, probably at her Napier St home, and father George was a Miller.

Selina's grand-mother, now Ann Crocker, told the officials of the birth and signed her name with her mark "X".

Selina was baptised on 26 May 1861 by the Rev J Long at the Primitive Methodist Church, Edwards Street, Auckland.

1884… Aged 23 Selina married **ROWLAND HILL** at Auckland on 25 December. They had a number of children, and three daughters were named Elsa, Ada and Ruby.

Rowland died before April 1921 when Selina signed her Will.

Rowland may have died in WW1 or they may have divorced before 1921.

1921… Selina signed her will on 13 April and granted administration of her estate to Angus MacDonald and Roderick Lewis.

Her daughter Elsa was married to Angus MacDonald. Angus was formerly a farmer at Taumaranui and in 1921 worked in Auckland as an Engineer.

Roderick was married to Selina's youngest sister Hilda and he was at that time an Auckland Confectioner.

The Will documents carry her signature with MacDonald's and Lewis's.

1932… Selina died at her daughter Elsa's home at Harrison Avenue, Belmont, Takapuna on 30 April, aged 71.

Basically, all her children participated equally in her estate which had a value of 1280 pounds.

No living descendants have been found to date.

--ooo0oo--

SELINA ANN THOMAS FAMILY TREE:

2nd Generation

SELINA ANN THOMAS .... married.......................		ROWLAND HILL
b 9 April 1861	25 Dec 1884	b
at Auckland.	at Auckland.	at
d 30 April 1932 (71)		d before 1921
bur		at

Rowland was the son of ......

Selina and Rowland had three children .. Ada, Elsie and Ruby.

++++++++++++++++++++++++++++++

3rd Generation	4th Generation	5th Generation	6th Generation
ADA ELLEN HILL			
b ref 3540 1885			
at Auckland.			
d			
bur			
ELSIE MAY HILL			
b ref 19076 1887 reg Elsa			
d			
bur			
m ref 6530 1907 reg Elsie			
at Auckland.			
ANGUS McINNES			
McDONALD			
b c 1879			
at			
d ref 29880 1963 (84)			
bur			
RUBY JANE HILL	**ROY CECIL DURHAM**		
b ref 4064 1889	b ref 3660 1910		
at Auckland.	at Auckland.		
d ref 32237 1970 (80)	m ref 9953 1940		
at	at		
m ref 7520 1908	**MADGE IRENE**		
at	**EDWARDS**		
MAJOR ALBERT	b ref 3660 1910		
RUGBY PRATT	at		
b			
d ref 19012 1946	**MAVIS MARY**		
	DURHAM		
Ruby married ========	b ref 17010 1912		
2nd ref 1999 1909	at		
JOHN WILLIAM			
DURHAM	**DONALD DURHAM**		
b ref 5969 1877	b ref 13401 1916		
at	at		
d ref 28256 1945 (67)			
at			
3 children			

ELIZABETH THOMAS

1864… Elizabeth was the third child of George and Jane Thomas, born 10 May while her parents were living at Napier St, Auckland Central. Elizabeth is a name long used in the Thomas family and she was the seventh, in six consecutive generations, to receive the name. Her grand-mother was Elizabeth Lewis. Five years earlier in Auckland her only NZ born 1st cousin was named Elizabeth too. Her birth certificate shows she was born at Low & Motions Flour Mill at Western Springs, Auckland and we can only assume that a mid-wife was available there. Jane would certainly not have been employed at the mill with two very small children under three years of age already in her care. Step-Grandfather Moses Crocker registered her birth and gave her father George's occupation as Miller. Elizabeth was known as Lizzie.

1881… MARRIAGE: Elizabeth married **GEORGE HENRY HARPER** at Auckland on 30 June. George was born at Bendigo (Aust or NZ ?) about 1859. We have found seven children … named… **Harold William John born 1883, Ivy May Jane b1885, Albert George b1887, Hilda Burnett b1888, Florence May 1891, Bertha Elizabeth 1893 & Allan Thomas born 1895.**

1934… GEORGE DIED: On 29 Nov, aged 75 at Auckland Hospital. The NZ Herald death notice says George & Elizabeth were living at 101 Crummer Rd, Grey Lynn, Auckland. He is buried at Waikumete Cemetery in plot 61, section 3, block A, Non Conformist. (J Weir & Co)

1951… ELIZABETH DIED: On 6 Feb 1951 aged 86. She was buried at Waikumete Cemetery alongside husband George. On her part of the headstone is the inscription …"IN SUMMER LAND."
Elizabeth's last address was at 103 Williamson Ave , Grey Lynn, Auckland, the home of Florence M Roseman… one of her daughters.

On 9 November 1964 John Pemberthy was interred with them but no headstone was erected for him. He was married (ref#1798 1906) to their daughter Ivy and in 1931 lived at 11 Crummer Rd, Grey Lynn.

WILLS: No will for Elizabeth or George has been found.

We present no family tree as insufficient detail has been obtained
and no living descendants have been found to date.

MARY ANN THOMAS:

1866... Mary was fourth child of George and Jane Thomas, born 12 March. Mary's birth certificate shows her date of birth as 6th March. (The family Bible has the 12th?) and it records that Mary was born at "North Road, Auckland." The only possible location in 1866 we have found with this address is George's brother's Star Flour Mill at Oakley Creek. George's occupation was recorded as Miller and the informant was Mary's step-grandfather, Moses Crocker.

1866... Mary was baptised on 11 May 1866 by the Rev William Colley at the Edwards St, Primitive Methodist Church, Auckland.
Her father George gave his occupation as "Whau Miller".

> Mary Ann was probably named after her mother's half sister
> Mary Ann Woods, nee Lowe.

1888... Aged 22, Mary Ann married **THOMAS JOHN STEWART** (Tom) aged 25, on the 22nd March. The Rev Robert Sommerville officiated at the Presbyterian Church in Avondale, Auckland. Witnesses were John Thomas, Carpenter of Avondale, and Katie Archibald of Avondale.
Tom gave his occupation as Butcher, living in Auckland and Mary's father George Thomas was at this time a Grocer.

Mary and Tom's Family Bible, now in the care of grand-daughter Aileen Gooder, shows that Tom was born at Coagh in County Tyrone in Ireland.

Tom's will states he was originally employed as a Butcher in Whangarei, but at the time of his marriage he operated a Butcher Shop in Ponsonby, Auckland. Some time after his marriage he took up farming at Brynderwyn, near Maungaturoto.

CHILDREN:
Mary and Tom had 7 children named Linda, Muriel, Myrtle, Olive, Algar, Doris and George.
The first three children (from 1889-1893) were born at Whangarei and the latter four children (1895-1903) were born at Auckland.
They were farming at Maungaturoto late in 1903.

DICK BUTLER:
We are grateful for the research of Dick Butler, who produced the 1963 book *"This Valley in the Hills"*.... A 100 year history of the Maungaturoto district of Northland and included Brynderwyn, where this Stewart family settled.

All the items from this book used here are coded (DB).

1903... DAIRY FACTORY:
Near page 48 in that book is a photo taken in the 1903 to 1904 season, outside the Dairy Factory at Maungaturoto.

TOM and MARY STEWART

Mr Butler names the people from left to right as.... suppliers Bob Cullen, Charles Judd, Norman Williams, Charles Underwood, Ned Cullen, Harold Flower, **Tom Stewart,** Mr Saunders and Major F Knight.
In the upper doorway is assistant Manager, Raglan Knight.   (DB)

The sequence of names puts Tom Stewart sitting on the cart, near the centre of the picture. He is wearing a wide brimmed hat and has his dark shirt sleeves rolled up. This Butler book is available in most Libraries.

1893... Tom organised his Will on 30 August and kept it very simple. All his real and personal estate (later valued at under 2000 pounds) went to his wife Mary Ann Stewart. The Will carries his signature.

1904... FARMLAND:

In September 1904 a large area of land was subdivided by Charles Otway, the surveyor and after it was brought under the Land Transfer Act, a Title was issued. The Lots on this subdivision were sold to:- Gilbert Calvert, Maungaturoto Co-op Dairy Co, John Mountaine, Otamatea County Council, John Robertson Rogers, Henry Worthington, William Jeffs, Thomas John Stewart, William Kerr, Edward William Drinkwater, Luke Langton, Thomas Taylor, Charles Underwood, Walter J Rowsell and John W Matthews, Charles Edward Ford & George Ford.   (DB)

We know from the picture above that Tom had a dairy herd.

WISES DIRECTORY: This paints a severe picture of Maungaturoto in 1880. It is described as 100 miles north by horse from Auckland, one Wesleyan Church and a population of 120. The nearest banks were at Dargaville, Whangarei and Auckland. Pahi and Waipu were Telegraph Stations and the nearest Post Office was at Pahi.

1908... SCHOOL:

The Brynderwyn School opened at the beginning of April 1908 with 21 pupils named as:- Annie, James, Gordon & George PORTER; John, William and Margaret JEFFS; Harold, Henry, Helen, Doris and Edna CULLEN; Florence, Olive, Algar and Doris **STEWART**; Alice UNDERWOOD; Prudence, Mabel & Beatrice TAYLOR; and Tyrell SNELLING: Full names are detailed by their teacher was Marion Sinclair who taught there until 1914.   (DB)

1907-11... Mary's sister Esther and her husband Joe Kimber were living in the district and had two children born in the Maungaturoto area.

We also know that Mary's brother William and family were farming in the district in 1914 and some were still living there until recently.

1910... FREEMASONS:

The Freemasons applied to the Grand Lodge of NZ for a charter to form a lodge. It was granted in 1910 and the installation meeting was attended by Wor Bro Albert H Curtis (Wor Master), Bro Tom Myers (Senior Warden) Bro Thomas John Stewart (Junior Warden).

Other members that day were L Nelson, D J Fraser, J B Fletcher, J Anderson, H McMurdo, R C White, W Leslie, W J Litten, J L Reid, W J Dell, M Fraser, W Collins, D McMillan and O Nicholson. (DB)

1911... DIRECTOR: Tom J Stewart served as a Director from 1911-17 on the Maungaturoto Dairy Co's Board. (DB)   Tom Stewart died in 1917.

1912... JERSEY COWS:
In 1912 a number of Maungaturoto farmers decided to purchase registered female Jersey cows. The first to do so were Alex Finlayson, W Collins, A H Curtis, **T J Stewart** and H & W Flower.
On 20 June, T J Stewart purchased "Lady Kensington" #1093, a daughter of the noted champion Flora 11, for 30 guineas. (DB)

1914... FARMERS UNION:
The inaugural meeting of the Maungaturoto branch of the Farmers Union was held on 23 Dec 1914. Part of the minutes read ..." It was proposed and carried that the following gentlemen be the committee for the ensuing year, Messrs N Finlayson (President), **T J Stewart**, W Thomas, W Bilton, N Jack, E Mason, J Anderson, (Sec / Treasurer)."
The following year T J Stewart was re-elected. (DB)
The W Thomas mentioned was Tom's brother-in-law, William.

1916... BOWLING:
The Maungaturoto Bowling Club was formed in 1913 and land was rented from Dr Mountaine for a green.
The list of members for 1916 included T Stewart. (DB)

1917... Son Algar told his daughter Heather that her grand-father Tom died from Peritonitis. When he took ill, a surgeon rode out from Whangarei and a Doctor from Waipu and they operated on Tom on the kitchen table at the farm. However, Tom died about two weeks later, at his residence at Brynderwyn aged 53 on 28 August and is buried at the Maungaturoto Congregational Cemetery.
Mary joined him twenty eight years later.
He was known to his Grandchildren as "Poppa".

A newspaper Obituary notes that he *"Farmed in the district for the past 14 years"* (arriving 1903) and that *"He took a leading part in everything pertaining to the welfare of the district, more especially sport"*….. *"His Cortege was preceded by a* *procession of Masons from the surrounding district and followed by a large concourse of mourners and friends. The Masons acted as pallbearers and conducted the graveside service."*

The members of <u>Lodge Marsden, Maungaturoto 169</u>, erected a plaque on his graveside as a token of their esteem.

1920... Daughter Olive died at Uncle Ernie's Mt Albert residence, aged 25 years, unmarried, and was buried with her father at Maungaturoto.

1938... On 20 June, Mary signed her Will while living with her daughter Muriel at 2 Thomas Ave, Mt Albert, Auckland. She appointed Muriel's husband, Stanley John Jones, a line foreman as her executor.

1945... MARY DIED on 24 May aged 79 at a private hospital in Auckland and left an estate valued at 280 pounds. She had moved from Mangaturoto, and lived for a while at Ruawai, but when she died had been living in Mt Albert.

Her Will left her shares in FTC and Farmers Fertilizer, to daughter Doris and all six living children divided the balance.

Heather Lock advises ...
She was known to all her Grand-children as "Ma". She was a tiny, gentle, kind little lady. She was a very talented needle worker. I have happy memories of being taught to crochet and she always seemed to have a crochet hook or sewing needle in her hands. We all loved her dearly."

MARY ANN STEWART in 1943

Her Family Tree follows ...

MARY ANN THOMAS FAMILY TREE:

2nd Generation

MARY ANN THOMAS............married......................THOMAS JOHN STEWART

b 12 March 1866	22 March 1888	b 23 June 1863
at Auckland.	at Auckland.	at Coagh, Tyrone, Ireland.
d 24 May 1945 (79)		d 28 August 1917 (53)
Bur Maungaturoto, Northland.		Bur Maungaturoto, Northland. (Plot 19)

Thomas was the son of...JOHN STEWART & JANE McKEOWN.

Mary and Thomas had 7 children, Linda, Muriel, Myrtle, Olive, Algar, Doris & George.

+++++++++++++++++++++++++++++++++++++

3rd Generation	4th Generation	5th Generation	6th Generation
LINDA ELIZA STEWART b 21 February 1889 at Whangarei. d 2 June 1977 (88) Bur Maungaturoto. m 16 May 1912 ===== at Maungaturoto. **FRANCIS LEOPOLD CULLEN** (Frank) b 17 July 1887 at Maungaturoto. d 25 June 1971 (84) Bur Maungaturoto. They had three children. (He was the son of Henry Cullen and Eleanor Jane Bailey)	**AILEEN LINDA CULLEN (B.E.M.)** b 10 April 1913 at Maungaturoto. m 8 October 1938===== at Auckland City. **ALLAN WILLIAM GOODER (C.B.E.)** b 16 February 1912 at Thames. d 17 Nov 1984 (72) Purewa Crematorium, Auckland.	**JANICE ANNE GOODER** b 25 November 1940 at Mt Albert, Auckland. m 7 March 1979 at === Finley N.S.W. Australia. **JOHN FRANCIS TUBB** b 15 May 1945 at Narrandera, NSW, Australia.	**MATTHEW ALFRED TUBB** b 28 January 1980 at Finley, N.S.W. **TIMOTHY JOHN TUBB** b 14 May 1981 at Finley, N.S.W. **ELIZABETH JAN TUBB** b 21 September 1982 at Finley, N.S.W.
		DONALD ALLAN GOODER b 1 December 1943 at Mt Albert, Auckland. m 6 May 1967 ======= at Waipu, Northland. **JILL GORDON** b 9 June 1945 at Paparoa, Northland.	**HAYDIE FRANCES GOODER** b 15 August 1971 at Downend near Bristol, England. **BRONWYN JANICE GOODER** b 22 August 1973 at Keynsham near Bristol, England. **CLAIRE LINDA GOODER** b 3 July 1977 at Mt Eden, Auckland.
	JEAN LORRAINE CULLEN b 10 July 1915 at Maungaturoto. d 27 May 1981 (65) Cremated North Shore, A RAYMOND next page..	**STEWART RAYMOND SPEED** b 13 December 1942 at Birkenhead, Auckland m 3 December 1966 === at Auckland City. PAULEEN next page...	**AMELIA GRACE SPEED** b 9 June 1968 at North Shore, Auckland. m at Sydney, Australia. DAVID next page...

240

3rd Generation	4th Generation	5th Generation	6th Generation

Linda & Frank cont.	Jean continued
	m 4 Sept 1939=======
	at Auckland City
	RAYMOND ARTHUR
	SPEED
	b 4 July 1914
	at Mt Eden, Auckland.
		Stewart married =====
		PAULEEN
		WATCHLIN
		b 14 December 1943
		at Auckland.
		    :
		    :
		    :
		    :
		2nd m 10 May 1991
		at Parnell, Auckland.
		GERALDINE
		FRANCES DONALD
		b
		at
			Amelia married
			DAVID KING
			b
			at
			
			REBECCA MARIA
			SPEED
			b 21 April 1970 at
			North Shore, Auckland.
			m
			at Sydney, Australia.
			DAVID BARTLEY
			b
			at

	ENID FRANCES **CULLEN** b 27 August 1918 at Auckland City. m 6 Feb 1943 ====== at Northcote, Auckland. **LLOYD WALTER** **LLEWELYN** b 12 March 1917 at Paeroa. d 29 August 1967 (50) Purewa Crematorium, Auckland.	**LYNNE PATRICIA** **LLEWELYN** b 26 December 1943 at Birkenhead, Auckland m 12 Feb 1972 ====== at Northcote, Auckland. **SATINI MATAIKA** b 5 February 1944 at Suva, Fiji. **KAYE FRANCES** **LLEWELYN** b 19 April 1946 at Birkenhead, Auckland m 13 July 1963 ====== at Devonport, Auckland. **JAMES RONALD** **ASKIN** b 8 September 1943 at Auckland.	**LITIA JOY** **MATAIKA** b 11 January 1977 at Auckland. **ANGELA** **FRANCES ASKIN** b 4 January 1964 at North Shore, Auckland. m 15 April 1989 at Auckland. **JAMES** **HERBERT JACOB** b 5 July 1951 at Hamilton. They have one 7th Generation child... **COURTNEY** **FRANCES JACOB** b 6 January 1993 at Auckland. **CARL LLOYD** **ASKIN** b 1 June 1968 at North Shore, Auckland.

3rd Generation	4th Generation	5th Generation	6th Generation
JANE **MURIEL** STEWART b 11 September 1891 at Whangarei. d 2 June 1970 (78) Cremated Purewa, A. Ashes at Maungaturoto. m 13 February 1923 at Maungaturoto. **STANLEY JOHN JAMES** b 9 August 1892 at Auckland. d 23 May 1978 (85) Cremated Purewa, A. Ashes at Maungaturoto. (no children)			
FLORENCE **MYRTLE** STEWART b 15 June 1893 at Whangarei. d 21 Sept 1973 (80) Cremated Purewa, A. 1st m 31 March 1915 = at Maungaturoto. **EDWARD KENNETH FINLAYSON** (Ted) b c1890 at d 29 June 1928 (38) Bur Waipu, Northland. : : : : : : : : : : 2nd m at **STANLEY VIVIAN SMERDON** b c1887 at d 11 May 1956 (69) Bur Purewa, Auckland. (no children)	**DAWN STEWART FINLAYSON** (a) b 16 December 1921 at Whangarei. m 7 Aug 1943 ====== at Mt Albert, Auckland. **COLIN RICHARD GOODER** b 18 February 1914 at Thames.	**CAMERON JOHN GOODER** b 19 July 1946 at Auckland. m ====== at b at **MAXEEN MAY GOODER** b 5 May 1950 at Auckland. m 6 February 1982 at Auckland. **TERRENCE JOSEPH ADAMS** b 5 June 1953 at Auckland. **ALWYN GAY GOODER** b 9 September 1951 at Paparoa, Northland. m 4 March 1979===== at Fiji. **JULIUS AH SAM** b 3 July 1949 at Fiji.	**GOODER** b at **KAYE ROBIN AH SAM** b 16 August 1979 at Fiji. **TRISH MAY AH SAM** b 9 August 1981 at Auckland.

Mary Thomas continued

3rd Generation	4th Generation	5th Generation	6th Generation
OLIVE MAY STEWART b 16 August 1895 at Auckland. d 17 Sept 1920 (25) Bur Maungaturoto. Remained Single.			
ALGAR THOMAS STEWART b 7 October 1899 at Morningside, Auckland. d 29 June 1985 (85) Bur Maungaturoto. m 6 June 1923 ====== at Parnell, Auckland. **MURIEL GWENDOLEN DORIS CAMBIE** b 18 February 1898 at Whangarei. d 4 August 1980 (82) Bur Maungaturoto. (Daughter of Herbert George Cambie and Jessie Matilda North)	**ALGAR STEWART** b 19 February 1925 Died in infancy. **RAE ALYSON STEWART** b 17 January 1926 at Auckland. m 18 Jan 1947 ====== at Auckland. **LEO NORMAN DOWLING** b 10 August 1925 at Te Aroha.	**JUDITH CHRISTINE DOWLING** b 20 April 1948 at Dargaville. m 20 Dec 1969====== at Auckland. **LUKE McDONNELL** b 10 September 1939 at Sydney, Australia. **BRIAR KAYE DOWLING** b 8 November 1952 at Hamilton. m 11 Jan 1973= ====== at Adelaide, Australia. **IAN RAMSAY** b 6 July 1944 at Adelaide, Australia. **CRAIG STEWART DOWLING** b 31 October 1962 at Auckland.	**BRIONY LEE McDONNELL** b 2 March 1972 at Adelaide, Australia. **DUANE ANTHONY McDONNELL** (a) b 6 July 1973 at Adelaide, Australia. **EMMAE NICOLE RAMSAY** b 21 March 1979 at Adelaide, Australia. **ALYCIA MEGAN RAMSEY** b 5 November 1980 at Adelaide, Australia.
	HEATHER PATRICIA STEWART b 31 December 1928 at Paparoa, Northland. m 18 Dec 1965===== at Auckland. ALLAN next page...	**GLENDA MARGARET LOCK** b 21 December 1966 at Auckland. ======= CAMPBELL next page..	**HONOR STEWART LOCK** b 7 March 1990 at Palmerston North.

3rd Generation	4th Generation	5th Generation	6th Generation
Algar and Doris Cont.	HEATHER married... **ALLAN LEONARD** **LOCK** b 12 July 1927 at Wellington.	**CAMPBELL ALLAN** **BRYCE LOCK** (a) b 14 June 1971 at Auckland.	
	BRYAN CLAYTON **STEWART** b 28 September 1931 at Paparoa, Northland. m 6 June 1958 ===== at Milford, Auckland. **PATRICIA** **LOU-ANN MILLER** b 30 March 1937 at Te Kuiti.	**ROBERT BRENT** **STEWART** b 17 March 1959 at Auckland.	
		LEANNE PATRICIA **STEWART** b 9 September 1960 at Auckland. m 21 March 1980===== at Takapuna, Auckland. **MALCOLM** **DAVID CLARK** b 17 February 1958 at Auckland.	**RACHAEL** **MELANIE CLARK** b 22 June 1985 at Helensville. **STEVEN** **MALCOLM CLARK** b 30 September 1987 at Helensville.
		GLENN BRYAN **STEWART** b 23 December 1961 at Milford, Auckland. m 1 Aug 1987 ===== at Auckland. **MONIQUE** **ELIZABETH** **JANSSEN** b 19 December 1964 at Brisbane, Australia.	**SHANNON LENY** **STEWART** b 31 August 1990 at Auckland.
		KIM ALLYSON **STEWART** b 5 December 1969 at Milford, Auckland.	

DORIS LENA
STEWART
b 11 September 1901
at Mt Albert, Auckland.
d 20 February 1980 (78)
Bur Maungaturoto.
(remained single)

3rd Generation	4th Generation	5th Generation	6th Generation
GEORGE WILLIAM STEWART b 30 March 1903 at Mt Albert, Auckland. d 8 August 1978 (74) Bur Waikumete, A. m 16 March 1926===== at New Lynn, Auckland. FREDA CONSTANCE GILLIAM b 21 October 1904 at Auckland City.	OLIVE JILL STEWART b 3 January 1928 at Morningside, Auckland. 1st m 9 Feb 1952 ===== at New Lynn, Auckland. COLIN WALLACE CAMPBELL b 17 November 1926 at Auckland. d 8 September 1960 (32) Bur Waikumete, A. :: 2nd m 2 March 1964=== at Henderson, Auckland. RONALD DAVID PLUMBLEY b 8 April 1937 at Liverpool, England.	JOHN STEWART CAMPBELL PLUMBLEY b 3 March 1953 at Glen Eden, Auckland. m 11 Aug 1973 ====== at New Lynn, Auckland. HEATHER JUNE BANKS b 31 May 1954 at Paparoa, Northland. -------- GRANT DAVID PLUMBLEY b 27 June 1966 at Henderson, Auckland.	PAUL COLIN PLUMBLEY b 17 January 1977 at Henderson, Auckland. SHARON KIM PLUMBLEY b 6 July 1979 at Henderson, Auckland.
	JACK GILLIAM STEWART b 16 October 1930 at New Lynn, Auckland.		
	WENDY ANNE STEWART b 30 March 1941 at Mt Albert, Auckland. m 20 Nov 1965 ===== at Henderson, Auckland. WILLIAM ROSS HAMILTON b 17 July 1936 at Whangarei.	MARTYN WILLIAM HAMILTON b 3 October 1967 at Epsom, Auckland. ANDREW ROSS HAMILTON b 12 March 1971 at Epsom, Auckland.	

ALGAR STEWART:

In 1921 Alf and Norman Leaf established a woodmill on the Snelling Farm, operating about 3 years. Two bullock teams were on big demand in the operation of this mill and these were in the hands of Tyrell Snelling and Alger Stewart ... one of Mary and Tom's sons. (DB)

JOHN (JACK) THOMAS:

1867... John, the fifth child of George and Jane (Polly) Thomas, was born on the 13 August at the Whau, Auckland. He was known as Jack. John is the most popular Thomas family name and he could be described as John V1. John V was his first cousin who was then aged 16 and working a Flour Mill at Oakley Creek because his father, John 1V, had recently died in NZ. At the time Jack was born his family were living at the Star Flour Mill site.

BAPTISM:
Jack was baptised on 12 May 1868 by the Rev W J Dean of the Edwards St, Primitive Methodist Church, Auckland. His father George gave their address as "Star Mills, Whau" and he was employed as a "Miller."
The two sisters, Polly Thomas and Mary Ann Woods arranged a double baptism, as William Morris Woods was baptised at the same time.

1894... MARRIAGE:
Jack married **ISABELLA MARY STEWART** in 1894, probably in Auckland. They had a family of 4, named Rita, Mabel, Leila & Norman.

Two brothers, Jack and Ernie Thomas married two sisters, Isabella and Cecelia Stewart. Isabella's father owned land in Mt Albert and when it was subdivided, Stewart Rd was named after him.

HOME:
Jack and Isabella lived on the eastern side of Great North Road at Avondale, about three doors from the Post Office. (MGL)

The 1918 PO Directory has Jack described as "A Carter" and gives their address as Great North Road, left hand side from Pt Chev, first house over Walton St...(now named Walsall St, Avondale.)

1914... ISABELLA DIED:
Isabella died on 28 August 1914 aged 45, and was buried in plot 170e at St Judes Cemetery, Rosebank Rd, Avondale.
Isabella signed her Will within hours of her death. Her very shaky mark "X" was witnessed by Evelena Laing of Onehunga. She left everything to her husband

but the estate value is not available. At this time Jack's occupation is recorded as "A Carter". Jack signed Isabella's Will using the phrase *"...having seen her die,"* on 21 October 1914.

Grand-daughter Marie Weston has a newspaper Obituary which reveals that Isabella was *"an active worker in religious and social circles and her cherry smile will be sadly missed by a host of acquaintances. She was a member of the Avondale Croquet Club, the Wesleyan Church and for many years an enthusiastic supporter of the Avondale Public School."*

1922... JACK's WILL:
Jack organised his will and signed it 29 September 1922.
He now described his occupation as "Baker".
He appointed his son Norman (of Otahuhu, Bus Driver) and son-in-law, David Stewart, as Executors. A Codicil dated 4 June 1937 appoints son-in-law Arthur Clarence Oldham of Pukekohe, a confectioner, as executor as David Stewart died before him. The documents carry the 3 signatures of Jack, Norman and Arthur.

Jack's estate was valued at 7755 pounds and his Will allowed for ......
"...My quarter share of land in Karangahape Rd, being Lots 3,4,17 and part of Lot 16 of section 1, allotment 9 of section 7, of Suburbs of Auckland... to his children, Rita, Mabel, Leila (Mrs Oldham) & Norman, in equal shares." Also his four children were to equally share all insurance policies and his three daughters to equally share the balance of the estate. In this regard the trustees could take as long as they liked but not to exceed 21 years.

1928... Living in the family residence at Avondale in 1928 was son Norman, described as "Motor Carrier" and it would seem he and his family shared the house with his father Jack.

1943... JACK DIED:
Jack died 3 September 1943 aged 76 and was buried with his wife at St Judes Cemetery in Avondale.
With them in the St Judes Plot is son-in-law Wm Steve Dodd, husband of Mabel, who died aged 40 while living at Manakau Rd, Epsom.

--oo0Ooo--

JOHN (JACK) THOMAS FAMILY TREE:

2nd Generation:

JOHN THOMAS (Jack)...............married........................**ISABELLA MARY STEWART**

b 13 August 1867	(ref #94) 1894	b (ref 10723) 1866
at Whau, Auckland.	at	at Auckland.
d 3 September 1943 (76)		d 28 August 1914 (48)
Bur St Judes, Avondale, Auckland.		Bur St Judes, Avondale, Auckland.

Isabella was the daughter of...   and sister of Cecelia.

John and Isabella had children named, Rita, Mabel, Leila and Norman.

++

3rd Generation	4th Generation	5th Generation	6th Generation
ETHEL RITA THOMAS			

ETHEL RITA
THOMAS
b 13 September 1895
at Avondale, Auckland.
d
Bur
m
at
RICHARD (Dick)
SANDHAM
b
at
d
Bur
No children.

JOHN (JACK) THOMAS

MABEL ISABELLA
THOMAS
b (ref 2355) 1898
at Auckland.
d 12 October 1978
Cremated Purewa, A.
m 4 Aug 1925 ======
at Auckland.
WILLIAM STEPHEN
DODD   (Steve)
b   c1889
at Scotland. UK.
d 25 Nov 1929 (40)
Bur St Judes, Avondale.
The son of John Dodd

ISOBEL DODD
b 14 January 1928
at Epsom, Auckland.
d 31 July 1993
Cremated Purewa, A.
m 22 November 1952
at Mt Eden, Auckland.
CYRIL ALBERT(Mac)
HUGH McKENNA
b
at
d 27 September 1953
at Auckland.
No children
         :
         :
         :
2nd married
BRIAN DOBBINS
no children

LEILA next page...   MARIE next page...   JOHN next page...   JEREMY next page...

Jack Thomas cont.

3rd Generation	4th Generation	5th Generation	6th Generation
LEILA FORBES THOMAS b 25 September 1903 at Avondale, Auckland. d 6 July 1976 (72) Cremated Purewa, A. m 4 May 1926 ====== at Avondale, Auckland. ARTHUR (Clarry) CLARENCE OLDHAM b 13 August 1901 at Tuakau, Auckland. d 18 Nov 1975 (74) Cremated Purewa, A.	MARIE BETH OLDHAM b 15 May 1930 at Mt Eden, Auckland. m 20 March 1954===== at Paerata, Auckland. FREDERICK (Snow) KINGSLEY WESTON b 28 May 1930 at Pukekohe, Auckland.	JOHN STEWART WESTON b 12 March 1955 at Waiuku, Auckland. 1st m 12 Jan 1980===== at Devonport, Auckland. LUISA MARIA D'ECA b 28 July 1956 at Hong Kong. : 2nd m 15 May 1993 at Wellington. THELMA MARY DICK b 11 October 1954 at Carterton. NZ.	JEREMY JOHN WESTON b 19 February 1985 at Wellington. BIANCA MARIA WESTON b 5 September 1987 at Wellington.
		PETER WILLIAM WESTON b 7 December 1957 at Pukekohe, Auckland. m 25 Oct 1980====== at Geelong, Victoria, Australia NGAIRE MURIEL MITCHELL b 1 June 1959 at Seymour, Victoria, Australia.	KERI JAN WESTON b 20 September 1984 at Middlemore, A. KATE SHIRLEY WESTON b 19 February 1986 at Greenlane, Auckland. MITCHELL PETER WESTON b 2 March 1990 at Greenlane, Auckland.
		JAN MARIE WESTON b 14 March 1959 at Pukekohe. Auckland. m 6 April 1990====== at Parnell, Auckland. DAVID PAUL GARMONSWAY b 15 August 1957 at Paparoa, Northland.	SAMUEL JOHN GARMONSWAY b 2 January 1992 at Greenlane, Auckland. MAXWELL CLARENCE GARMONSWAY b 28 April 1993 at Greenlane, Auckland.
		MARY BETH WESTON b 14 March 1959 at Pukekohe, Auckland. continued...	THOMAS WESTON MARTIN b 25 December 1992 at Greenlane, Auckland.

Jack Thomas cont.

3rd Generation	4th Generation	5th Generation	6th Generation
Leila and Clarry cont.	Marie and Snow cont.	Mary continued m 16 Nov 1993 ====== at Mission Bay, A. **GRAEME FRASER** **MARTIN** b 14 June 1958 at Napier.	**JACK WESTON** **MARTIN** b 14 June 1993 at Greenlane, Auckland.
		ROBERT KINGSLEY **WESTON** b 1 July 1961 at Epsom, Auckland.	
	ANNETTE CLARICE **OLDHAM** b 7 March 1941 at Pukekohe, Auckland. m 25 May 1992 at Pakuranga, Auckland. **MICHAEL JOHN** **WATSON** b 14 August 1936 at Essex, England.		
NORMAN JOHN **THOMAS** b at Mt Albert, Auckland. d 19 July 1971 Cremated Purewa. A. m ====== at **AGNES BARKLEY** b at d 10 September 1979 Cremated Purewa. A. Norman died at home 590 Mt Wellington Highway, Auckland. Norman served in WW1 #13142 Mounted Rifles.	**NORMA ISABEL** **THOMAS** b 7 June 1922 at Avondale, Auckland. m ====== at Otahuhu, Auckland. **JAMES RENWICK** **EASTMAN** (Jim) b at d b4 1971 Bur	**STUART JAMES** **EASTMAN** b 15 September 1949 at Te Awamutu. m ====== at **MARY** **BERNADETTE** **LALLOLI** b at	1st **EASTMAN** b at 2nd **EASTMAN** b at 3rd **EASTMAN** b at 4th **EASTMAN** b at
		SUZANNE NOELENE **EASTMAN** b 11 July 1953 at Te Awamutu. m 1 Nov 1974 ====== continued...	**NICHOLAS** **RENWICK** **ANDERSON** (twin) b 21 March 1975 at Auckland. continued...

Jack Thomas continued.

3rd Generation	4th Generation	5th Generation	6th Generation
Norman and Agnes cont.	Norma and Jim cont.	Suzanne married at Auckland========== PHILIP WILLIAM ANDERSON b 23 October 1952 at Dunedin.	MATTHEW JAMES ANDERSON (twin) b 21 March 1975 at Auckland. JOEL DAVID ANDERSON b 22 May 1982 at Auckland. IAN PHILIP ANDERSON b 3 July 1984 at Howick, Auckland.
	BRIAN THEODORE THOMAS b 4 October 1924 at Auckland. d 1978 (54) Cremated and ashes scattered at sea. m ===== at NOELINE PEGGY DEMLER b 19 July 1927 at Auckland. d 5 February 1971 (43) Cremated Purewa, A.	CHERYL-ANNE THOMAS b 8 November 1954 at Auckland. m ===== at LUCIO PALAZZO b at	LUKA PALAZZO b 26 August 1990 at Milan, Italy. (Family live in Italy)
		GRANT DEMLER THOMAS b 9 September 1956 at Auckland City. m ===== at KATHRYN JOANNE STOREY b 8 March 1960 at Auckland.	MELISSA LUCY THOMAS b 28 September 1987 at Auckland. EDWARD LLOYD DEMLER THOMAS b 30 March 1992 at Auckland.
		ROBYN MAREE THOMAS b 22 March 1960 at Mt Eden, Auckland. m 20 May 1988 ===== at Auckland City. PETER MICHAEL STEEL b 5 January 1958 at Howick, Auckland.	SAMANTHA LOUISE STEEL b 22 November 1989 at Greenlane, Auckland. THOMAS BENSON STEEL b 18 December 1991 at Greenlane, Auckland.
		MALCOLM EASTMAN THOMAS b 18 April 1966 at Auckland.	

251

WILLIAM THOMAS:

1869... WILLIAM was the sixth child of George and Jane Thomas, born 23 July while the family was living at Great North Road, Whau. (Star Mill)
> William received another popular Thomas name and could be referred to as William V1. First cousin William V, was aged 21 and also living at Whau when this William was born.

William is thought to have been baptised on 9 April 1871 by the Rev C Waters at the Primitive Methodist Church, Edwards St, Auckland.
The Rev forgot to fill in the Thomas child's name but William's birth is the closest.

1898... 1st MARRIAGE:
William married **BERTHA WINNIFRED BICKNELL** (Bignall in the Family Bible) in April 1898 (ref #2465).
They had two sons named ERNIE and GEORGE.
The family advise that Bertha died at the age of 24 whilst trying to give birth to a female child. The child did not live either and is probably buried with her mother, although not mentioned in the burial records. Bertha is buried with her parents at the St Michael's & All Angels Anglican Church Cemetery at Puketapu near Napier.

1906... 2nd MARRIAGE:
William remarried to **LILY DAVIES** of Maungaturoto in 1906 (ref #5843) and she gave William another son known as STANLEY. William's son Ernie named a daughter Bertha Lillian Thomas after both wives.

HOMES:
William and family seem to have lived all over the North Island. He was born at Avondale, Auckland. Two of his children were born at Hastings. He started out as a ploughman on the Tamona Estate at Hastings and then farmed for a while at Waipukurau.
After Bertha died, he shifted to the Maungaturoto district where his married sisters Mary and Esther were now living. He then married Lily, moved into a new farm and soon Stanley arrived. He operated two farms in Northland, at Maungaturoto and Otonga, and later retired to Mt Albert, Auckland.

1914… MAUNGATUROTO: The minutes of the inaugural meeting of the Maungaturoto branch of the Farmers Union held on 23 December, show that Mr W Thomas was on the 1915 Committee. (DB)

1920… RETIREMENT:

Son Stanley advises that William and Lily purchased 5 acres in Mt Albert and that these were subdivided in the late 1920's.

We first found William in the 1924 PO Directory. There were very few houses in Lloyd Avenue then and they were closest to the railway line.

In 1933 their house was number 15 Lloyd Ave and in 1943 had been renumbered 18 Lloyd Ave West, situated on the right hand side from New North Road and on the corner of Thomas Avenue. We wonder if Thomas Ave was named after the first occupant, William Thomas.

1945… WILLIAM's WILL:

William signed his will on 23 June with his name in full. He appointed as Trustees, his son George Arthur Thomas of Maungaturoto and Cyril A Huband, his solicitor. His estate was later valued at 11,317 pounds.

Briefly he had five properties to leave.

a. Freehold house 18 Lloyd Ave West, Mt Albert Lots 8 & 9 on DP19048, part Allotment 34, parish of Titirangi.. to his son Davie Stanley Thomas he left his half interest. The other half was owned by Lily.

b. Freehold house 16 Lloyd Ave West, Mt Albert. After Lily's death the property went to his son George Arthur Thomas.

c. Freehold house 14 Huia St, Onehunga. After Lily's death the Property went to his grandchildren Laurel Marguerite Thomas and Bertha Lillian Thomas.

d. Farm property at Otonga. Sections 11 and 28 of Block X11 in Hukerenui District went to his grandsons Douglas William Thomas and Rex Colston Thomas.

e. Farm property at Maungaturoto went to his son Davie Stanley Thomas, described as Lot 2 DP25251 Part Allotment 148, Wairau Parish.

All residue of estate to his wife Lily.   William died two months later.

1945… WILLIAM DIED:

He died on 10 August 1945, aged 76, at his residence 18 Lloyd Ave West, Mt Albert, and was buried in plot 214e, St Judes Cemetery, Rosebank Rd, Avondale.

1945... LILY's WILL:

Lily signed her Will on 21 July and left everything to her son Davie Stanley Thomas, Maungaturoto farmer. When she died nearly 10 years later her estate was valued at under 4000 pounds

She signed her name – Lily Thomas. (Note, not Lillian)

1955... LILY DIED:

Lily died 7 March aged 79 and joined William at St Judes. There is no headstone on the plot today in 1993.

BERTHA & WILLIAM THOMAS at Napier.

The Church records show that buried with William and Lily in this plot are Frederick Thomas and Kate Thomas. Although their death dates are given (8 Sept 1921 and 7 March 1938) no age has been mentioned. They are not part of William's family and we have been unable to resolve this mystery before going into print but feel they may be children of William's cousin John Coates Thomas.

WILLIAM THOMAS FAMILY TREE:

2nd Generation

WILLIAM THOMAS................1st married..........................BERTHA WINNIFRED BICKNELL

b 23 July 1869	April 1898	b c1881
at Auckland	at Taihape. NZ.	at (poss Napier)
d 10 August 1945 (76)	:	d September 1905 (24)
Bur St Judes, Avondale.	:	Bur at Puketapu, Napier.
	:	
	2nd married	LILY DAVIES
	(ref #5843) 1906	b February 1876
	at Maungaturoto,	at Maungaturoto, Northland. NZ.
	Northland, NZ.	d 7 March 1955 (79)
		Bur St Judes, Avondale.

Bertha was the daughter of ELIZABETH RACHEL (Betsy) and JOHN BICKNELL.
William & Bertha had three children named Ernie, George and a daughter who died at birth.
Lily was the daughter of..
William and Lily had one child they named Stanley.

++

3rd Generation	4th Generation	5th Generation	6th Generation
ERNEST WILLIAM THOMAS (Ernie) b 25 July 1900 at Hastings. d 13 October 1938 (38) Bur Kauri, Northland. m 27 March 1923 ==== at Whangarei. MARGARET HELEN TEAL b 6 August 1899 at Opuawhanga, Northland. d 10 April 1989 (89) Bur Kauri, Northland. (the daughter of John Teal and Margaret Colston Dempster)	DOUGLAS WILLIAM THOMAS b 13 October 1924 at Whangarei. m 19 June 1948 ===== at Te Puke. JOYCE EDNA RUSSEL b 4 August 1925 at Whangarei. (Daughter of William Smith Russel and Eileen Alma Steadman)	NOLA EILEEN THOMAS b 30 March 1949 at Whangarei. m 24 Oct 1970====== at Te Puke, BOP, NZ. TREVOR RICHARD ALLEN b 5 September 1948 at Morrinsville. ALISON JOYCE THOMAS b 4 March 1951 at Tauranga. BOP. NZ m 9 Dec 1972 ===== at Te Puke, BOP, NZ. MICHAEL JOHN HALTON b 24 September 1947 at Cygnet, Tasmania, Australia.	BRAD ALLEN b 8 July 1973 at Tauranga. RAELENE ALLEN b 11 July 1975 at Tauranga. LAUREN ALLEN b 14 December 1977 at Tauranga. SCOTT BRENNEN HALTON b 4 December 1973 at Sydney, Australia. TRENT DOUGLAS HALTON b 26 January 1976 at Hobart, Tasmania, Australia. TODD WILLIAM HALTON b 24 November 1978 at Te Puke, BOP, NZ. JOSHUA KARL HALTON b 8 November 1983 at Te Puke, BOP, NZ.

William Thomas cont.

3rd Generation	4th Generation	5th Generation	6th Generation
Ernie & Margaret cont.	Douglas & Joyce cont.	**RUSSELL ERNEST THOMAS** b 13 June 1953 at Te Puke, BOP, NZ. m 14 July 1973 ===== at Pukehina, BOP, NZ. **MARGARET JEAN KERELUK** b 27 October 1952 at Quesnel, BC. Canada.	**LEANNE MARY THOMAS** b 17 February 1975 at Tauranga. **WAYNE PHILIP THOMAS** b 16 October 1977 at Tauranga.
		BARBARA HELEN THOMAS b 17 June 1961 at Te Puke, BOP, NZ. m 23 May 1987 ===== at Cairns, Australia. **BRYAN DOUGLAS ANDREW GARDINER** b 17 September 1960 at Dubbo, Queensland, Australia.	**KIRRI JOY GARDINER** b 10 September 1987 at Cairns, Australia. **BECKY MAREE GARDINER** b 13 September 1990 at Tauranga, BOP, NZ.
		SHIRLEY ELIZABETH THOMAS b 20 July 1966 at Te Puke, BOP, NZ.	
	REX COLSTON THOMAS b 19 December 1925 at Whangarei. m 10 Aug 1946 ===== at Otonga, Northland. **BEATRICE** (Judy) **EVELINE MOODY** b 16 February 1927 at Manurewa, Auckland.	**MARGARET EVELYN THOMAS** b 26 February 1947 at Whangarei. 1st m Dec 1965 ===== at Whangarei. **KEITH JAMES NICHOLAS** b 7 July 1944 at Whangarei. : : : : : : : :	**CYNTHIA MARGRIT NICHOLAS** b 10 June 1966 at Whangarei. (She has a son of the 7th Generation) **COREY JAMES NICHOLAS** b 29 May 1991 at Whangarei. **JAMES CAMERON NICHOLAS** b 1 November 1967 at Whangarei. m 20 May 1989 at Whangarei. STACEY next page...

256

William Thomas cont.

3rd Generation	4th Generation	5th Generation	6th Generation
Ernie & Margaret cont.	Rex and Judy cont.	Margaret & Keith cont.	JAMES married **MARY STACEY ROGERS** b 30 April 1967 at Whangarei. (They have two girls of the 7th Generation) **LETISHA DENE EVELYN NICHOLAS** b 29 May 1990 at Whangarei. and
		2nd married **CLIFFORD NELSON ROBINSON** b 12 September 1942 at Canada. (no children)	**ADALEENA HAYLEE ROSE NICHOLAS** b 31 Auguast 1991 at Whangarei.
		BRIAN REX THOMAS b 5 July 1949 at Whangarei. m 4 March 1972===== at Whangarei. **SHARYN DONALDSON** b 20 May 1954 at Whangarei.	**JOHN WILLIAM THOMAS** b 6 June 1974 at Whangarei. **MEGAN JANE THOMAS** b 26 February 1976 at Whangarei. **JOLENE EVELYN THOMAS** b 1 January 1978 at Whangarei. **BRONWYN LEA THOMAS** b 22 July 1981 at Whangarei.
		JUDITH THOMAS b 5 January 1951 at Whangarei. m Oct 1970===== at Whangarei. **NORMAN KEIGHTLY HILL** b at	**RENEE HILL** b 15 April 1971 at Whangarei. (She has one child of the 7th Generation) **SHAUN HARLOW** b 4 September 1988 at Whangarei. NORMAN next page...

257

William Thomas cont.

3rd Generation	4th Generation	5th Generation	6th Generation
Ernie & Margaret cont.	Rex and Judy cont.	Judith & Norman cont.	**NORMAN ROBERT HILL** b 7 June 1973 at Whangarei. d 17 November 1990 Bur Maunu, Whangarei.
	LAUREL MARGUERITE THOMAS b 25 October 1927 at Whangarei. m 7 Nov 1953======= at Whangarei. **ERIC TIMOTHY SMITH** b 27 March 1927 at Takapuna, Auckland.	**JANINE LAUREL SMITH** b 8 February 1955 at Whangarei. m 27 March 1982 at Auckland. **MICHAEL JEFFERY WILLIAMS** b 16 May 1944 at Tonypandy, Rhondda Valley, Wales.	
	BERTHA LILLIAN THOMAS b 4 September 1931 at Whangarei. m 23 June 1956===== at Whangarei. **RICHARD GERALD CARR** b 19 July 1930 at Waitara, Taranaki. d 17 December 1977 Bur Whangarei.	**BRENDA MARGARET CARR** b 8 November 1959 at Whangarei. m 15 May 1982===== at Whangarei. **RICHARD CHARLES DOUGLAS SMITH** b 24 August 1940 at Masterton. **DAVID GERALD CARR** b 10 February 1965 at Whangarei.	**SUANNA HELEN JANE SMITH** b 16 September 1984 at Whangarei. **EMMA MARY GRACE SMITH** b 4 June 1988 at Whangarei.
GEORGE ARTHUR THOMAS b 7 February 1903 at Hastings. d 1 February 1979 (76) Bur Maungaturoto. NZ. m 2 May 1934 ===== at Maungaturoto. **ALICE FULLER UNDERWOOD** b 14 December 1900 at Auckland.	**ELVA MARGARET THOMAS** b 12 April 1937 at Greenlane, Auckland. d 25 August 1990 (53) Bur Maungaturoto. NZ. m 14 Nov 1959===== at Maungaturoto. **LESLIE JOHN HODSELL** b 23 January 1934 at Te Kopuru, Northland.	**CRAIG JOHN HODSELL** b 20 August 1961 at Paparoa, Northland. m 8 April 1989 ===== at Otorohanga. **GAEWYN PAMELA LITTIN** b 21 January 1962 at Warkworth. Robyn next page...	**DEKLAN JOHN HODSELL** b 14 October 1990 at Whangarei. **SAM HENRY HODSELL** b 3 August 1992 at Whangarei. Kate next page...

258

William Thomas cont.

3rd Generation	4th Generation	5th Generation	6th Generation
George & Alice cont. (Alice was the daughter of Charles Henry Underwood and Elizabeth Clarke Ford)	Elva & Les continued	**ROBYN MICHELLE HODSELL** b 28 May 1963 at Paparoa, Northland. m 25 March 1988===== at Parnell, Auckland. **CRAIG BRETT CHARLES WAALKENS** b 13 October 1963 at Paparoa, Northland.	**KATE ALICE WAALKENS** b 19 December 1990 at Greenlane, Auckland. ? **WAALKENS** due Sept 1993 at
		BRIAR LEANNE HODSELL b 25 May 1966 at Paparoa, Northland. m 11 Nov 1989===== at Maungaturoto. **STEPHEN MALCOLM JAQUES** b 11 September 1965 at Warkworth.	**ZOE ELVA JAQUES** b 7 November 1991 at Whangarei. **GEORGIA MARY JAQUES** b 12 June 1993 at Whangarei.
		KERRY LISA HODSELL (twin) b 30 August 1971 at Paparoa. Northland. **LYNDSAY ALLISON HODSELL** (twin) b 30 August 1971 at Paparoa, Northland.	
	BEVERLEY FULLER THOMAS b 14 November 1939 at Greenlane, Auckland. m 6 April 1963 ===== at Maungaturoto. **JAMES THOMAS PATON** b 26 October 1938 at Te Aroha.	**GRANT THOMAS PATON** b 8 November 1964 at Matamata.	
		JAN MAREE PATON b 19 September 1966 at Matamata. m 25 Oct 1986 ===== at Matamata. **NEVILLE CLIFFORD ROWLAND** b 10 July 1963 at Tolaga Bay. NZ.	**KRISTY MAREE ROWLAND** b 17 March 1989 at Hamilton. **SARAH JANE ROWLAND** b 18 October 1990 at Hamilton.

259

3rd Generation	4th Generation	5th Generation	6th Generation
George & Alice cont.	Beverley & James cont.	Jan & Neville continued	KATIE JESSICA ROWLAND b 9 July 1993 at Hamilton.

1905 Unnamed daughter THOMAS....stillborn.

3rd Generation	4th Generation	5th Generation	6th Generation
DAVIE STANLEY THOMAS b 3 December 1916 at Otonga, Northland. m 9 March 1938 ==== at Maungaturoto. ETHEL MARY CULLEN b 13 September 1917 at Maungaturoto. (The daughter of George Cullen and Emma Nellie Drake)	EUNICE NELLIE THOMAS b 19 January 1939 at Paparoa, Northland. m 1 Oct 1957======= at Maungaturoto. ROBIN THOMAS FITNESS b 19 September 1937 at Paparoa, Northland.	SHEREE JAN FITNESS b 6 May 1958 at Paparoa, Northland. m 24 Nov 1977 ===== at Wellington. DEAN MALCOLM CRERAR b 13 February 1956 at Lower Hutt.	GRANT MALCOLM CRERAR b 27 February 1981 at Lower Hutt. GREGORY THOMAS CRERAR b 13 February 1984 at Auckland.
		DELWYN KAY FITNESS b 1 October 1960 at Paparoa, Northland. m 6 Oct 1979====== at Waipukurau. HAMISH JACKSON b 3 December 1955 at Napier.	MATHEW ROBERT JACKSON b 26 August 1982 at Waipukurau. NICHOLAS TIMOTHY JACKSON b 24 September 1983 at Waipukurau.
	ROY KEVIN THOMAS b 11 May 1941 at Paparoa, Northland. d 18 July 1984 (43) Bur Maungaturoto. m 10 June 1962===== at Matakohe, Northland. JUNE STRACHAN b 19 June 1946 at Wanganui.	PHILLIP DEAN THOMAS b 9 June 1963 at Whangarei. JANET MARGARET THOMAS ======== b 5 October 1965 at Paparoa, Northland. BRYCE THOMAS b 22 March 1967 at Whangarei. MICHAEL THOMAS b 29 October 1970 atWhangarei.	JESSICA LEAH THOMAS b 6 December 1989 at Auckland.

260

William Thomas cont.

3rd Generation	4th Generation	5th Generation	6th Generation
Stan and Ethel cont.	**WILLIAM GEORGE THOMAS** b 17 July 1944 at Warkworth. d 18 July 1977 (33) Bur Maungaturoto. m 15 June 1968 ====== at Maungaturoto. **SHARLENE MARGARET LAMBERT** b 18 May 1949 at Paparoa, Northland.	**CORRINE LESLEY THOMAS** b 2 November 1969 at Whangarei. m 28 March 1992 at Whangarei. **BRETT ANTHONY DUNN** b 12 November 1966 at Whangarei. **JODI MAREE THOMAS** b 23 April 1972 at Paparoa, Northland. m 6 February 1993 at Whangarei. **TREVOR WAYNE BARNES** b 3 December 1969 at Kawakawa.	
	PETER DAVIE THOMAS b 24 August 1955 at Warkworth. m 24 April 1976====== at Maungaturoto. **ANGELA DALLAS** b 30 October 1957 at Te Kopuru, Northland.	**TRACEY MARIE THOMAS** b 28 August 1979 at Whangarei. **BEVAN WILLIAM THOMAS** b 21 November 1982 at Whangarei.	

261

GEORGE THOMAS:

1871... George's birth certificate states he was "born 2 Sept 1871 at the Whau". His parents were living at The Star Mill on Oakley Creek, where we found his father was Manager from 1865 till at least 1874.

He was George and Polly's 7th child and received his father's name.

He is George the third, in our Index of Family members.

SCHOOL:
All of his schooling would have been at the Whau (Avondale) School.

1895... MARRIAGE:
George, aged 23, was first married on 1 May 1895 at the Auckland Registry Office to **MARY ANN "Minnie" MORGAN** aged 20. She was born at Ballarat, Australia about 1875 to Thomas Morgan (Railway employee) and Harriet Louisa Robins. See page 271 for photo of Minnie. When witnessing this marriage her mother signed "X" over the reference "Harriet Louisa Pascoe... Mother of the bride".

We are advised she had two sisters, Lilly and Ette and a brother George.

1901... MINNIE DIED: After giving George three sons (Albert, Victor and Ernest) Minnie died on 19 February 1901 whilst the family was living in Henderson. Aged 26, she died of complications after giving birth to daughter Victoria about 19 January 1901. She was in hospital most of that time and would have known her daughter had died 9 February at only three weeks of age. Ten days after Victoria, Minnie also died.

Victoria and Minnie were buried in the same Waikumete Cemetery plot (Nonconformist block C, Section 11, Plot 16) but there is no headstone for Victoria. Minnie's son Victor, son Albert and his wife Maida have since joined Minnie in this large family plot. Minnie's headstone has the notation ...

> *"A precious one from us has gone*
> *A voice we loved is stilled."*

1895... ALBERT BRITTON THOMAS was the first child of George and Minnie Thomas. He was born in the Sexton's house at Waikumete Cemetery. The Sexton's wife was a midwife. Eighty six years later Albert was laid to rest at Waikumete within 150 yards of his birth place.

GEORGE the BLACKSMITH:

His family remembers that George loved horses.

The informative and well written 1977 book "Henderson's Mill" by Anthony G Flude should be read by all George Thomas descendants.

It is a history of the Henderson district covering the years 1849 to 1939 and pages 63-65 mention George the Blacksmith.

In brief his son Albert advised Mr Flude that George bought two and a half acres of land at this corner site for 12 pounds 10 shillings and with local townsfolk's help he cleared the land of Ti-Tree etc. The house he erected faced the Great North Road and the Blacksmith's shop faced Railside Avenue. Soon George built a second blacksmith shop at Hobsonville and travelled each week to do the horses of that locality.

Depicted in the book is one of George's Invoices to Mr Corban the grape grower and wine producer of Henderson, for services rendered up to 10 December 1908, and this carries George's signature showing the account was settled on 11 January 1909.

Also included is a delightful story of how George shod the horse of a warring Maori leader on his way to the Waikato while his 50 odd fully armed followers waited, and how he assisted in stopping their advance, and in their ultimate return, peacefully, to Northland.

There is a sketch done by Albert...not to scale...of the position of his father's Blacksmith's shop and his first home in Henderson 1902-1914.

Mr Flude makes a very grateful acknowledgement (page 101) of Albert Thomas's untiring assistance which ends *"without his help this publication would not have been possible"*.

From these comments we have been able to obtain accurate records of the five properties George owned in the Henderson area.

HENDERSON PROPERTY (A)

1896... Vol 76/192 George purchased on 16 Jan, Lot 8 (37.2 perches) from the BNZ Estates Co. Situated on the south east corner of Great North Rd and Emma St. Emma St was renamed Rata St, then George St, then Station Rd and is now Railside Avenue, in Henderson, Auckland.

Here George built a house facing the Great North Rd.   Photo next page.

Transfer #17628 says he paid 10 pounds and described himself "Settler".
Purchase was registered at Lands and Deeds on 18 Feb 1896 and became Vol 77/168. During the eight years George owned this property there were no mortgages recorded against it.

> **1904…** Vol 77/168 George sold on 7 Sept, Lot 8 with house, to
> Arthur William Metcalf and Edgar Christopher Metcalf, both
> Grocer's Assistants of Avondale for 275 pounds.
> George signed transfer #34419. Sale was registered on 19 Sept
> 1904. George left money in the sale a Mortgage #22678 but
> Details have been destroyed. Mortgage discharged 3 Feb 1906.
>
> --

1900… HOUSE:

The photo below was probably taken mid year 1900 showing George and Minnie and the three boys standing on the front veranda of their home at this address. We select this time because Ernest was born March 1899 making him aged one and a half by the middle of 1900 and Minnie does not yet show the arrival of Victoria who was born January 1901.

1900 The RATA St HOME OF MINNIE & GEORGE THOMAS:

HENDERSON PROPERTY (B)

1898... Vol 82/58 George purchased on 29 Dec, Lot 7 (39 perches) on Emma St, Henderson, from the Asset Realisation Board. This joined Lot 8 where his home was. On Lot 7 George built his Blacksmith Shop and it faced onto Emma Street.
Transfer #22188 records he paid 8 pounds 10 shillings and now described himself as "Blacksmith".
This purchase was registered 4 Feb 1899 and became Vol 91/123.

1912... Vol 91/123 George divided Lot 7 into two pieces, each of 19.5 perches. On 15 August ... sale A: George sold the most southern half vacant land to Annie Jane Leach, wife of David Leach, Karangahake Storekeeper. Sale registered 2 Sep 1912 and became Vol 197/122.

1912... At the same time he sold her two more sections of 1 rood 33 perches that joined this half of Lot 7.
Transfer #68198 says he received a total price of 412 pounds.
(Vol 197/122 Annie Leach sold this half to J A Thorne on 19 Sep 1918 and he owned it until 15 May 1940.)

1913... Vol 91/123 Sale (B). George sold the 19.5 northern half of Lot 7, with the Blacksmith's Shop on 23 April to Joseph Alfred Thorne for 250 pounds. In 1913 Emma St was known as Rata St. Transfer #73342 is signed by George. The sale was registered 2 June 1913 and became Vol 208/21.

George left money in the sale as Mortgage #54155 but details have been destroyed. Mortgage discharged on 20 Feb 1919.
(Vol 208/21 Joe Thorne remained Blacksmith until 10 July 1947 when the sale of the Blacksmith property was recorded to Murray Becroft.
We are informed that the original Anvil used by George on these premises still exists and is with Mr Becroft today in Henderson.)

**SKETCH MAP ON PAGE 266 SHOWS THE
LOCATION OF THESE FOUR PROPERTIES.**

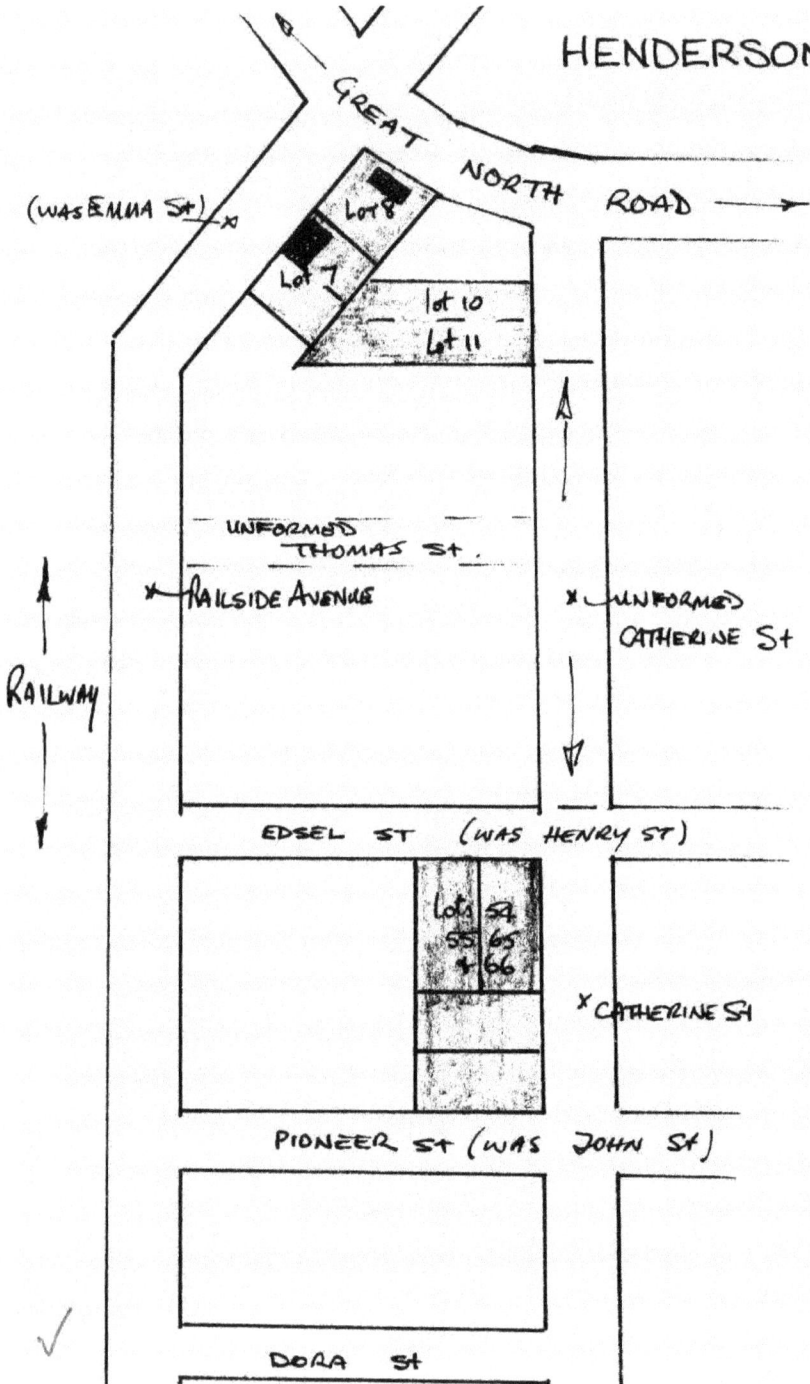

HENDERSON:

(WAS EMMA St)

Lot 8

Lot 7

lot 10

Lot 11

GREAT NORTH ROAD →

UNFORMED THOMAS St.

RAILSIDE AVENUE

× UNFORMED CATHERINE St

RAILWAY

EDSEL ST (WAS HENRY ST)

Lots 54, 55, 65 & 66

× CATHERINE St

PIONEER St (WAS JOHN St)

DORA St

266

HENDERSON PROPERTY (C)

1899... Vol 91/233 George purchased from John Platt Lot 10 & Lot 11 of 1 rood 30 perches, on 28 November. Both faced Catherine St, Henderson and backed onto Lot 7 which had the Blacksmith Shop. Transfer # 23760 shows George paid 16 pounds for these. Purchase registered 28 Nov 1899, remained Vol 91/233.

1912... Vol 91/233 George sold Lots 10 & 11 to Annie Jane Leach on 15 August as part of Transfer #68198.

HENDERSON PROPERTY (D)

1899... Vol 76/191 George purchased from the Asset Realisation Co, Lots 54, 55, 65, & 66 (1 acre 3 perches) on 29 May. These faced three streets in Henderson........Henry St, (now known as Edsel St) Catherine St and John St (now known as Pioneer St) Transfer #22930 shows George paid 18 pounds total. Purchase registered 26 June 1899 and became Vol 93/28.

1904... Vol 93/28 ON 26 August George sold all four Lots to Peter Lawson of Henderson, a Railway employee, for 125 pounds. Transfer #34295 is signed by George and registered 2 Sep 1904. George appears to have mortgaged these four sections to Eliza, wife of Robert Cranwell a Henderson Orchardist. She signed the sale document giving her consent to the sale. Mortgage document #20674 has been destroyed.

BLACKSMITH: Grandson Bob has saved an item that appeared in the *'Western Leader'* in April 1987 written by a Mrs Freeman, a satisfied customer of George Thomas the Blacksmith. In part she says ... *"Mr George Thomas was the first Blacksmith that I remember. That was 80 or more years ago. When I took our Pony to him to be shod, he always made a fuss of me, calling me Lassie ... He had three boys going to the Henderson school. In his latter years there, another blacksmith set up in Henderson but as he was elderly, he did not last long at the job ... Years ago children coming home from school, would look at the open door, and then the fireplace to see the flaming forge and sparks and hear the bellows roar. After many years of toil, Mr Thomas sold out to a Mr Vic Elder... How well I remember the village blacksmithy."*

1897... VICTOR GEORGE ALEXANDER THOMAS was the second child of George and Minnie Thomas. He was born in the Old Stone Jug, an Inn then situated near todays Chamberlain Park Golf Course on the Great North Road at Pt Chevalier.

George's grandchildren in Victor's family called him...... **"TomTom"**.

1899... ERNEST EDWARD THOMAS was the third child of George and Minnie Thomas.

1901... VICTORIA MINNIE MAY THOMAS was the fourth child of George and Minnie, but died aged 3 weeks, on February 9.

CEMETERY: George purchased two side by side plots at Waikumete Cemetery in Nonconformist section C11, numbers 16 & 18. He paid 3 pounds on 30 March 1901. This became the Thomas Family grave, where Victoria and Minnie were the first interred.

1901... MINNIE DIED aged 26 on 19 February. (more detail p262)

1904... FARMER:
In this year, and now aged 33, George became a Farmer in Sturgess Road, Henderson. He had Allenley Builders erect a large house on the 15 acre block he purchased from the Sturgess Estate and 89 years later this house still stands at the corner of Sturgess Road and Geordie St, Henderson.

STURGESS ROAD PROPERTY:
1903... Vol 99/147 George purchased on 15 June, from John Roderick and Edward Henry Holt, Part of Lot 31 (22 acres) land facing Sturgess Rd, Henderson.

George later built a new home here and started farming the land. His descendants still live on and own some of those 22 acres in 1993. Transfer #31119 shows he paid 190 pounds. The purchase was registered 26 June and became Vol 114/224.

1903... George gained a Mortgage with Eliza Cranwell 23 July and documents number 20674 was discharged 11 Feb 1908. All details have been destroyed.

1919... Vol 114/224 George subdivided this land into two parts....
One of 15 acres, 1r, 11.2p ... the other of 6 acres, 2r, 14.8p.
(A) George sold the 15 acres on 29 Dec to Charles Edward Grainger,
a farmer, for 2,825 pounds. Signatures were finally put on Transfer
#129549 in March 1920 and registration was completed on 14 July
1920. These 15 acres became Vol 309/335.

THIS IS GEORGE'S SIGNATURE ON THIS DOCUMENT.

1920... Vol 309/335 15 acres Lot 31. George left money in the sale to Charles
Grainger as Mortgage #98761 on 14 July 1920. This was discharged on
21 October 1925 but details have been destroyed.

Charles Grainger tried to remortgage with NZI Insurance Co
but at the last moment this was cancelled.

George came to his rescue and Mortgage #158800 replaced #98761.
It was signed in 1925 and discharged 13 March 1929 after the sale of
the property.

Transfer #229484 shows that Charles Edward Grainger sold these 15
acres to Victor George Thomas (son of George the Blacksmith) on 15
March 1929 for 2,225 pounds. Victor's second wife Daisy and his son
Laurie live on or have an interest in part of this land in 1993.

1924... Vol 114/2249 **(B)** George sold these 6 acres to Frederick Henry Manson
Shepherd, a school teacher of Henderson, for 600 pounds on
3 October 1924. Transfer #182998.
Sale was registered 8 October 1924 and became Vol 401/60.
No Mortgage given on this sale.

--ooo0ooo--

The STURGESS Rd HOME OF GEORGE THOMAS.

1906... MARY PARNELL PURCHON became George's second wife on 12 February at New Plymouth. A widow, her maiden name was Wills. Her father Albert was a Methodist Minister and Maori Interpreter and her Grandfather was named Samuel Wills.

Mary married James Purchon at Nelson when she was aged 22. She was 44 when she married George aged 34 in 1906 and brought her daughter Alice Mary Purchon to join the Thomas family. Mary died at their home aged 87 on 9th March 1949, on the eve of her 88th birthday and was buried with George.

MARY and GEORGE on a visit to ROTORUA.

GEORGE THOMAS and first wife MINNIE

GEORGE and MINNIE'S 3 sons
ERNIE standing   *VICTOR at Left*   *ALBERT at right*

FARM PROPERTY at TE PUA: near HELENSVILLE.

1920...   Vol 100/54 #137932. On 1 October Percy James McLeod sold
          Lots 2 and 3 in the Kaipara District called Te Pua Tangihua to
          George Thomas, Henderson Blacksmith for 1716 pounds 8/- and
          it was registered in his name on 21 December 1920. The property
          measured 33 acres 3 roods 5 perches, fronted the Main Highway
          just south of Helensville and had an exit onto Te Pua School Rd
          via a planned but unformed road at the rear.
          Charles Henry Spinley owned this property from 1900 to 1919.

The book *"Men Came Voyaging"* by Colleen Sheffield is a history of the Helensville area and in part it mentions Mr C H Spinley *"...shifting his Blacksmith and Foundry business to beyond the north railway station, adjacent to the river. The new house he erected here was later shifted to Te Pua when Mr Shipley farmed there"*. That house is still on the land today in 1993.

George had a number of Mortgages on the property over the years and all except the last was discharged by George. He died Aug 1958 during a Mortgage term and the Public Trust took control on 18 September 1958.

1959...   On 10 February Transfer #616847 records the Mortgage
          being paid off and George's son, Ernest Edward Thomas,   .
          Helensville Farmer, became the new owner *".... in pursuance of
          the provisions of the last Will and Testament of George Thomas,
          Retired Farmer, now deceased...."*

**GEORGE'S
TE PUA
FARM
LOCATION.**

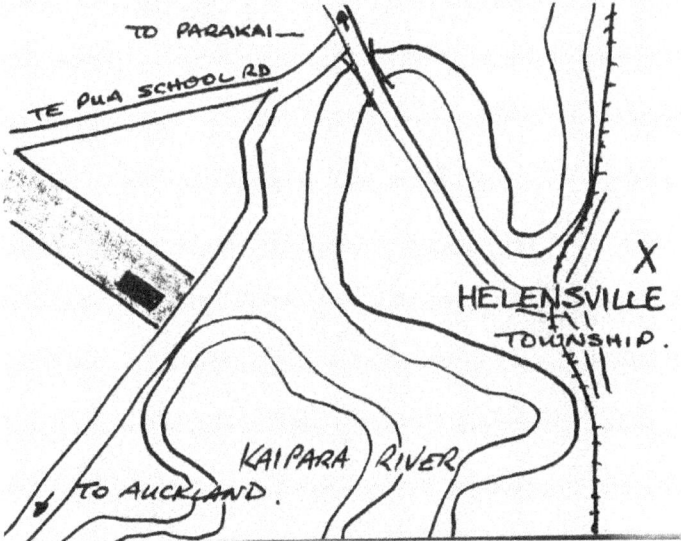

1920... MARRIAGES:
George's three sons all married in the early 1920's.

273

VICTOR THOMAS and MYRTLE .... 1921 wedding day

RETIREMENT PROPERTY:

1919... Vol 98/241 #116134. George purchased this land on 29 August. Lot 8 plan 2270 of Part Allotment 57 of 1 acre, was known as 874 New North Road but known in 1993 as number 1184 New North Road. He paid 400 pounds and it was registered in his name on 11 September 1919 becoming Vol 294/207.

1929... Vol 294/207 George Thomas, Farmer of Henderson on 11 Sept took a Mortgage #172047 with Emily Marriage which was discharged 7 May 1930, but details have been destroyed.

Transfer #403029 dated 4 July 1946 shows George subdivided this acre and sold 1 piece of 2 Roods 39.3 perches as Lot 2 part of Lot 8 of plan 33562 to Gerald Ernest Wright & Dulcie Blanch Wright. He received 300 pounds from the sale.
The balance of land was registered to George as Vol 855/56.

1946... Vol 855/56 Lot 1, part of Lot 8, part of Lot 57 was registered to George Thomas 26 July 1946.

1952... 30 July "Proclamation #13576 defining middle-line of Railway."
George died in August 1958.
20 February 1959 Transmission to Public Trustee.
20 February 1959 Transfer #616846 to Albert Britton Thomas,
retired mechanic, and George Albert Thomas of Frankton,
Engineer, as tenants in common in equal shares.

1959... 22 December #Transfer 632260 to HRH Queen Elizabeth 11 for
Railway purposes.

In 1993 this section remains unused "for Railway Purposes".
The house has been removed and only George's wooden, single car
sized garage remains on it.

--oo00oo—

1923... GRANDCHILD: George Albert Thomas VIII was their first Grandchild, born 25 January 1923. Due to a stroke, his mother could not adequately
raise both George and his sister Doreen, so his grandparents, George and Mary
took care of him until he was 16 years of age.

1938... PLOTS:
On 2 May 1938 George, whilst living at 874 New North Road, Mt Roskill,
purchased at Waikumete Cemetery, Wesleyan burial plot C30, #83 and another
receipt shows Alice Purchon purchased burial plot C30, #81 next door. They each
paid 4 pounds for their single plot. These plots were later joined together and
became the final resting places for George and Alice's mother, Mary.
Alice, at this date was not living with her mother but with another spinster at
1654 Great North Road, Avondale.

1949... MARY DIED: George's second wife Mary died in March of this year.

GEORGE's WILL: No will was found for either of George's wives.

George III (Blacksmith/Farmer) signed his Will on 18 July 1947.
The Public Trust acted as executor of the estate valued at 9620 pounds.
When George III died his Will gave the 1184 New North Road house and land
to son Albert and grandson George VIII, the latter having been raised by his
grandparents.

275

Son Victor gained the Sturgess Road farm property.

Son Ernest inherited the Helensville farm property, including the house, crops, stock and farm implements and the Kaipara Dairy Co shares.

The balance of his estate went equally to his sons Albert and Ernest.

HEIRLOOMS:

There are numerous items that belonged to George Thomas treasured today by descendants. Granddaughter Doreen has a Clock and a number of Cups and Saucers. There is also a collection of World War 1 Postcards.

1958... GEORGE DIED:

George died 26 August 1958 aged 87.

Both he and Mary were residing at 1184 New North Road, Mt Roskill, at the time of their deaths.

He was buried with second wife Mary at Waikumete Cemetery, Auckland. Wesleyan block C, Section 30, Plot 81/83.

Comment on their headstone reads ....   "Peace Perfect Peace:"

--ooOOoo--

GEORGE THOMAS FAMILY TREE:

2nd Generation:

GEORGE THOMAS .... married		MARY ANN (Minnie) MORGAN
b 2 September 1871	1 May 1895	b c1875
at Whau, Auckland.	at Auckland City.	at Ballarat, Australia.
d 26 August 1958 (87)	"	d 19 February 1902 (26)
bur Waikumete , Auckland.	"	bur Waikumete, Auckland.
	"	
	2nd married	MARY PARNELL PURCHON
	12 Fenruary 1906	10 March 1861 (nee Wills)
	at New Plymouth.	at New Plymouth.
		d 9 March 1949 (87)
		bur Waikumete, Auckland.

Minnie was the daughter of THOMAS MORGAN and HARRIETTE LOUISA ROBINS
George and Minnie had 4 children named Albert, Victor, Ernest & Victoria.
Mary was the daughter of ALBERT WILLS and ANN JOLL
George and Mary had no children. May's daughter was named Alice Mary Purchon.

++

3rd Generation	4th Generation	5th Generation	6th Generation
ALBERT BRITTON THOMAS	GEORGE ALBERT THOMAS	KEVIN GEORGE THOMAS	ADRIANNA THOMAS
b 9 November 1895 at Waikumete, Auckland	b 25 January 1923 at Auckland City.	b 15 October 1945 at Hamilton.	b 5 Oct 1971 (a) at Henderson, Auckland
d 18 Dec 1981 (86)	d 9 May 1986 (63)	m 29 March 1969 =======	m 26 Feb 1993 at
bur Waikumete, A.	bur Waikumete, A.	St Andrews, Auckland.	Herne Bay, Auckland
m 5 Oct 1921 ========	1st m 5 July 1945 ====	ROBYN ANN WHEELER	CRAIG RICHARD THORNTON AUSTEN
at Newton, Auckland	at Hamilton.	b 14 November 1947	b 1 June 1960
MURIEL MAIDA SAVAGE	NOLA AUDREY REMNANT	at Auckland City.	at Leeds, England.
b 6 May 1901 at Hikuai, east of Thames	b 1 April 1924 at Raetihi, NZ.	3 children ... Adrianna Sasha and Rebecca.	2 children ... 7th Gen
d 16 August 1938 (37)	d 6 June 1973 (49)		
bur Waikumete, A.	bur Newsread Cem.		Sidney Wheeler Austin
(She was daughter of	Hamilton.		b 31 May 1997
Bejamin Savage a	Geo & Nola issue = 5		at White Rock, B.C.
farmer of Irish descent..	(Nola was daughter		Canada.
& Janet Lennan Black)	Elliot Vernon		
	Remnant & Frances		Georgia Thomas
Savage equals Tepene	Amy Morley)		Austin
in Maori. She was of	"		b 13 April 1999
the Arawa tribe.	2nd m 9 Nov 1973		at White Rock,
Albert and Maida had	at Hamilton.		Canada.
two children named	NGAIRE COWLEY		
George and Doreen.	b 5 December 1925		
	at Ohakune, NZ.		SASHA THOMAS
	(Ngaire's children are		b 8 August 1973 (a)
	Paul, Lindy and		at Henderson, A.
	Deborah Thomson)		

3rd Generation	4th Generation	5th Generation	6th Generation
Albert & Maida contin ..	George & Nola contin..	Kevin & Robyn continue	
			REBECCA THOMAS b 6 February 1975 at Henderson, A. partner **PETER SEYMOUR** b at 2 children ... 7th Gen
			Austin Thomas Seymour b 21 April 1999 at Henderson, A.
			Mackenzie Geoffrey Seymour b 12 June 2006 at Henderson, A.
		ROBYN MARIE **THOMAS** b 16 March 1947 at Hamilton. d 24 Aug 2008 (61) bur Mt Manganui, NZ m 30 March 1968 ===== at Hamilton. **SELWYN GERALD** **COX** b 15 July 1945 at Paeroa, NZ.	**MICHELLE MARIE** **COX** b 19 September 1968 at Hamilton. 1 child ... 7th Gen **DOMINIQUE COX** b 9 July 1992 at Hamilton.
			JASON MICHAEL **COX** b 13 February 1970 at Hamilton.
			MATTHEW DAMON **COX** b 10 October 1973 at Hamilton.
			MICHAEL BRENT **COX** b 20 Sept 1977 (a) at Hamilton.

George Thomas cont.

3rd Generation	4th Generation	5th Generation	6th Generation
Albert & Maida cont.	George & Nola cont.	MARGARET NOLA THOMAS b 11 Feb 1952 at Hamilton. m 7 July 1975 ======== at Manurewa, A. VALENTINE TUREIA IRWIN b 7 July 1950 at Wairoa, NZ (son of John Paul Irwin & Parehuia Whaanga. Descendants from Tuhoe and Kahungunu Maory tribes respectively.) divorced 1998. 4 children ... Rachel, Francesca, Terewai, and Valandra. "	RACHEL THOMAS b 3 May 1975 at Otahuhu, A. adopted by Peter & Jill Shaw & known as ROWENA SALLY SHAW at Paterangi, NZ m 21 July 2001 at Bristol, England. PAUL HOWARTH b 3 Sept 1976 Bristol, England. 2 children 7th G Alexander Joseph (AJ) Howarth b 14 Jan 2008 at Bristol. E Naimh Aroha Howarth b 20 July 2010 at Bristol, E. FRANCESCA (Fran) MEREAIRA TIAKE IRWIN b 17 Nov 1978 at Otahuhu, A m 13 Feb 2009 at Christchurch, NZ JOHN JASON WINIATA b 6 Sept 1976 at Auckland. 1 child 7th G Brianna McCord Winiata b 18 April 2016 at Christchurch, NZ Terewai next page

279

3rd Generation	4th Generation	5th Generation	6th Generation
Albert & Maida cont..	George & Nola cont..	Margaret & Valantine continue	
		"	TEREWAI MAKERE IRWIN
		"	b 17 April 1980
		"	at Otahuhu, A.
		"	m 10 Feb 2007
		"	at Christchurch, NZ
		"	SHAUN VAN HALEWYN
		"	b 20 March 1973
		"	at Nelson, NZ
		"	divorced 2017
		"	2 children 7th G
		"	
		"	Willem Rangi
		"	van Halewyn
		"	b 22 Feb 2012
		"	at Christchurch.
		"	
		"	Pieter Tureia
		"	van Halewyn
		"	b 31 March 2014
		"	at Christchurch.
		"	
		"	VALANDA (Will)
		"	TE RANGI
		"	PAONGATAI IRWIN
		"	b 6 Dec 1981
		m 2 Feb 2008	at Wairoa, NZ
		at Rakaia, NZ	m 29 July 2017
		KEVIN PATRICK BREEN	at Martinborough, NZ
		b 6 May 1950	JASMINE DWYER
		at Gore, NZ	b 9 Feb 1992
		d 30 June 2013	at Auckland.
		bur Rakaia, NZ	2 children 7th G
		"	
		"	Theodore
		"	Tawhake
		"	Xiao-Long Irwin
		"	b 15 April 2018
		m 16 Jan 2016	at Upper Hutt, NZ
		NEIL JOSEPH DAVIS	
		(Charlie)	Milena Terewai
		b 17 Jan 1955	Yuet-Ying Irwin
		at Waikari, NZ	b 7 April 2022
			at Upper Hutt, NZ
		Lesley next page	

280

George Thomas continues

3rd Generation	4th Generation	5th Generation	6th Generation
Albert & Maida cont..	George & Nola cont..	LESLEY JEAN THOMAS b 23 Aug 1955 at Hamilton, NZ m 13 Nov 1976 ======= at Browns Bay, A. JOHN EDWARD THOMPSON b 20 Jan 1954 at Hamilton, NZ 3 children	CARL JAMES THOMPSON b 5 Sept 1980 at Greenlane, A. JAMIE JOHN THOMPSON b 25 May 1984 at Greenlane, A. ALASTAIR THOMPSON b 30 June 1986 at Greenlane, A.
		Lyall next page ...	Bevan next page ...

MAIDA M SAVAGE
and
ALBERT B THOMAS
on 5th October 1921

George Thomas cont.

3rd Generation	4th Generation	5th Generation	6th Generation
Albert and Maida cont.	George nd Nola cont.	**LYALL DALE THOMAS** b 7 May 1958 at Hamilton. m 19 May 1979===== at Paterangi, Waikato. **GAY SHERYL DENCH** b 23 September 1958 at Te Awamutu, NZ. (daughter of Roy William Dench and Joycelyn Louise Dench)	**BEVAN LYALL THOMAS** b 31 May 1980 at Te Awamutu. **RICHARD GEORGE THOMAS** b 1 May 1982 at Te Awamutu.
	DOREEN MAIDA THOMAS b 16 March 1924 at Auckland City. d 5 November 2012 bur **1st marriage 1948 ====** at Mt Roskill, A. **HAROLD FRANCIS BREWER** b 11 October 1924 at Wiri, Auckland. : : : : : : : 2nd m 16 Nov 1963 at Auckland City. **RONALD EDWARD THOMAS** b 11 May 1933 at Helensville, A. No children. (He was the son of Ernest Edward Thomas and Ivy Trylsson)	**DAVID WILLIAM HAROLD BREWER** b 9 August 1949 at Greenlane, Auckland. 1st m 23 Jan 1971===== at Mt Roskill, Auckland **GILLIAN RUTH GREY** b 19 May 1950 at Auckland. 2nd married======== at Auckland to **JENNIFER ANNE WOOD** b 25 July 1957 at Auckland. **MICHELLE JEANETTE THOMAS** (a) b 8 January 1968 at Greenlane, Auckland. **LORRAINE ROSALEA THOMAS** (a) b 14 October 1969 at Greenlane, Auckland. Single mother ======	**DEBRA GILLIAN BREWER** b 18 July 1973 at Henderson, Auckland. **JOANNE MARIE BREWER** b 1 July 1975 at Henderson, Auckland. **JASON DAVID BREWER** b 29 June 1979 at Mt Albert, Auckland. **CHERYL LEA THOMAS** b 27 December 1986 at Mt Albert, Auckland.

Victor next page...   Laurie next page...   Selwyn next page   Shaun next page

George Thomas cont.

3rd Generation	4th Generation	5th Generation	6th Generation
VICTOR GEORGE ALEXANDER THOMAS b 9 May 1897 at Pt Chevalier, A. d 9 May 1982 (85) Bur Waikumete, A. 1st m est 1921 ====== at Auckland. **MYRTLE MARY ANN ELIZABETH LARDER** b 10 September 1897 at Auckland City. d 31 May 1942 (44) Bur Waikumete, A. There were 7 children. (She was daughter of William Thomas Larder and Eden Emily Miller.) :	**LAWRENCE (Laurie) VICTOR THOMAS** b 4 July 1923 at Grey Lynn, Auckland. m 23 February 1946 === at Pitt St Methodist, A. **KATHLEEN PATRICIA BARTON** b 1 August 1923 at Henderson. (Pat is the daughter of Charles Arthur Barton and Jessie Platt.) (Pat is a sister of George Barton who married Laurie's sister Avis)	**SELWYN LAWRENCE THOMAS** b 6 June 1947 at Auckland. m 24 Oct 1970====== at Auckland. **LORRAINE IVY NEWLOVE** b 14 May 1952 at Riverhead, Auckland. ―――――― **GRANT RUSSELL THOMAS** b 26 October 1953 at Auckland. married ======= at New Lynn, Auckland. **MERVIL MASON** b August at Auckland.	**SHAUN SELWYN THOMAS** b 12 June 1973 at Auckland. **JOANNE THOMAS** b 21 October 1975 at Auckland. **TONY MASON THOMAS** b 7 August 1981 at Mt Albert, Auckland.
	ROBERT WILLIAM THOMAS (Bob) b 25 January 1925 at Onehunga, Auckland. m 27 Jan 1951 ====== at St Mathews, A. City. **MERLE EILEEN JOYCE LOWE** b 6 August 1929 at Auckland. (daughter of Tasman (Tassy) Francis Lowe & Violet Ellen McCabe)	**CHRISTINE MERLE THOMAS** b 23 September 1953 at Glen Eden, Auckland. m 2 Nov 1974====== at Oratia, Auckland. **ARTHUR RONALD MURRAY** b 19 February 1954 at Epsom, Auckland. ―――――― **RUSSELL BRUCE THOMAS** b 3 December 1955 at Pt Chevalier, A. m 2 February 1983 at Auckland City. **MOIMAI TAURUA==** b 23 October 1961 at Auckland. (divorced 1991)	**GAVIN STEWART MURRAY** b 29 July 1977 at Mt Albert, Auckland. **GRAHAM THOMAS MURRAY** b 11 September 1980 at Mt Albert, Auckland. **MICHELLE LOUISE MURRAY** b 19 October 1984 at Mt Albert, Auckland. **MAC ALEXANDER ELLIS** b 8 August 1975 at Auckland. (step son) ----------------- **BRETT WILLIAM THOMAS** b 19 February 1982 at Auckland.

George Thomas cont.

3rd Generation	4th Generation	5th Generation	6th Generation
Victor & Myrtle cont. : : : : : : : : :	Bob and Merle cont.	**GAIL JOY THOMAS** b 29 August 1957 at Greenlane, Auckland. m 3 February 1979 === at Oratia, Auckland. **DAVID WILLIAM** **SPREADBURY** b 31 May 1957 at Auckland.	**HELEN MARIE** **STREADBURY** b 4 March 1982 at Mt Albert, Auckland. **MARK BRENDON** **SPREADBURY** b 17 February 1984 at Mt Albert, Auckland.
: :	**AVIS MYRTLE** **THOMAS** b 7 August 1927 at Remuera, Auckland. m 10 September 1949== at Henderson, Auckland. **FREDERICK** **GEORGE BARTON** b 22 September 1925 atHenderson, Auckland. (son of Charles Arthur Barton and Jessie Platt.)	**JUDITH ANN** **BARTON** b 7 March 1953 at Pitt St, Auckland. m 25 October 1975=== at Oratia, Auckland. **ROBIN ANTHONY** **STOKES** b 28 May 1942 at Auckland City. **WARREN GEORGE** **BARTON** b 20 February 1956 at Pitt St, Auckland. m 23 April 1976===== at Oratia, Auckland. **RHONDA PENELOPE** **BETTS** (Penny) b 14 September 1955 at Pitt St, Auckland.	**NATASHA MARIE** **STOKES** b 19 February 1978 at Henderson, Auckland. **KATRINA** **ELIZABETH** **STOKES** b 16 February 1979 at Henderson, Auckland. **CARL ANTHONY** **BARTON** b 30 September 1983 at Henderson, Auckland. **DEAN GEORGE** **BARTON** b 16 December 1986 at Henderson, Auckland.
: : : : : : : : : : : : : : : :	**MALCOLM ERNEST** **THOMAS** (Snowy) b 12 February 1930 at Onehunga, Auckland. m 26 June 1954 ===== at Mt Roskill, Auckland. **PATRICIA EVELYN** **BRICE** b 17 March 1935 at Grey Lynn, Auckland. (daughter of George Alfred Brice and Beatrice Mary Tittle)	**LYNNETTE ANNE** **THOMAS** b 2 April 1960 at Mt Albert, Auckland. m 26 June 1982 ===== at Hillsborough, A. **CHRISTOPHER** **CARLYLE** **TORCKLER** b 8 July 1958 at Henderson, Auckland. JANINE next page...	**KEITH ADAM** **TORCKLER** b 23 November 1987 at Tweed Heads, NSW, Australia.

284

3rd Generation	4th Generation	5th Generation	6th Generation
Victor and Myrtle cont.	Malcolm & Patricia cont	**JANINE PATRICIA THOMAS** b 23 November 1962 at Grey Lynn, Auckland. m 19 April 1986 ===== at Mt Roskill, Auckland. **PHILIP WILFRED REYNOLDS** b 16 November 1953 at Malta.	**BOWAN JAMES REYNOLDS** b 29 July 1990 at Greenlane, Auckland. **JULIA PATRICIA LILLIAN REYNOLDS** b 18 October 1992 at Greenlane, Auckland.
:	:	**PHILLIP MALCOLM THOMAS** b 9 April 1964 at Grey Lynn, Auckland. m 16 April 1988 ===== at Kumeu, Auckland. **NATASJA CATHERINA LENARDA VAN OORSHOT** b 10 September 1967 at Brabant, Den-Bosch, Holland.	**JORDAN PHILLIP THOMAS** b 9 July 1993 at Henderson, Auckland.
:	:	**STEPHANIE SHARYN THOMAS** b 15 July 1967 at Mt Eden, Auckland.	
:	**VALERIE JOY THOMAS** b 3 August 1931 at Onehunga, Auckland. m 12 August 1950 ==== at Glen Eden, Auckland. **WILLIAM (Bill) RAYMOND MATHEWS** b 24 June 1925 at New Plymouth. (son of Kenneth Wilfred Mathews and Amy Eilleen)	**GEOFFREY RAYMOND MATHEWS** b 17 November 1951 at Tokoroa m 1 Dec 1992 ======= at Auckland. **ADELE LESLEY SCOTT** b 2 November 1951 at Dunedin. **HOWARD WAYNE MATHEWS** b 23 November 1953 at Tokoroa. continued next page	**NICHOLAS SCOTT MATHEWS (a)** b 1 April 1991 at Ukraine. **EMILY CHELSEA MATHEWS (a)** b 18 February 1993 at Matamata. **JOY MARIE MATHEWS** b 12 June 1973 at Matamata. continued next page

285

George Thomas cont.

3rd Generation	4th Generation	5th Generation	6th Generation
Victor and Myrtle cont. :	Valerie & Bill continued	Howard continued. m 1972====== at Matamata. **MAUD FALLON** b 10 September 1954 at Matamata.	**LIANNE MELLISSA MATHEWS** b 2 January 1975 at Matamata. **KENNETH GRAHAM MATHEWS** b 16 November 1980 at Matamata. **GRAEME DANIEL MATHEWS** b 3 August 1982 at Matamata.
:		**RUSSELL OWEN MATHEWS** b 3 March 1955 at Tauranga. m 25 Sept 1975 ===== at Tauranga. **ROSEANNE MARY EVEMY** b in England.	**NEAL OWEN MATHEWS** b 1976 at Tauranga. **STEPHAN RICHARD MATHEWS** b at Tauranga. **ELLENOR MARY MATHEWS** b at Tauranga.
:		**KENNETH GRAHAM MATHEWS** b 26 April 1957 at Whakatane. d 26 November 1976 Bur Tauranga. (19)	
:		**GWENDOLINE JOY MATHEWS** b 7 January 1959 at Auckland. m 9 June 1979====== at Tauranga. **EDWARD JAMES HEREKIUHA** b 27 October 1946 at Paeroa. continued next page...	**NADIA JOY HEREKIUHA** b 4 August 1979 at Tauranga. **MARCIA MIRIA HEREKIUHA** b 1 February 1984 at Hamilton. JOEY next page...

286

George Thomas cont.

3rd Generation	4th Generation	5th Generation	6th Generation
Victor and Mertyl cont.	Valerie and Bill cont.	Gwen and Edward cont.	**JOEY DANE** **TEKURA** **HEREKIUHA** b 30 May 1987 at Hamilton.
		RICHARD WILFRED **MATHEWS** b 15 April 1960 at Tauranga. **BRUCE DAVID** **MATHEWS** b 12 April 1962 at Tauranga. **SUZANNE VALERIE** **MATHEWS** (Sue) b 3 May 1964 at Tauranga.	
	JUNE EDEN **THOMAS** b 19 October 1932 at Auckland d 1 October 1987 (54) bur Waikumete, A m 14 Sept 1951 ====== at Auckland City **LEWIS TEMPLE** **JONES** (Buddy) b 30 November 1929 at Auckland City (He was son of Lewis Victor Hawke Jones and Winnie Carr) (Buddy is the brother of Margaret who married June's brother Joe .. G G Thomas)	**MERVEN LEWIS** **JONES** b 24 March 1952 at Henderson, Auckland m 6 March 1993 ======= at Glen Eden, Auckland **YIN PHENG CHIN** b 3 October 1958 at Teluk Intan, Malaysia **CAROL OLLWEN** **JONES** b 1 December 1953 at Henderson, Auckland m 2 December 1972 ==== at Oratia, Auckland **BRIAN RONALD** **DAHLBERG** b 16 December 1944 at Ashburton, NZ **DAVID LARSING** **JONES** b 12 November 1954 at Henderson, Auckland JULIE next page ..	**SEAN MERVEN** **JONES** b 11 August 1994 at Auckland. **HUDSON MARK** **DAHLBERG** b 28 August 1974 at Whangarei **LYNDON JAMES** **DAHLBERG** b 22 December 1975 at Whangarei Julie brought to the family LENA MARIE KENNY b 17 July 1978 at Henderson, Auckland

George Thomas cont.

3rd Generation	4th Generation	5th Generation	6th Generation
Victor & Myrtle cont.	June and Buddy cont.	DAVID continued... m 10 Nov 1984===== at Mt Albert, Auckland. **JULIE MARIE** **EVERSON** b 31 December 1960 at Greenlane, Auckland.	**CLIFFORD DAVID** **JONES** b 9 July 1985 at St Lukes, Auckland. **STEVEN MICHAEL** **JONES** b 22 October 1987 at St Lukes, Auckland.
		KENNETH **WILLIAM JONES** b 7 October 1955 at Henderson, Auckland. m 11 Oct 1975 ====== at Henderson, Auckland. **SUSAN LEE** **BRANDON** (Sue) b 14 January 1957 at Grey Lynn, Auckland.	**PHILLIP KENNETH** **JONES** b 11 February 1977 at Mt Albert, Auckland. **KYLE DOUGLAS** **JONES** b 7 November 1978 at Mt Albert, Auckland. **CASIE MARIE** **JONES** b 30 September 1982 at Mt Albert, Auckland.
		DIANNE **ELIZABETH JONES** b 23 December 1960 at Glen Eden, Auckland.	
		GAY MICHELLE **JONES** b 26 December 1961 at Glen Eden, Auckland. m 30 Oct 1980 ====== at Henderson, Auckland. **NEIL DESMOND** **GRIGG** b 27 August 1956 at Henderson, Auckland.	**AMBER MICHELLE** **GRIGG** b 7 July 1979 at Henderson, Auckland. **SHANNON MARIE** **GRIGG** b 22 April 1981 at Henderson, Auckland. **TAMMY** **MARGARET GRIGG** b 9 February 1984 at Henderson, Auckland.
	JOE next page...	JENNIFER next page...	RACHEL next page...

288

George Thomas cont.

3rd Generation	4th Generation	5th Generation	6th Generation
Victor & Merte cont. : : : : : : : : : :	GRAHAM GEORGE THOMAS (Joe) b 6 October 1934 at Auckland City. m 26 June 1953===== at Auckland City. MARGARET SYBIL JONES b 11 August 1936 at Avondale, Auckland. (the daughter of Lewis Victor Hawkes Jones and Winnie Carr)	JENNIFER WYNN THOMAS b 18 February 1954 at Auckland. m 5 December 1972== at Orewa, Auckland. FREDERICK JAMES SMITH b 9 March 1949 at Auckland. There were 5 children.	RACHEL NELDA SMITH b 10 February 1971 at Australia. TIMOTHY ASHTON (Rachel & Timothy have two 7th Generation children....... EMILY WINIFRED ASHTON b 8 August 1989 atTasmania, Australia. and WILLIAM GEORGE ASHTON b 12 August 1991 at Tasmania, Australia. Jennifer's four other children.... MARGARET KAREN SMITH b 27 July 1973 at Takapuna, Auckland. TERESA JEAN SMITH b 17 September 1977 at Takapuna, Auckland. LARISSA JOY SMITH b 12 September 1977 at Takpuna, Auckland. DANIEL WAYNE SMITH b 12 June 1986 at Australia.
:		GRAHAM THOMAS b 10 August 1955 at Whangarei. m 10 July 1976 ===== at Avondale, Auckland. KAREN MARGARET WATTS continued...	GRAHAM GEORGE THOMAS b 16 March 1979 at Auckland. MICHAEL BRETT THOMAS b 5 June 1981 at Auckland.

289

George Thomas cont.

3rd Generation	4th Generation	5th Generation	6th Generation
Victor & Myrtle cont.	Joe and Margaret cont.	KAREN continued... b 27 September 1957 at Auckland City.	COLLIN GLENN THOMAS b 28 July 1985 at Adelaide, Australia. ALANA MAY THOMAS b 12 May 1987 at Adelaide, Australia.
		KAREN RUTH THOMAS b 8 June 1959 atTakapuna, Auckland. 1st m 24 Sept 1977 === at Orewa, Auckland. ROYDON PARKIN b at : : : 2nd M 10 Feb1990 at Whangaparaoa. KENNETH GRAY b at	LAURA KAREN PARKIN b 30 May 1980 at Greenlane, Auckland. JESSICA ROSE PARKIN b 19 December 1981 at Helensville. MICHAEL LEWYS PARKIN b 20 December 1985 at Helensville.
		WENDY MARGARET THOMAS b 4 January 1967 at Takapuna, Auckland. m 8 March 1986 ===== at Whangaparaoa. GREGORY CAMP b 8 August 1962 at Helensville.	SARAH WENDY CAMP b 4 November 1987 at Helensville. MATHEW GREGORY CAMP b 27 July 1989 at Helensville.
	John and Dorothy next page...	Belinda and Michael next page...	

290

George Thomas cont.

3rd Generation	4th Generation	5th Generation	6th Generation
VICTOR remarried on 21 April 1944 at Auckland City.==== DAISY ISABEL WARD b 20 December 1920 at Stratford, NZ. There was 1 child, John. (Daisy was daughter of John Henry Ward and Edith Ann Knight.)	HAROLD JOHN THOMAS b 25 November 1945 at Avondale, Auckland. m 29 January 1966==== at Mt Albert, Auckland. DOROTHY MARGARET WHYTE b 13 April 1946 at Tokomaru, near Palmerston North. (daughter of Joseph Andrew Whyte and Linda Maureen Moody)	BELINDA KAROLINE THOMAS b 4 July 1968 at Henderson, Auckland. m 29 May 1993 at Nara, Gold Coast, Australia. MICHAEL JAMES CAREY b 1960 at Yass, NSW. Australia. VAUGHAN ANDREW THOMAS b 6 January 1972 at Henderson, Auckland.	
ERNEST next page.	RONALD next page		

WEDDING DAY of DOROTHY & JOHN THOMAS Jan 1966
L-R... VAL, BOB, MERL, JOE, PAT, JOHN, DOROTHY, LAURIE
AVIS, GEORGE, DAISY & VICTOR.
Front... MARGARET, JENNIFER, CAROL, BUDDY, JUNE & BILL.

291

George Thomas cont.

3rd Generation	4th Generation	5th Generation	6th Generation

ERNEST EDWARD THOMAS
b 2 March 1899
at Henderson, Auckland.
d 2 October 1987 (88)
Bur Otahuhu, Auckland.
1st m   1921
at
EVELYN REID
(nee SILVIA)
b   1895
at Matakana, Northland.
d 6 Dec 1926   (31)
Bur Waikumete ,
Auckland.
(Evelyn, brought her
daughter Mavis Reid to
join the family but had
no children with Ernest)

:
:

2nd m 18 June 1932 ===
at Mt Eden, Auckland.
IVY TRYLSSON
b   (ref #2730) 1904
at Auckland.
d 9 January 1966 (61)
Bur Otahuhu, Auckland.
(daughter of John Nils
Trylsson and Georgina
Elizabeth Ellis)

VICTORIA MINNIE MAY THOMAS
b c19 January 1901
(ref #58) at Auckland.
d 9 February 1901
(aged 3 weeks)
Bur Waikumete
Cemetery, Auckland.

RONALD EDWARD THOMAS
b 11 May 1933
at Helensville.
m 16 November 1963
at Auckland City.
DOREEN MAIDA THOMAS
b 16 March 1924
at Auckland City.
(She was daughter of
Albert Britton Thomas
and Muriel Maida
Savage = Tipene)
(Ronald and Doreen
raised Doreen's son
David and two adopted
daughters named
Michelle and Lorraine)

KEITH ERNEST THOMAS
b 8 July 1936
at Helensville.

ERNIE THOMAS

ERNIE THOMAS and IVY

ESTHER THOMAS

1875... **ESTHER** was the third child of George and Jane Thomas, born 2nd October while her parents were living at the Star Flour Mill site at Oakley Creek, Waterview. The family Bible records her name as Hester at the time of her birth but records her as Esther when she married.

She was the third girl to receive the name Hester.

She was baptised Esther on 11 January 1876 by the Rev W Harris at the Primitive Methodist Church, Edward St, Auckland. The family's address was given as... 'Waterview' and her father was 'a Miller'.

1901... MARRIAGE:
On 24 April, Esther married **(JOE) JOSEPH SEARLE KIMBER**.
(marriage ref #1495). He was born in 1872 (ref #212) at Auckland.
They had four children named Gordon, Dora, Myrtle and Norman.
Their birth dates and full names are recorded in the family Bible.

1902... GORDON SEARLE KIMBER. He was born 5 June 1902 at Ponsonby, Auckland.

1903... DORA MAY KIMBER. She was born 23 July 1903 at Ponsonby, Auckland. She married a Mr McKenzie.

1907... MYRTLE FRANCES KIMBER. She was born 23 April 1907 at Maungaturoto. She married a Mr Webb.

1910... NORMAN SYDNEY KIMBER was born 31 December 1910 at Maungaturoto but died aged 11 on 3 February 1921.

MAUNGATUROTO:
Also living in Maungaturoto at the time Esther and Joe were there, were Esther's brother William and family, and Esther's sister Mary Ann Stewart and family. The Kimber's were not in the district long and Joe may have worked on either of William or Mary's farms.

1909... KIMBER CAT:

A small story in the Maungaturoto *"Literary & Social Club"* magazine under the heading "Coursing" read...

"Quite a good coursing match was seen here the other evening. Mr A Curtis's dog, instead of chasing the cows, chased Mrs Kimber's cat, the latter only escaping the former's fangs by a hairs breadth. Mr Curtis had to chase the cows himself and it was good sport seeing and listening to him." (DB)

1943... ESTHER DIED:

Esther died on 14 February aged 67 and we are still trying to locate her resting place and a copy of her Will has not been found.

1947... JOE's WILL:

Joe signed his Will on 15 July and kept it simple. It states that he was formerly from Putaruru but was then a retired builder of Papakura.

He appointed his son Gordon, a Timber worker of Te Awamutu as his executor, and left all his estate (value under 600 pounds) equally between his son Gordon and his two daughters, Frances M Webb and Dora M McKenzie.

1954... JOE DIED:

On 1st June 1954, Joe died aged 81 and the family had him cremated at Waikumete Cemetery and his ashes were taken away. We do not know where they reside or where they were scattered.

His last known address was 10 Queen St, Papakura, Auckland.

We have not found a living descendant to date.

--ooo0oo—

EDWARD ERNEST THOMAS   (1877-1953)

1877... ERNEST was the name the tenth child of George and Jane Thomas was known by. He was born 9 August while the family was living at Great North Road, in the township of Whau (now Avondale), four months after his father became Post Master there.

1900... MARRIAGE:
Aged 23 Ernest married **CECILA MARY STEWART** on 12 December. She was known as Celia and her name at birth registration was Mary Cecilia Stewart.

In fact, everywhere we looked their names seemed to differ. Edward Ernest, or Ernest Edward...Earnest or Ernest...Cecelia May or Cecilia Mary, or Celia.

Their family have had "Ernest" and "Celia" printed on their headstones.
They had 1 son, Allan, and 3 daughters named Dulcie, Muriel and Jean.
        Ernest's brother Jack married Celia's sister Isabella.

BOWLS: Ernest's nephew M G Lewis advises that Ernest was a keen and good Bowls player.

1950... 50 YEARS:
Ernest and Celia celebrated their 50th Wedding Anniversary with their family at daughter Jean Holdsworth's home at 56 Allendale Rd, Mt Albert, Auckland.

1952... ERNEST's WILL:
On July 17th Ernest signed EE Thomas to his Will. He appointed wife Celia and son-in-law John Colin Vinson as Trustees. His total estate (later valued at under 10,000 pounds) was left for administration to his Trustees but his wife had full use of the property and income.

        a, The property 837 New North Rd, Mt Albert (then occupied by Mrs Ward) to be held in trust for the children of his daughter Jean Isabella Holdsworth.

        b, The remainder of his estate (which must have included 845 New North Rd where his wife lived) to his daughters Muriel and Jean.

1953... ERNEST DIED:

On the 21 April, Ernest died aged 75 and was buried at Waikumete Cemetery, plot 36/38, section 21, block C, Non Conformist.

Ernest's burial records state he was a retired Coach Builder and that he resided at 845 New North Road, Mt Albert.

1953... CELIA's WILL:

This Will was signed CM Thomas on 15 December and Celia appointed her solicitor Russell Tonson Garlick as executor. Her estate, later valued at under 6,000 pounds, was divided as follows .....

The Mahogony Bedroom Suite, Rosewood Table, Crystal Vase and Breadknife to daughter Jean. The string of pearls to daughter Muriel. A sum of 200 pounds each to grand-daughter Mary Dene Vinson and Merle Kirkup.

The residue to be equally divided between her two daughters.

1956... CELIA DIED:

Celia died 14 May aged 81 and was interred with Ernest at Waikumete.

Their headstone carries the inscription:-

> "Swift to it's close....Ebbs out life's little day."

Buried with them is their son Allan who passed away aged 22.

ERNEST and CELIA THOMAS.

ERNEST THOMAS FAMILY TREE:

2nd Generation:

EDWARD ERNEST THOMAS.....married..........................CECILIA MARY STEWART

b 9 August 1877	12 December 1900	b ref #545 1875
at Auckland.	(ref # 4209)	registered Auckland.
d 21 April 1953 (75)		d 14 May 1956 (81)
Bur Waikumete, Auckland.		Bur Waikumete, Auckland.

Cecilia was the daughter of...   & sister of Isabella.

Earnest and Cecilia had 4 children named: Dulcie, Muriel, Allan and Jean.

+++

3rd Generation	4th Generation	5th Generation	6th Generation
DULCIE THOMAS	**MERLE KIRKUP**	**VICTORIA JANE**	
b 3 February 1902	b 14 February 1930	**CAULFIELD**	
at Mt Albert, Auckland.	at Auckland.	b 21 October 1961	
d 22 November 1949	m 5 March 1957 =====	at Auckland.	
Bur Purewa, Auckland.	at Auckland.		
m 21 March 1928=====	**WILLIAM JOHN**	**LOUISE MAREE**	
at Mt Albert, Auckland.	**STEWART**	**VERITY**	
THOMAS JAMES	**CAULFIELD**	b 26 November 1959	
KIRKUP	b 27 April 1931	at Auckland.	
b 12 October 1902	at Te Aroha.		
at Auckland.			
d 19 March 1981			
Cremated Purewa.			
MURIEL GRACE	**MARY DENE**	**JULIENNE MARY**	
THOMAS	**VINSON**	**GIBBS**	
b 1 September 1903	b 24 January 1931	b 24 February 1967	
at Mt Albert, Auckland.	at Mt Albert, Auckland.	at Hastings.	
d 3 February 1985	m 27 Sept 1966 =====		
Cremated Waikumete.	at Mt Albert, Auckland.		
m 27 April 1930=====	**GEORGE GILBERT**		
at Mt Albert, Auckland.	**GRAY GIBBS**		
JOHN COLIN	b 1 July 1920		
VINSON	at Stratford.		
b 10 March 1904			
at Pokeno.			
d 14 September 1975			
Cremated Purewa, A.			
ALLAN EDWARD			
THOMAS			
b ref #2805 1904			
at Mt Albert, Auckland.			
d 31 October 1926 (22)			
Bur Waikumete, A.			

JEAN next page...   John next page...   Karen next page...   Alex next page...

Ernest Thomas cont.

3rd Generation	4th Generation	5th Generation	6th Generation
JEAN ISABELLE THOMAS b 14 July 1914 at Mt Albert, Auckland. m 3 June 1939 ===== at Mt Albert, Auckland. **GORDAN CAMPBELL HOLDSWORTH** b 28 November 1916 at Auckland. d 12 April 1990 (77) Cremated at Waikumete. (He was son of William John Holdsworth and Annie Briggs.)	**JOHN STEWART HOLDSWORTH** b 26 September 1941 at Mt Albert, Auckland. m 20 Nov 1965 ===== at Mt Roskill, Auckland. **NOELINE ENID CAIRN** b 22 December 1942 at Auckland City.	**KAREN LEIGH HOLDSWORTH** b 4 June 1966 at Mt Albert, Auckland. m 2 March 1989===== at Mt Eden, Auckland. **PAUL DAVID WILSON** b 15 May 1966 at Pakaranga, Auckland.	**ALEX JOHN WILSON** b 8 September 1992 at Greenlane, Auckland.
		RHONDA ANNE HOLDSWORTH b 17 November 1968 at Mt Albert, Auckland.	
		SUSAN DEBRA HOLDSWORTH b 27 October 1972 at Mt Albert, Auckland.	
	BARRY GORDAN HOLDSWORTH b 25 September 1943 at Mt Albert, Auckland. 1st m 12 Dec 1964 ==== at Wanganui. **JACKIE ADELE MacDONALD** b 14 August 1946 at Christchurch.	**JEFFREY GORDAN HOLDSWORTH** b 1 July 1965 at Greenlane, Auckland. **MURRAY JOHN HOLDSWORTH** b 29 September 1967 at Greenlane, Auckland. **GRANT WILLIAM HOLDSWORTH** b 8 September 1971 at Greenlane, Auckland.	
	TONY OWEN HOLDSWORTH b 7 May 1952 at Mt Albert, Auckland.		

ALFRED SAMUEL THOMAS: (1880 – 1942)

1880... Alfred the eleventh child of George and Jane (Polly) Thomas, was born 7 June while the family were living in the Whau township.

MARRIAGES: 1903... The Thomas family Bible shows that Alfred married **HELENA MARGARET (Maggie) BURKE** in 1903. (Unable to find her death)

1919... Alfred married (ref 2703) **ISABELLA MCMAHON** (born at Cambridge NZ, about 1884). Alfred is buried with his wife Isabella.

1920... BIRTH of son **TREVOR OWEN THOMAS**, on 23 March 1920.
Trevor died 14 Sept 2009 (89) buried North Shore Memorial Park, Silverdale.

1937... WILLS:
On 21 April he signed his Will...A S Thomas and described himself as of 95 Williamson Ave, Grey Lynn, occupation...Milk Vendor. He left his estate valued at 1226 pounds to his wife Isabella as sole Executrix and Trustee. No children were detailed, nor a list of assets given.
On 27 January 1942 Isabella signed the Will and noted her birth place.

WILLIAMSON AVE: Number 95 was in the PO Directory of 1918 occupied by Captain T Wolfenden...a Dairyman and 1921 is the first year Alfred is mentioned...as Dairyman. Maybe it was a shop, a Dairy and not a Milk Run which I initially thought a "Milk Vendor" was.

1942... ALFRED DIED: He died at his home on 4 January aged 61 and is buried at Waikumete Cemetery, Anglican Block, Section 1, Plot 36.
A comment on the headstone reads "AT REST"

1952... The PO Directory advises that Mrs Isabella Thomas was still living at 95 Williamson Avenue, Grey Lynn.

1976... ISABELLA DIED:
Isabell died on 8 May 1976 aged 92 and rests with Alfred at Waikumete. The headstone mentions her twice...as both Isobella and Isabella.
We present no Family Tree for Alfred as insufficient detail obtained.

HILDA JANE THOMAS: (1883-1958)

1883... **HILDA** was the twelfth child of George and Jane (Polly) Thomas, born 28 February whilst the family were living in the Whau Township.

1912... Hilda married **RODERICK FORRESTER LEWIS** on 13th March at Waipu, Northland (ref#1384) and had two sons, Neville and Maurice.

Hilda, from the age of 18, played the organ twice each Sunday at the Waterview Methodist Church and father George saw that all the family attended all the services that day. (MLG)

The Church still stands in 1993 at the corner of Fir St and Great North Road at Waterview, not far from the family home at Whau (Avondale). This Church was built in 1875 and unfortunately no historical documentation has survived.

Her parents George and Jane Thomas had a dog named Bruce and it was Hilda's pleasant duty to keep it fit and fed. (MLG)

One of Hilda's fondest memories were of Easter Friday. Her father would rise about 2am and bake the Easter Buns and later sell them for 1 shilling a dozen and we are advised he placed the traditional 13 buns into the bags. Hilda used to sit on the stairs and watch her father until she was old enough to help, by putting the buns into the bags. (MGL)

1879... **RODERICK** was born on 8 July 1879 at Tintinallogy in New South Wales, Australia and travelled with his parents to live in Paraguay.

After a brief stop in England, he came to NZ in 1905 aged 25.

His parents were Mary Ann and Alexander Forrester Lewis.

Alexander was a shearer and Union Organiser and farmed for a while at Maungaturoto. While there he served on the board of the Maungaturoto Dairy Company from 1907 to 1914 and was it's Chairman for the years 1911-14. (DB)

During 1915-16 Alexander served on the NZ Farmers Union Committee at Maungaturoto. (DB)

Roderick was a regular and keen Cricket player for the Maungaturoto team during 1909-14. He specialised in bowling and his best figures have been recorded as.... 6 wickets for 16 runs. (DB)

His last occupation before he retired was Star Agent from c1930.

1971... RODERICK DIED He died 28 July 1971 aged 92. Rev O R Bambury, an Anglican,   conducted his funeral at the Purewa Crematorium.

1916... NEVILLE RODERICK LEWIS was born 29 October 1916 and married May MacDougall. They named a daughter Myrna. When May died, Neville married Inez Walker. He Died on 26 April 1988.

1921... MAURICE GEORGE LEWIS was born 27 June 1921 at Balmoral, Auckland and married Doreen Emily Pearson. Doreen brought Carolyn and Denise Pearson to join the family. At the time of his father's death Maurice was aged 50 and living at 68 Gifford Ave, Mt Roskill. Maurice still lives in Avondale in 1993, one of the last three living grandchildren of George and Polly Thomas. He was born after they died but his mother Hilda passed on some memories to him.

1958... HILDA DIED. Aged 75 in the ambulance on the way to Auckland Hospital on 7 September 1958. Her funeral was conducted by the Rev Wesley Parker, a Methodist, at the Purewa Crematorium. Hilda and Roderick were living at Flat 5, 692 New North Road in Mt Roskill at the time of their deaths. Son Maurice received both lots of ashes which he scattered on the grounds of the Waterview Methodist Church.

HILDA and RODERICK LEWIS.

HILDA THOMAS FAMILY TREE:

2nd Generation:

HILDA JANE THOMAS...............married......................RODERICK FORRESTER LEWIS

b 28 February 1883	12 March 1912	b 8 July 1879
at Avondale, Auckland.	at Waipu, in	at Tintinallogy, NSW, Australia.
d 7 September 1958 (75)	Northland, NZ	d 28 July 1971 (92)
Purewa Crematorium, Auckland.		Purewa Crematorium, Auckland.

Roderick was the son of ALEXANDER FORRESTER LEWIS and
MARY ANN FORRESTER LEWIS.

Hilda and Roderick had 2 children named Neville and Maurice.

+++

3rd Generation	4th Generation	5th Generation	6th Generation
NEVILLE RODERICK LEWIS	MYRNA ANN LEWIS	WAYNE ANTONY WHYMAN	KIM LOLA WHYMAN
b 29 October 1916	b 20 May 1942	b 18 June 1961	b 19 August 1988
at Maungaturoto.	at Auckland.	at Auckland.	at Perth, Australia.
d 26 April 1988 (71)	m 3 Dec 1960 =======	m ======	
Cremated, Auckland.	at Auckland.	at Perth, Australia.	LUKE ERIC
1st m 28 Aug 1936 ===	ELSDEN	IRIS VAN DER POEL	WHYMAN
at Auckland City.	WHYMAN	b 17 March 1953	b 19 January 1993
MAY	b 27 May 1940	at Capetown, South	at Perth, Australia.
MacDOUGALL	at Levin.	Africa.	
b 30 May 1912			
at Auckland.			
d 23 March 1968 (56)			
Bur Auckland.		ERIC ELSDEN	
(She was daughter of		WHYMAN	
Duncan MacDougall		b 8 April 1963	
and Flora McKenzie)		at Auckland.	

2nd m 23 March 1978
at Auckland City.
INEZ PAMELA
WALKER
b 26 May 1928
at Stratford, NZ.
(daughter of Twentyman
Wilson Walker and
Pearl Grace Willing)
There were no children.

MAURICE next page...

Hilda Thomas cont.

3rd Generation	4th Generation	5th Generation	6th Generation
MAURICE GEORGE LEWIS b 27 June 1921 at Balmoral, Auckland. m 30 March 1959===== at Auckland City. DOREEN EMILY PEARSON b 10 August 1928 at Ngaruawahia, Waikato, NZ (Doreen was daughter of George Pearson and Charlotte Pope.)	JULIE JANE AILSA LEWIS She was born the day the Auckland Harbour Bridge opened b 30 May 1959 at Greenlane, Auckland. 1st m 4 Jan 1980 ===== at Auckland. ROGER REECE THOMAS b 9 December 1939 at Auckland. : : 2nd m 26 June 1987 at Kohimarama, Auck. PETER GEOFFREY BUCK b 12 August 1951 at Palmerston North.	HAYLEY AMELIA THOMAS b 28 May 1981 at Auckland.	
Doreen brought two children to the family. Carolyn Emily Pearson who married Brendon Crawford.......and........ Denise Muriel Pearson who married Brian Stewart.	(This family is living in Hong Kong) SCOTT GEORGE RODERICK LEWIS b 25 September 1962 at Greenlane, Auckland.		

--ooOOoo--

303

ACKNOWLEDGEMENTS:

Other Writings,
A.H. WALKER............ "The Story of Point Chevalier." 1861-1961.
D.N. HAWKINS.......... "Rangiora."
W.H. SCOTTER........... "Ashburton Country."
A.G. FLUDE............... "Henderson's Mill."
DICK BUTLER (DB).... "This Valley in the Hills."

Thanks to,
Takapuna Family History Centre.
Takapuna Public Library staff.
Auckland City Library staff, NZ Room.
Auckland Museum Library staff.
Canterbury Museum Library staff.
Invercargill Public Library staff.
Coromandel & Thames Library staff.
Ilfracombe Museum staff, Devon England.
Lands & Deeds, Auckland. Archives section.
National Archives, Wellington.
Auckland Archives staff.
Ashburton Library staff.
Ashburton Council staff.
Ashburton Guardian, Mr Ray McCausland.
Justice Dept, Levin House, Lower Hutt.
Methodist Church Archives, Auckland.
Primitive Methodist Archives, Auckland.
NZ Postal Archives & Postal History Society.

Special Thanks to,
Elizabeth Newcombe and May Verney and family in Devon.
Michael Stanley Thomas for help during early research years.
Peggy Meikle for early computer help in compiling the family trees.
Lilian and Nelson Price, my parents who answered many questions.
All Grand-children of John and Phebe Thomas.
All Grand-children of George and Polly Thomas.
My wife Jill, for tremendous patience and willingness to travel all over NZ and England in research for this book and for doing lots of typing.
Richard Somerville, for invaluable help in the proof-reading area.
Tony and Xanthe Price for production assistance.

*The following pages include details found since publication
of the original 1993 'The THOMAS family' book.*

--oo0Ooo--

Page 8 .. JOANNA THOMAS born 1852 in Devon, England.
All details have been removed because of an error by the author.
Her parents are also John and Jane Thomas, but not our John & Jane Thomas.

Page 8 and 9 .. **Alterations to the BRIEF TREE** make it more easily understood.

1860... Page 45 .. **The STAR MILLS** advertisement of August 3 is possibly the
first advert placed by John Thomas who was now ready for customers.

To Wheat and Flour Dealers, &c.

THE undersigned is prepared to take Wheat, &c.,
to grind, in any quantities, at 1s. per bushel,
smutted, ground, and dressed; Grain cracked for
horses, 4d. per bushel.

P.S.—All Flour made from good wheat will be
guaranteed by a Star brand. Any parties not re-
quiring the offal can get 40 lbs. of best flour free of
charge. Wheat can be conveyed from Queen-street
Wharf and back for about 1½d. per bushel if in large
lots by boat, or 3d. by land.

A partner would be accepted if an equivalent of
means could be given; a judge of wheat preferred.

For particulars apply by post or on the premises.

JOHN THOMAS,
Star Mills, Oakley's Creek.

August 3d, 1860.

Pages 47-49 In this book is a longer article than in the original book, about the
trials of John Thomas' venture into making **BRICKS** and **NZ WARS of 1864.**
More details appeared when researching for The William Thomas book.   (T)

1864... page 47 .. BRICK BURNER advertisement .. January 12, 1864.

To Brick Burners.

WANTED, a competent BRICK BURNER.—Apply to C. ARTHUR, Queen-street; or to JOHN THOMAS, Star Mills, Oakley's Creek.

1864... June 8th LOST WHEAT: (*'The New Zealander'* newspaper)
John Thomas wants COMPENSATION.

SUPREME COURT.—YESTERDAY.

CIVIL SITTING.
[Before His Honor Chief Justice Sir G. A. ARNEY.]

The Court opened at eleven o'clock, at which hour his Honor took his seat on the Bench.

THOMAS v. CASEY.

This was an action brought by Mr. John Thomas, of Oakley's Creek, against Mr. Jeremiah Casey, of Auckland, for the recovery of £200 damages, sustained by loss of a cargo of wheat in course of transit in defendant's boat from Auckland to Oakley's Creek.

A special jury was sworn in this case, James Williamson, Esq., foreman.

Mr. Wynn, instructed by Mr. Hill, appeared for plaintiff; Mr. Merriman, instructed by Mr. J. B. Russell, for the defendant.

Issues:—Plaintiff alleged and defendant denied that he contracted for the conveyance in a certain cargo-boat of a cargo of wheat from on board the barque *Nightingale*, alongside the Queen-street wharf, to Oakley's Creek; plaintiff alleged, and defendant denied, that the defendant agreed to deliver the same at Oakley's Creek in good order and condition; that the defendant had failed in the delivery of the wheat at Oakley's Creek in accordance with the terms of the contract; that the non-delivery or damage of the wheat was caused by the act of God and the Queen's enemy, perils of the sea, or uncontrolable means, and not by neglect on the part of the defendant. Was the cargo upset by overloading on the part of the defendant, or his servants; or, did the accident happen in consequence of such alleged overloading?

306

This cutting from the newspaper, page 306, is the start of the case but it goes on for 10 A4 pages in the 8 June 1864 issue. Briefly ... John Thomas bought 110 bags of wheat carried to Auckland by ship from Adelaide and paid 183 pounds for it. He hired Casey to transport it to the Mill by sea. Ship was very deep when laden. The wind got up strength and the boat sank. Casey claimed it was a 'hand-shake deal' and 'no contract' applied. Many witnesses were called but John Thomas lost and had to also pay costs of the special jury.

1865... Page 52 .. Star Flour Mill's mention in sale of land advertisement
In *The Daily Southern Cross* newspaper many times during May 1865.
(Good and free advertising for Star Mill. T)

SUBURBS, AT POINT CHEVALIER, GREAT NORTH ROAD, KARANGAHAPE ROAD, NEWTON.

2 VALUABLE ALLOTMENTS, containing about Five Acres each, having large frontages to the Waitemata River and to a road. This property is admirably adapted for Brick-making, Lime-burning, or other manufacturing purpose, being approachable by both land and water, having a constant supply of fresh water at all times running through the property, and adjoining extensive shell banks, with an unexhaustible supply of sand, &c

To capitalists, or as a villa residence, a more desirable opportunity for investing is not likely again to occur, the Allotments being situate in the neighbourhood of a rapidly advancing district, in close proximity to the Northern Hotel, Oakley's Creek, Star Flour Mill, and about equidistant from Auckland and the new townships of Windsor, Whau, Waterview, &c.

1865... page 52 .. BRICK YARD for RENT .. June 30, *New Zealand Herald*.
With John Thomas' death, no family member wanted to continue making bricks, so their yard and equipment were offered for rent. We could not find a record of anyone taking up this offer.

TO LET—A BRICK YARD, at OAKLEY'S CREEK, four miles from Town, on the Great North Road. Apply to J. S. MACFARLANE & Co.; or to Mrs. THOMAS, at the Yard.

John Thomas, PETITION for compensation after Brick losses ....

AUCKLAND PROVINCIAL COUNCIL.

TUE-DAY. FEBRUARY 28.

The SPEAKER took the chair at ten minutes past three o'clock, with only twelve members in the House.

PETITIONS.

Mr. KING presented a petition from John Thomas, a mill owner on the North Road, prayin · for redress on account of himself and his men being embodied in the militia against a gnarantee that had been previously given by the Government, whereby he broke down in the fulfilment of his contract for supplying the Lunatic Asylum, and was mulcted in consequence.

Petition was received and laid on the table.

Mr Walker's condensed version of this Court Case is accurate from newspaper accounts of the occasion. John Thomas' case went before the Auckland Provincial Council and was deferred many times but after he died (8 April) they brought the matter to an end. *The New Zealander* newspaper, starting on February 28, 1865 (above), through March and into June 1865, has mention of the case, but April 13, 1865 has the greatest detail of what was considered. The matter was completed on 8th June 1865 with John not winning compensation.

1893... p55 ..   JANE THOMAS' last residence before 1893.

COSTLEY HOME as it was about 2000

1870... page 54 .. THOMAS & BARRACLOUGH advertisement of 13 July

MAIZE MEAL.

Messrs. Thomas and Barraclough, Star Flour Mills, will supply the above at 11s. 6d. per 100lb., Net Cash, in quantities from 100lb., upwards.—Mr. Lavers, Seedsman, Wyndham-street, will receive orders.

N.B.—Bags or Sacks charged for.

1872... page 69 .. JOHN THOMAS & PHEBE WOODS MARRIAGE

They married on 31 December 1872 ... the newspaper has the wrong date.

THOMAS—WOODS—On January 1, at the Whau Presbyterian Church, by the Rev. David Hamilton, John Thomas, of the Star Mills, to Phœbe Woods, of Auckland. This being the first marriage celebrated in the Whau Presbyterian Church, the Rev D. Hamilton presented the newly-married couple with a handsomely-bound Bible, and the settlers of the district presented an album bearing an appropriate inscription, as a token of esteem and in commemoration of the first wedding celebrated in the church.

DAILY SOUTHERN CROSS 22 JAN 1873

1874... THOMAS & BARRACLOUGH DISSOLVE PARTNERSHIP

notice .. **September 30, NZ Herald.** (book page 54)

NOTICE.

The Partnership hitherto existing between John Thomas and Thomas Barraclough, as Millers, was dissolved by mutual consent, on the 26th instant.

All debts owing to the late firm will be collected by George and John Thomas.

JOHN THOMAS.
THOS. BARRACLOUGH.

Witness—GEORGE HARPER.

Auckland, 28th September, 1874.

GEORGE THOMAS,
OF STAR MILLS,

BEGS to intimate to the bakers and the public that he has OPENED a FLOUR STORE opposite the Wheatsheaf.

G. T., being a practical Miller, will be able to guarantee a first-class article, and as cheap as any mill in town.

N.B.—Mr. G. OUGHTON will cease to act as his agent from this date.

GEORGE THOMAS.

August 14, 1867.

1867... August 14 .. advert for STAR MILLS with **George Thomas in charge**. Mention of this advert on page 217 of book.

--oo0Ooo--

1874... October 10 .. GEORGE & JOHN THOMAS jnr advertisement. Originally inserted September 29, the advert was still running in October.

GEO. AND J. THOMAS,
STAR MILLS, WHAU.

WHOLESALE PRICES CURRENT.

	Per ton.		
Best Star Flour, from Adelaide wheat	15	0	0
From Selected Oamaru Wheat	14	0	0
Silk-dressed Flour	13	0	0
Maize Meal	14	10	0
Wheat Meal	13	0	0
Sharps	8	0	0
Bran	7	10	0

P.S.—Any orders for Flour, Gristing, etc., left with Mr. G. H. Lavers, Wyndham-street, will be strictly attended to.

September 29, 1874.

LILLIAN ELSIE THOMAS and SCHOOL:

Soon after their arrival in Invercargill late in January 1925, Percy and Elsie's children Lillian and Leslie started a new school. However, son Hector began work at the Nursery with his father.

Lillian and Les were both enrolled at the Waikiwi School, by their father on 31 March 1925., He was noted as ... Mr Thomas, The Nursery, Waikiwi.
Lillian became pupil number 1523 with birthday noted as 3 August 1912.
Lesley became pupil number 1522 with birthday noted as 23 January 1915.
They had attended the East Ashburton School before this date.

> Lesley spent three years there leaving on 16 December 1927 gaining his **School Leaving Certificate,** and continued his education at Southland Boys High School.
> Lillian spent two years at Waikiwi Primary, left on 17 December 1926 with the **School Leaving Certificate**, and moved to the Southland Technical College in 1927.

The *"Southland Times"* newspaper on 18 December 1926 page 10 records the Waikiwi Schools prizes presented at their breaking-up ceremony. Ten of the Standard 6 pupils were awarded the Proficiency Certificate and one of these was Lillian Thomas.
The **'Teachers Annual Exam Reports'** for each year, 1925 and 1926 are near impossible to read but Lillian's are available at the Invercargill Public Library.
I did note that under Proficiency she scored a 6. Pupils received grades starting at 1 and 6 seemed to be the maximum possible.

> The staff at the Invercargill Public Library found these facts while hunting the newspapers of those years for detail of a medal Lillian may have won at Swimming ... but sadly nothing showed up at either of these school newspaper mentions and those for the local Swimming Clubs .. Murihiku Swimming Club and the Municipal Tepid Baths Club. (T .. 2021/22)

More of Lillian's life's facts appear in other books I have put together, including her husband's ... Nelson Price .. World War 2 Diary.

--ooo0oo—

Headstone for Lillian's brother
LESLIE and parents PERCY & ELSIE THOMAS'
grave at Invercargill's St John Cemetery

Page 8 Brief Tree .... MORE NAMES ADDED

Since printing the original THOMAS FAMILY book, we have found descendants of WILLIAM THOMAS, the brother of JOHN (Chapter 4).

The names of William and Eliza's children have been added to the page 8 tree. Their personal life histories and families' details are now recorded in the "WILLIAM THOMAS family" book.

--ooO0oo—

INDEX of THOMAS FAMILY MEMBERS

Name	Ref
THOMAS	
Adrianna	277
Albert John (I)	8+111
Albert Britton (II)	277
Albert Peter (III)	8
Alfred Edward (I)	8+118
Alfred Samuel (II)	9+291
Alice Agatha	8
Alison Joyce	255
Allana May	290
Allan Edward (I)	297
Allan Bertram (II)	170
Alexander Roy	8+209
Amanda Megan	129
Andrea Jane	123
Ann	9+12
Anne	8+14
Anne	184
Arthur Gordon (I)	8
Arthur Hamilton (II)	8+111
Arthur Raymond (III)	138
Audrey Jean	172
Avis Myrtle	284
Aynslie Ruth	209
Barbara Helen	256
Beatrice May	31
Belinda Karoline	291
Bertha Maud (I)	8+111
Bertha Lillian	258
Bessie Thirza T	25
Bevan Lyall (I)	282
Bevan William (II)	261
Beverley Dawn (I)	124
Beverley Fuller (II)	259
Brian Theodore (I)	251
Brian Rex (II)	257
Brent John	123
Brett William	283
Bronwyn Lea	257
Bryce	260
Charles (I)	8+12
Charles (II)	9+14
Charles Ernest (III)	8+198
Cheryl-Anne	259
Cheryl Lea	282
Christene Merle	283
Clarence Matthew	139
Collin Glenn	290
Corrine Lesley	261
Darrin Karl	157
David Stanley (I)	260
David Bertram (II)	171
Dean Graham	157
Deborah Kaye	125
Desmond John	122
Doreen Maida	282
Doris Ophir	128
Dorothy Amelia	173
Douglas William	255
Dulcie	297
Edith May	8
Edward Ernest	9+297
Edward Lloyd D	251
Eleanor Rose	8
Eliza (I)	8
Eliza (II)	8
Eliza Jane (III)	8+215
Elizabeth (I)	8+11
Elizabeth (II)	8+12
Elizabeth (III)	8+12
Elizabeth (IV)	9+17
Elizabeth (V)	8+24
Elizabeth (VI)	9+66
Elizabeth Jane (VII)	8
Elsie May	173
Elva Margaret	258
Emma Louise	139
Enid Lorraine	126
Ernest Edward (I)	292
Ernest William (III)	255
Ethel Isabel (I)	8
Esther	28
Ethel Rita (II)	248
Eunice Nellie	260
Frederick Palmer (I)	9+26
Frederick William (II)	8+137
Frederick John (III)	139
Gail Joy	284
Gary Roydon	173
Gavin Wayne	157
George (I)	9+17
George (II)	9+210
George (III)	9+277
George Alexander (IV)	8
George Bertram (V)	8+170
George Arthur (VI)	258
George Harry (VII)	184
George Herrick (VIII)	137
George Morris (IX)	173
George Albert (X)	277
Grace	9+14
Grant Demler (I)	251
Grant Russell (II)	283
Graeme Hector (I)	157
Graeme Edward (II)	129
Graham Geo. (Joe) (I)	289
Graham (II)	289
Graham George (III)	289
Harry	184
Hayley Amelia	303
Hector Percival	156
Hester (I)	8+11
Hester (II)	9+14
Hester (Esther) (III)	9+285
Hilda Jane	9+302
Hope Elizabeth (Betty)	173
Ian Russell (I)	138
Ian Wayne (II)	129
Ivy Gladys	8
James Sydney	8+184
Jan Margaret	209
Jane Kate	139
Janet Margaret	260
Janine Patricia	173
Jared Norman Ray	209
Jean Isabelle	298
Jennifer Wynn	289
Jessica Leah	260
Jessie Elizabeth	8+140
Jill Annette	139
Joanna	8
Jocelyn Margaret	127
Jodi Marie	261
John (I)	8+11
John (II)	8+12
John (III)	9+17
John (IV)	8+35
John (V)	8+68
John (Jack) (VI)	9+248
John Coates (VII)	8
John Woods (VIII)	8+111
John H (Jack) (IX)	8+197
John Hunter (X)	122
John Harold (XI)	291
John William (XII)	257
Jolene Evelyn	282
Jordan Phillip	285
Judith	257
June Eden	287
Karen Ruth	290
Karene Jeanetta	170
Karl Brendon	127
Karyn Mary	269
Kay Dawn	124
Keith Ernest	292
Kentley Sydney	25
Kevin Lees (I)	157
Kevin George (II)	277
Laurel Marguerite	9+210
Lawrence Victor	283
Leanne Mary	256
Leila Forbes	249
Leonard Palmer	9+33
Lesley Jean	281
Leslie Walter	161
Lillian Elsie	152
Lois Margaret	156
Lorraine Rosales	282
Lyall Dale	282
Lynnette Anne	284
Mabel Rita	248
Malcolm (Snowy) (I)	284
Malcolm Eastman (II)	251
Maree Ann	125
Margaret Elsie (I)	209
Margaret Evelyn (II)	256
Margaret Nola (III)	279
Marion Lois	123
Mary (I)	9+14
Mary Ann (II)	9+240
Mary Ann (III)	8
Mary Jane (IV)	8+111
Megan Jane	257
Melissa Lucy	251
Mervyn Roy	209
Michael (I)	260
Michael Stanley (II)	173
Michael Ian (III)	138
Michael Brett (IV)	289
Michelle Jeanette	282
Morva Sybil	184
Muriel Grace (I)	297
Muriel Joan (II)	137
Murray Bruce	127
Nathan David	173
Neil Hunter	125
Neville William	122
Nichola Elizabeth	283
Noeline Elizabeth	138
Nola Eileen	255
Norma Isabel	250
Norman John	250
Patricia Merle	138
Peter Davie	261
Phillip Dean (I)	260
Phillip Malcolm (II)	285
Phillipa Jane	138
Phyllis Eva	197
Phoebe Elsie (I)	8+185
Phoebe Elsie (II)	118
Rachael	279
Rachel Joy	127
Raelene Annette	126
Rebecca (I)	278
Rebecca Helen (II)	129
Rebekah-Jane	173
Reginal John	127
Rex Colston	256
Rhonda Anne	126
Richard (I)	9+17
Richard George (II)	282
Richard Henesey (III)	9+215
Richard (IV)	9+31
Richard James (V)	123
Robert (I)	9+14
Robert William (II)	8+283
Robyn Marie (I)	278
Robyn Marie (II)	251
Roger Lee (I)	139
Roger Reece (II)	303
Ronald Claude (I)	126
Ronald Edward (II)	292
Roy Kevin	260
Russell Ernest (I)	256
Russell Bruce (II)	283
Sasha	277
Selina Ann	9+233
Selwyn Lawrence	283
Shane Francis	299
Shaun Selwyn	283
Shirley Margaret (I)	137
Shirley Elizabeth (II)	256
Steffan Mark	129
Stephanie Sharyn	285
Susan Kay	122
Suzanne Mary	170
Tony Mason	283
Tracy Marie	261
Una Miles	184
Unnamed	260
Valerie Joy	285
Valmai Agnes	175
Vaughan Andrew	291
Vernon Neil	125
Victor George Alex	283
Victoria Minnie May	292
Vivian Athol Sinclair	127
Walter Percival (I)	8+156
Walter Brown (II)	9+33
Walter James (III)	8
Warren James (I)	127
Warren James (II)	127
Wayne Philip	256
Wendy Margaret	290
William (I)	8+11
William (II)	8+12
William (III)	8+17
William (IV)	8+17
William (V)	8+58
William (VI)	9+255
William (VII)	255
William Fred. (VIII)	9+31
William George (IX)	9+261
William Henry (X)	8
Wyvern Ian	129
THOMPSON	
Alastair	281
Carl James	281
Jamie John	281
John Edward	281
TITTLE Beatrice M	284
TOOLEY Myra P M	209
TOOMEY Cynthia M	124
TOPP	
Brendon M David	127
David Benjamin	127
Deborah Marie	127
Tracey Jane	127
TORCKLER	
Christopher Carlyle	284
Keith Adam	284
TRYLSSON Ivy	292
John Nils	292
TUBB Elizabeth J	240
John Francis	240
Matthew Alfred	240
Timothy John	240
TULLEY Louisa M	184
UNDERWOOD	
Alice Fuller	258
Charles Harvey	259
VAGLE Henny	158
Van HALEWYN	
Pieter Tureia	280
Shaun	280
William Rangi	280
Van OORSHOT	
Natasja Catherina	158
VERITY Louise M	297
VINSON John Colin	297
Mary Dene	297
VOICE Rhonda M	137
VOS Irene	209
Livinia Gladys	209
VINCENT Brent J	128
Craig Alexander	128

318

THE FOLLOWING PAGES HAVE BEEN SUPPLIED SO THAT NEW INFORMATION AND NEW BIRTH, MARRIAGE, DEATH & BURIAL DETAILS IN YOUR FAMILY, CAN BE RECORDED FOR FUTURE GENERATIONS TO KNOW.

www.ingramcontent.com/pod-product-compliance
Lightning Source LLC
LaVergne TN
LVHW010315070426
835509LV00029B/3497